Advanced Mathematic
for Economists

Static and Dynamic Optimization

Advanced Mathematics for Economists

Static and Dynamic Optimization

PETER J. LAMBERT

Basil Blackwell

© Peter J. Lambert, 1985

First published 1985

Basil Blackwell Ltd
108 Cowley Road, Oxford OX4 1JF, UK

Basil Blackwell Inc.
432 Park Avenue South, Suite 1505,
New York, NY 10016, USA

British Library Cataloguing in Publication Data
Lambert Peter J.
 Advanced mathematics for economists: static
 and dynamic optimization
 1. Economics, Mathematical
 I. Title
 510′.2433   HB135
 ISBN 0-631-14138-3
 ISBN 0-631-14139-1 Pbk

Library of Congress Cataloging in Publication Data
Lambert Peter J.
 Advanced mathematics for economists.
 Bibliography: p.
 Includes index.
 1. Economics, Mathematical.   2. Mathematical
optimization.   I. Title.
HB135.L35   1985   510′.24339   85-6199
ISBN 0-631-14138-3
ISBN 0-631-14139-1 (pbk.)

Filmset by Advanced Filmsetters (Glasgow) Ltd
Printed in Great Britain by Billing & Son, Worcester

To Jane, with love

Contents

Preface

This book is aimed at final-year undergraduates doing mathematics for economists courses and postgraduate students. It contains a compact, accessible treatment of the main topics encountered in mathematical courses at these levels, moving from basic material into the twin areas of static and dynamic optimization.

The prerequisites for using the book effectively are fairly minimal. It is assumed that the reader has an understanding of economics at the undergraduate level, and is mathematically able and familiar with basic concepts such as sets, functions and limits.

Some readers, notably graduate students with quantitatively strong first degrees, will be able to focus on Part II of the book, on optimization, using Part I only to review and refresh their existing knowledge of familiar topics. For others, Part I will provide the necessary foundation of basic material. With sufficient motivation, and sympathetic encouragement, all mathematically competent students can master the optimization techniques which form the *raison d'etre* for the book.

Nearly half of the book is devoted to a treatment of the univariate calculus, matrix algebra and multivariate calculus. Sufficient matrix theory is surveyed to enable a self-contained treatment of linear differential and difference equations to be given within Part I of the book; there is also enough matrix material to form an input to courses in econometric theory. The chapters on the calculus are made vigorous by the inclusion of a variety of applications.

Part II of the book focuses on the Lagrange multiplier technique: when it will work, why it works and what economic insights it yields. Thus in the later chapters we derive, and illustrate the significance and practicability of, the Kuhn–Tucker conditions for constrained static optimization, and the Pontryagin (Hamiltonian) conditions for dynamic problems in the optimal control format. Properties of maximum value functions and duality are explored in detail. Brief expositions of the calculus of variations and dynamic programming approaches to economic problem-solving are also given, and the book ends with an Appendix.

The Appendix describes non-rigorously a recent mathematical development in optimization theory. F. H. Clarke's *generalized gradient vector* approach both extends and synthesizes the static and dynamic Lagrangean methods which are our main theme. It provides, at an advanced level, a central organizing concept for constrained optimization. We bring this to the readers' notice.

Much of the discussion in the main text proceeds at a heuristic level and by means of plentiful worked examples and inter-linked exercises. But the theorems and proofs required by the most analytical user are also given (as are solutions to the exercises).

There is an underlying message that should come across from the study of mathematics at the level of this book. It is that the language of mathematics can be *productive*, giving expression to ideas, and facilitating lines of approach from which insights flow. No other justification can (or need) be given for involving the student in the upper reaches of the subject.

I hope that this book plays a part in bringing advanced mathematics to a wider economist audience. It has grown out of several years' experience of teaching a mathematics course to graduate students of economics at the University of York. I must acknowledge in this respect a debt to Jim Malcolmson: I inherited the course from him, and some of his ideas and approaches will have filtered through. In a similar vein I am pleased to admit the influence upon me of the books by Intrilligator (1971) and Dixit (1976): these have been (for perhaps too long) the central and only texts on economic optimization both for lecturers and students. Alan Ingham provided a stream of invaluable comment upon the manuscript; this has led to many improvements; I hereby absolve him from responsibility for remaining shortcomings. Andy Tremayne generously provided computer-drawn graphs for Chapter 3. Finally I want to put on record the heavy cost that fell upon my wife, during my preparation of this book. Over the months that it took me to assemble the main body of material, there were very many late nights and lost weekends. With great pleasure I dedicate the book to her.

Peter J. Lambert
University of York

Glossary

$[a, b]$	closed interval with end-points a and b
(a, b)	open interval with end-points a and b
$\begin{bmatrix} a \\ b \end{bmatrix}, \begin{bmatrix} a & b \\ c & d \end{bmatrix}$	2×1 column vector, 2×2 matrix, etc.
adj A	adjoint of square matrix A
A^{-1}	inverse of square matrix A
A^t	transpose of square matrix A
CF	complementary function associated with a differential or difference equation
det A	determinant of square matrix
dy/dx	derivative of y with respect to x
d/dx	operator for differentiation
$[dy/dx]^-, [dy/dx]^+$	left, right derivative of y with respect to x
d^2y/dx^2	second derivative of y with respect to x
$\partial y/\partial x_i$	partial derivative of y with respect to x_i
$\partial/\partial x_i$	operator for partial differentiation
$[\partial y/\partial x_i]^-, [\partial y/\partial x_i]^+$	left, right partial derivative of y with respect to x_i
$\partial^2 y/\partial x_i^2, \partial^2 y/\partial x_i \partial x_j$	second partial derivatives of y
dx	infinitesimal increment to variable x
dy	total differential of function y of one or more variables
$d(\underline{x}, \underline{z})$	Euclidean distance between $\underline{x}$ and $\underline{z}$
$\partial h(\underline{x}_0)$	generalized gradient vector of function $h(\underline{x})$ at $\underline{x} = \underline{x}_0$

$\exp(x), e^x$	exponential function of x
$e_{Y,X}$	instantaneous elasticity of Y with respect to X
$E(\underline{p}, u)$	expenditure function
$f(a)$	value at $x = a$ of function $f(x)$
$f'(a), f''(a), f'''(a), f''''(a)$	value at $x = a$ of first, second, third and fourth derivative of function $f(x)$
$f(x \mid x > a)$	conditional frequency density function for variate x given $x > a$
$f_i; f_{ij}$	partial derivative of $f(\underline{x})$ with respect to x_i; second partial derivative with respect to x_i and x_j
GS	general solution to a differential or difference equation
$H, H(\lambda, t, x, u)$	Hamiltonian for optimal control problem
$H(\underline{a})$	Hessian matrix of function $f(\underline{x})$ at $\underline{x} = \underline{a}$
H_i	ith sub-determinant of Hessian matrix
I, I_n	$n \times n$ identity matrix
$K', \dot{K}$	derivative of variable $K = K(t)$ with respect to time t
K–T conditions	Kuhn–Tucker conditions
$\lim_{z \to a}; \lim_{z \nearrow a}; \lim_{z \searrow a}$	limit as z approaches a; as z approaches a from below; as z approaches a from above
$\ln(x)$	natural logarithm of x
$L(\underline{\lambda}, \underline{x}); L(\underline{\lambda}, \underline{x}, \underline{a})$	Lagrangean function; Lagrangean function given parameter value $\underline{a}$
L^*	modified Lagrangean (not incorporating non-negative variables constraints)
$\max_{\underline{x} \in X} f(\underline{x})$	(find the) maximum value of $f(\underline{x})$ such that $\underline{x} \in X$ (etc.)
$\min_{K,L} rK + wL$	(find the) minimum value of $rK + wL$ over all values of K and L (etc.)
$0, 0_{m,n}$	$m \times n$ null matrix
$\underline{0}$	zero (column) vector

PS	particular solution to differential or difference equation
rk A	rank of matrix A
$\mathbf{R}^m$	set of all m-tuples of real numbers
st	such that, or subject to. Thus, $\max f(\underline{x})$ st $\underline{x} \in X$
tr A	trace of square matrix A
$V; \tilde{V}$	maximum value; maximum value with added constraints
$V[s, x \mid T, y]$	maximum value for optimal control problem (p. 201)
$|x|$	modulus of real number x
$x^{(i)}$	ith derivative with respect to time t of function $x = x(t)$
$\bar{x}$	fixed value of variable x (etc.); also mean of distribution of x
$\hat{x}, x^*$	optimal value of variable x (etc.)
$\|\underline{x} - \underline{z}\|$	Euclidean norm (length) of vector $\underline{x} - \underline{z}$
$\in$	belongs to
$\doteq$	approximately equal to
$\equiv$	identically equal to
$\Rightarrow$	implies
$\not\Rightarrow$	does not imply
$\rightarrow$	approaches
$\vert_a^b$	evaluated between a and b: thus $f(x)\vert_a^b = f(b) - f(a)$
$\int_a^b f(x)\,dx$	integral from $x = a$ to $x = b$ of $f(x)$
$\Sigma_i; \Sigma_{i=1}^n$	summation over i; from $i = 1$ to $i = n$
	derivative of variable, often with respect to time t. Thus x', m', K' when $x = x(t)$, $m = m(t)$, $K = K(t)$ (etc.)
$\Delta x, \Delta f$	small finite increment to variable x, to value of function $f(x)$
$\nabla f(\underline{a})$	gradient vector of $f(\underline{x})$ at $\underline{x} = \underline{a}$

$\lambda; \lambda(t)$ Lagrange multiplier; costate variable in optimal control theory

θ number between 0 and 1 used in Taylor's theorem

$\theta(p)$ Lorenz curve $(0 \leqslant p \leqslant 1)$

Part I

Basic Material

1 Univariate Calculus

Differentiation and integration are perhaps the most useful and basic techniques in the economist's mathematical tool-kit. If a variable y is functionally related to another variable x, we use differentiation to examine the responsiveness of y to changes in x, and integration to add ys across a distribution or continuum of xs. In this first chapter we set out the main results in the calculus of functions of a single variable ('univariate' functions) that will be necessary for the rest of the book; and we apply them, as we go, in a variety of directions to illustrate the power of the calculus to give formal expression to ideas in economics.

1.1 THE DERIVATIVE

Let $y = f(x)$ be a function which is *continuous*: by this we mean that its graph has no vertical jumps or gaps. See, for example, figure 1.1 where, as x changes, the slope of the curve changes.

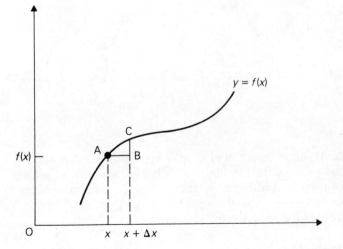

Figure 1.1

1

The function that defines the slope at each point, say at A with co-ordinates $(x, f(x))$, is called the *derivative* of $f(x)$ and is denoted $f'(x)$. It is determined as $\lim_{\Delta x \to 0} BC/AB$, i.e. as

$$f'(x) = \lim_{\Delta x \to 0} \frac{f(x + \Delta x) - f(x)}{\Delta x} \tag{1.1}$$

if this limit exists.

There are some alternative notations for the derivative. Most commonly we may write $f'(x)$ as

$$\frac{dy}{dx} \quad \text{or} \quad \frac{d}{dx}[f(x)] \quad \text{or} \quad \frac{df}{dx}. \tag{1.2}$$

In the case of a function of *time*, e.g. if capital stock at time t is $K(t)$, a frequently adopted convention is to write $dK/dt = K'(t) = \dot{K}$, the 'dot' conveying everything (see Example 1.5.2, p. 17).

The symbol d/dx is an 'operator', denoting the act of *differentiating* the function $y = f(x)$. If the limit does not exist for some value(s) of x, then the function is not differentiable at that/those values.

If $f'(a) > 0$ then $y = f(x)$ is an increasing function of x around ('in a neighbourhood of') $x = a$; if $f'(a) < 0$ then $y = f(x)$ is decreasing around $x = a$. A value of a for which $f'(a) = 0$ is a *turning point*. It may be a maximum, a minimum or a point of inflection (see figure 1.2).

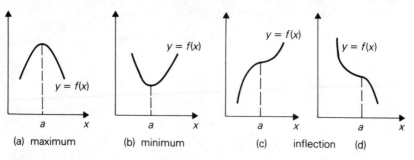

(a) maximum   (b) minimum   (c)   inflection   (d)

Figure 1.2

The right-hand side of equation (1.1) may approach $\pm\infty$; in such a limiting case the graph of the function evidently becomes vertical, either upwards or downwards. Another possibility is that the limit in equation (1.1) may not be well-defined (see Example 1.1.1(b), p. 3).

Some properties of the derivative are given below:

1. if $y = c$ (constant) then $dy/dx = 0$
2. if $y = x^n$ then $dy/dx = nx^{n-1}$

3. $d/dx[cf(x)] = cf'(x)$ for all constants c
4. $d/dx[f(x)+g(x)] = f'(x)+g'(x)$
5. $d/dx[f(x)g(x)] = f'(x)g(x)+f(x)g'(x)$
6. $d/dx[f(x)/g(x)] = [f'(x)g(x)-f(x)g'(x)]/[g(x)]^2$ if $g(x) \neq 0$.

1.1.1 Examples

(a) We prove property 5 above. By definition

$$\frac{d}{dx}[f(x)g(x)] = \lim_{\Delta x \to 0} [f(x+\Delta x)g(x+\Delta x)-f(x)g(x)]/\Delta x$$

$$= \lim_{\Delta x \to 0} \{[f(x+\Delta x)-f(x)]g(x+\Delta x)$$

$$+[g(x+\Delta x)-g(x)]f(x)\}/\Delta x$$

$$= \lim_{\Delta x \to 0} [f(x+\Delta x)-f(x)]/\Delta x . \lim_{\Delta x \to 0} g(x+\Delta x)$$

$$+f(x) . \lim_{\Delta x \to 0} [g(x+\Delta x)-g(x)]/\Delta x$$

using an elementary property of limits. Since g is differentiable, it is continuous, and $g(x+\Delta x) \to g(x)$ as $\Delta x \to 0$. The result follows.

(b) The function

$$y = f(x) = |x| = \begin{cases} +x & x \geqslant 0 \\ -x & x \leqslant 0 \end{cases}$$

is not differentiable at $x = 0$; its derivative if $x \neq 0$ is

$$f'(x) = \begin{cases} +1 & x > 0 \\ -1 & x < 0. \end{cases}$$

From the definition,

$$f'(x) = \lim_{\Delta x \to 0} [f(x+\Delta x)-f(x)]/\Delta x = \lim_{\Delta x \to 0} (|x+\Delta x|-|x|)/\Delta x$$

if this limit exists. If $x > 0$ and Δx is very small, then $x+\Delta x > 0$ also. Hence

$$(|x+\Delta x|-|x|)/\Delta x = (x+\Delta x-x)/\Delta x = 1$$

whilst, similarly, if $x < 0$ then for very small Δx, $x+\Delta x < 0$ also, and we have

$$(|x+\Delta x|-|x|)/\Delta x = [-(x+\Delta x)+x]/\Delta x = -1.$$

Hence, in the limit, $f'(x) = +1$ or -1 according as $x > 0$ or $x < 0$. If $x = 0$ then the limit that defines $f'(0)$ would be $\lim_{\Delta x \to 0} |\Delta x|/\Delta x$; but

$$|\Delta x|/\Delta x = \begin{cases} +1 & \Delta x > 0 \\ -1 & \Delta x < 0, \end{cases}$$

and so the limit as $\Delta x \to 0$ is not defined.

The function $y = |x|$ has a *kink point* at $x = 0$: although it is *continuous*, it is not *smooth*, i.e. *continuously differentiable* (see figure 1.3).

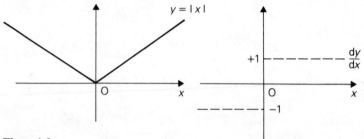

Figure 1.3

An economic example of a function with a kink point is provided by the typical income tax schedule, with an ascending sequence of fixed marginal tax rates. If an income x attracts a tax-free allowance of a, and taxable income $x-a$ is subject to tax at rate m_1 for taxable income up to a threshold b_1, m_2 for taxable income between b_1 and b_2, etc., then we have a *piecewise linear* functional relationship between income x and tax paid $t(x)$, as in figure 1.4. The slope $t'(x)$ is the individual's highest marginal rate of tax; if his taxable income is at a threshold b_j then the tax to be paid on a unit *increase* in income is m_{j+1}, greater than the reduction in liability m_j for a unit *decrease* in income.

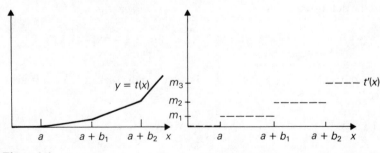

Figure 1.4

At a kink point on a piecewise linear function $y = f(x)$, in fact quite generally, we may define the *left* and *right* *derivatives* of $f(x)$, as:

$$[dy/dx]^- = \lim_{\Delta x \nearrow 0} [f(x + \Delta x) - f(x)]/\Delta x \qquad (1.3)$$

and

$$[dy/dx]^+ = \lim_{\Delta x \searrow 0} [f(x + \Delta x) - f(x)]/\Delta x \qquad (1.4)$$

respectively. These measure the responsiveness of the function $y = f(x)$ to small *decreases* and *increases* in x respectively.

An alternative notation for the (ordinary) derivative of $y = f(x)$, at a point $x = a$, is

$$f'(a) = \lim_{z \to a} [f(z) - f(a)]/(z - a) \qquad (1.5)$$

(put $x = a$, $x + \Delta x = z$ in equation (1.1)). For the left and right derivatives at $x = a$, which are of course equal if $f(x)$ is differentiable at $x = a$, we use $\lim_{z \nearrow a}$ and $\lim_{z \searrow a}$ respectively.

Another very useful property of the derivative is known as the *chain rule*:

1.1.2 Theorem   The chain rule

$$\frac{d}{dx}\{f[g(x)]\} = f'[g(x)]g'(x).$$

Proof   The proof of this rule follows from equation (1.1):

$$\frac{d}{dx}\{f[g(x)]\} = \lim_{\Delta x \to 0} \{f[g(x + \Delta x)] - f[g(x)]\}/\Delta x$$

$$= \lim_{\Delta x \to 0} \{f[g(x + \Delta x)] - f[g(x)]\}/[g(x + \Delta x) - g(x)]$$

$$\times \lim_{\Delta x \to 0} [g(x + \Delta x) - g(x)]/\Delta x.$$

Since g is differentiable, it is continuous, and $g(x + \Delta x) \to g(x)$ as $x \to 0$. Letting $g(x) = u$, $g(x + \Delta x) = u + \Delta u$ we have

$$\frac{d}{dx}\{f[g(x)]\} = \lim_{\Delta u \to 0} [f(u + \Delta u) - f(u)]/\Delta u$$

$$\times \lim_{\Delta x \to 0} [g(x + \Delta x) - g(x)]/\Delta x$$

$$= f'(u)g'(x) = f'[g(x)]g'(x)$$

as claimed.

The chain rule makes differentiating composite functions very straight-forward. Consider for example the derivative of $y = (x^2 + 2x + 3)^{22}$ with respect to x. Let $f(u) = u^{22}$ and $u = g(x) = (x^2 + 2x + 3)$. Then

$$\frac{d}{dx}\{f[g(x)]\} = f'[g(x)]g'(x) = 22(x^2 + 2x + 3)^{21} \cdot (2x + 2).$$

We can treat the derivative dy/dx as a fraction. The chain rule makes this clear. If $y = f(u)$ and $u = g(x)$, so that $y = f[g(x)]$, then $dy/dx = f'[g(x)]g'(x) = f'(u)g'(x)$. This could be written

$$\frac{dy}{dx} = \frac{dy}{du} \cdot \frac{du}{dx}. \tag{1.6}$$

It is just as if the dus cancel.

Further, suppose that two functions f and g are *inverses*, so that $f[g(x)] = x = g[f(x)]$: application of one, and then the other, to a value x returns us to the value x. Again using the chain rule, we find that $f'(x) = 1/g'(y)$, i.e.

$$\frac{dy}{dx} = \frac{1}{dx/dy} \tag{1.7}$$

just as for reciprocals of fractions. In fact we may interpret dx as an infinitesimal shift in x, and dy as the resultant infinitesimal shift in $y = f(x)$ when $x \to x + dx$. These infinitesimal shifts are related by the equation $dy = f'(x)dx$, whence the derivative is indeed a fraction of infinitesimal numbers:

$$f'(x) = \frac{dy}{dx} = dy \div dx. \tag{1.8}$$

We discuss this further in chapter 3.

1.2 THE SECOND DERIVATIVE AND CURVATURE

Having differentiated $y = f(x)$ and obtained $dy/dx = f'(x)$ we can do the same again, and obtain $d^2y/dx^2 = f''(x)$. Just as the first derivative measures the slope or rate of change of $y = f(x)$, so the second derivative measures the rate of change of the slope.

If $y = f(x)$ has the property that $d^2y/dx^2 = f''(x) > 0$ for all x, then *the slope increases as x increases*: see figure 1.5(a), (b). In figure 1.5(a) the large negative slope becomes less negative, which counts as an increase even though the curve is getting flatter. Such a function is said to be *convex*. If

$f''(x) < 0$ for all x the function is *concave*: *its slope decreases as* x *increases*, as in figure 1.5(c), (d).

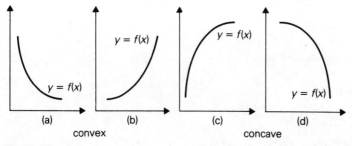

Figure 1.5

If there are ranges of values of x for which $f''(x)$ is positive, and others for which $f''(x)$ is negative, then $y = f(x)$ has convex and concave portions. The second derivative is a useful indicator of curvature (see Exercise 1.2.3(b), p. 9).

Another property that distinguishes concave and convex functions concerns chords drawn to the curve. The chord joining any two points P and Q on the curve in figure 1.5(a) or (b), lies *above* the curve; for figure 1.5(c) and (d) chords lie below the curve. If the co-ordinates of P and Q are $[x, f(x)]$ and $[x', f(x')]$ then points on PQ have co-ordinates which can be parameterized as weighted averages, of the form $[kx + (1-k)x', kf(x) + (1-k)f(x')]$ for $0 < k < 1$. For example $k = \frac{1}{2}$ determines the mid-point of PQ, $k = \frac{1}{3}$ specifies the point one-third of the way from Q to P, etc. See figure 1.6. The point on the graph of the function which lies vertically above/below this parametric point on PQ has co-ordinates $[kx + (1-k)x', f(kx + (1-k)x')]$.

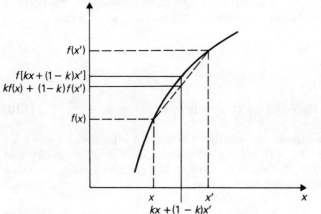

Figure 1.6

This leads to the following characterizations of convexity/concavity:

1.2.1 Definition

$y = f(x)$ is convex if and only if

$$f[kx + (1-k)x'] \leqslant kf(x) + (1-k)f(x')$$

for all x, x' and for all k such that $0 < k < 1$.

1.2.2 Definition

$y = f(x)$ is concave if and only if

$$f[kx + (1-k)x'] \geqslant kf(x) + (1-k)f(x')$$

for all x, x' and for all k such that $0 < k < 1$.

Both of these definitions admit the possibility of equality between $f[kx + (1-k)x']$ and $kf(x) + (1-k)f(x')$. If for two values x and x', $f[kx + (1-k)x'] = kf(x) + (1-k)f(x')$ for every k such that $0 < k < 1$, then $f(.)$ is linear on the interval between x and x'. Thus, according to Definitions 1.2.1 and 1.2.2, linear functions are both concave and convex, and functions with linear portions may be concave or convex. Note that linearity implies a *zero* second derivative. In fact the earlier second derivative criterion needs to be weakened slightly.: if $f''(x) \geqslant$ (respectively, $\leqslant$)0 for all x, then $f(x)$ is convex (respectively concave). An advantage of Definitions 1.2.1 and 1.2.2 is that they apply to non-differentiable functions (see Exercise 1.2.3(c), p. 9); also they generalize readily to functions of several variables (see chapter 3, section 3.7).

We return to second derivatives. A turning point of $y = f(x)$ is a point $x = a$ at which $f'(a) = 0$. It may be a maximum, a minimum or a point of inflection. It is clear from a comparison of figures 1.2 and 1.5 that

$$f'(a) = 0 \quad \text{and} \quad f''(a) < 0 \Rightarrow \text{a maximum at } x = a \tag{1.9}$$

whilst

$$f'(a) = 0 \quad \text{and} \quad f''(a) > 0 \Rightarrow \text{a minimum at } x = a. \tag{1.10}$$

If $f''(a) = 0$ we cannot say whether there is an inflection at $x = a$ or not (see Exercise 1.2.3(a), below). We can derive the full necessary and sufficient conditions for maxima, minima and points of inflection using *Taylor's theorem*, to which we turn next.

1.2.3 Exercises

(a) Sketch the graphs of $y = x^3$, $y = x^4$ and $y = -x^4$ for $-1 \leqslant x \leqslant 1$.

Find d^2y/dx^2. Are any of these functions concave/convex? Deduce that in general, if $x = a$ is a turning point of $y = f(x)$ and $f''(a) = 0$, the turning point could be a maximum, minimum or inflection.

(b) Use derivatives to show that the function $y = x^3 - 9x^2 + 24x + 1$ is increasing for $x < 2$ and $x > 4$, decreasing for $2 < x < 4$, concave for $x < 3$ and convex for $x > 3$. Sketch its graph for $0 \leqslant x \leqslant 5$. What are its maximum and minimum values on this range (take care)?

(c) Convince yourself that the function $y = |x|$ is convex, as is the piecewise linear income tax function $t(x)$ in figure 1.4. What are the second derivatives of these functions, in the ranges where they can be differentiated twice?

1.3 TAYLOR'S THEOREM AND THE TAYLOR SERIES

Suppose that the first n derivatives $f'(x), f''(x), f'''(x)\ldots$ of $f(x)$ exist and are finite in an interval $b < x < c$ (we denote this by $x \in (b, c)$) and that the $(n-1)^{st}$ derivative $f^{(n-1)}(x)$ is continuous for $b \leqslant x \leqslant c$ (denoted $x \in [b, c]$). *Taylor's theorem* says that we may write

$$f(x+a) = f(a) + xf'(a) + x^2f''(a)/2! + \ldots + x^{n-1}f^{(n-1)}(a)/(n-1)! + R_n$$
$$(1.11)$$

whenever $a \in [b, c]$ and $x + a \in [b, c]$, and where

$$R_n = x^n f^{(n)}(a + \theta x)/n! \tag{1.12}$$

for some $\theta \in (0, 1)$.

   Equations (1.11) and (1.12) in Taylor's theorem approximate a function that is n-times-differentiable by a polynomial of degree n, and specify the error R_n that arises in making this approximation. Of course, if f is not once-differentiable (as was the case for $y = |x|$ and the piecewise linear tax function) then we cannot make any such approximation. On the other hand if f is infinitely differentiable we can make the approximation for any n we choose. Furthermore, if

$$\lim_{n \to \infty} R_n = 0 \tag{1.13}$$

whenever $a \in [b, c]$ and $x + a \in [b, c]$ then we may write $f(x+a)$ as a convergent infinite series:

$$f(x+a) = f(a) + xf'(a) + x^2f''(a)/2! + \ldots + x^n f^{(n)}(a)/n! + \ldots. \tag{1.14}$$

The right-hand side of equation (1.14) is known as a *power series* in x, and equation (1.14) itself is called the *Taylor series expansion* of $f(x+a)$ about $f(a)$.

1.3.1 Exercises

(a) Suppose that $f(x)$ is continuous on the interval $[b,c]$ and differentiable on (b,c). Show that there exists a $d \in (b,c)$ such that $[f(c)-f(b)]/(c-b)=f'(d)$. (This result is known as the *intermediate value theorem*: it says that the slope of the chord joining two points on the curve $y = f(x)$ at $x = b$, $x = c$ equals the slope of the function at some intermediate point $x = d$).

(b) Let $t(x)$ be the income tax paid on income x. Assume that $t(0) = 0$ and (unlike the piecewise linear case) that $t(x)$ is twice-differentiable for all x. Suppose further that the marginal tax rate $t'(x)$ increases with income (i.e. $t''(x) > 0$ for all x). Show that the average tax rate $t(x)/x$ increases with income, by noting that $t(y)/y > t(x)/x$ if and only if $[t(y)-t(x)]/(y-x) > t(x)/x$ and applying the intermediate value theorem to $[t(y)-t(x)]/(y-x)$ and to $t(x)/x = [t(x)-t(0)]/(x-0)$.

One of the most important applications of the Taylor expansion of $f(x+a)$ about $f(a)$ occurs when x is very small. Putting $x = \Delta a$, we can approximate the value of the function near to $f(a)$ by ignoring the high powers of Δa which occur in the expansion equation (1.14).

A *first-order approximation* neglects the terms involving $(\Delta a)^2, (\Delta a)^3, \dots$ and simply says:

$$f(a+\Delta a) \doteq f(a)+\Delta a \cdot f'(a) \tag{1.15}$$

which may be re-arranged more recognizably as

$$f'(a) \doteq \frac{f(a+\Delta a)-f(a)}{\Delta a}. \tag{1.16}$$

This is merely an approximate version of the definition of the derivative (see equation (1.1)).

If there is a turning point at $x = a$, then $f'(a) = 0$ and the first-order approximation (1.15) becomes uninformative. We could then go to a *second-order approximation* of the Taylor series:

$$f(a+\Delta a) \doteq f(a)+\Delta a \cdot 0+(\Delta a)^2 f''(a)/2! \tag{1.17}$$

by ignoring only the third- and higher-order terms, the ones involving $(\Delta a)^3$, $(\Delta a)^4$, etc. We see from approximation (1.17) that *the value of the function near the turning point is greater/lower than the turning point value* f(a) *according as* f''(a) *is positive/negative.* Thus we have a minimum/

maximum at $x = a$ according as $f''(a)$ is positive/negative. This confirms conditions (1.9) and (1.10) above: it also offers us an avenue for further exploration of the nature of the turning point if $f''(a) = 0$. For then approximation (1.17) is uninformative, and we may go to the *third-order approximation* of the Taylor series about the turning-point value $f(a)$:

$$f(a+\Delta a) \doteqdot f(a) + (\Delta a)^3 f'''(a)/3!. \tag{1.18}$$

If $f'''(a) \neq 0$ then we cannot have a maximum *or* minimum at $x = a$: for (ignoring $(\Delta a)^4$ etc.) $f(a+\Delta a) - f(a)$ changes sign when Δa changes sign, i.e. depending on whether $x = a + \Delta a$ is to be left or right of $x = a$. Thus $x = a$ must be a point of inflection (as in figure 1.2, case (c) or (d)). If $f'''(a) = 0$ the approximation (1.18) becomes uninformative and we may go to a *fourth-order approximation* of the Taylor series about the turning point value:

$$f(a+\Delta a) \doteqdot f(a) + (\Delta a)^4 f''''(a)/4!. \tag{1.19}$$

As with the second-order approximation, we have a maximum/minimum if $f''''(a)$ is negative/positive (since $(\Delta a)^4$ cannot change sign). If $f''''(a) = 0$ we may go on to consider a *fifth-order approximation*, and so on.

What emerges is a result called the nth *derivative rule*, which we express as a theorem:

1.3.2 Theorem

Suppose that $f'(a) = 0$ and that the first non-zero derivative of $y = f(x)$ at $x = a$ is the nth, $f^{(n)}(a) \neq 0$. If n is *odd* then $x = a$ is a point of inflection; if n is *even* then $x = a$ is a minimum/maximum according as $f^{(n)}(a)$ is positive/negative.

1.3.3 Exercises

(a) What is the nature of the turning point at $x = 0$ of each of the functions $y = \pm x^n$ for $n = 2, 3, 4, 5, 6, 7, \ldots$?

(b) Obtain the Taylor series expansion for $y = \sqrt{x}$ when $a = 100$. Derive an approximate value of $\sqrt{103}$.

The first-order Taylor series approximation of $f(x+a)$ in expression (1.15) simply estimates $f(x+a)$ by linear projection from $f(a)$, taking account of the slope: see figure 1.7. The second-order approximation, namely

$$f(x+a) \doteqdot f(a) + xf'(a) + x^2 f''(a)/2! \tag{1.20}$$

incorporates an allowance for curvature, through the term $f''(a)$. The

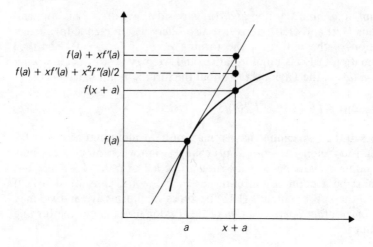

Figure 1.7

higher the order of approximation we take, the closer we get to $f(x+a)$. The residual after an nth-order approximation is R_n, and this approaches zero as $n \to \infty$ if the infinite Taylor series expansion upon which we base these approximations is valid.

1.4 THE EXPONENTIAL AND LOGARITHM FUNCTIONS

Two important functions for economics are the *exponential* and *logarithm* functions. Indeed they are the only algebraic functions used regularly in Part II of this book. The exponential function, $y = \exp(x)$, may be defined in several ways. One approach is via limits:

$$\exp(x) = \lim_{n \to \infty} \left(1 + \frac{x}{n}\right)^n. \tag{1.21}$$

Then $\exp(x) > 0$ for all x (if $x < 0$, the right-hand side of equation (1.21) becomes positive for $n > |x|$, and thus is positive in the limit). Also

$$\exp(ab) = \lim_{n \to \infty} \left(1 + \frac{ab}{n}\right)^n = \lim_{mb \to \infty} \left(1 + \frac{a}{m}\right)^{mb}$$

$$= \left[\lim_{m \to \infty} \left(1 + \frac{a}{m}\right)^m\right]^b = \exp(a)^b,$$

writing $n = mb$; therefore $\exp(x) = \exp(1)^x$. Writing $\exp(1) = e \; (\doteq 2.718281828)$ we have $\exp(x) = e^x$. Expanding the right-hand side of equation (1.21) and taking limits, term by term, we get the convergent series

$$y = \exp(x) = e^x = 1 + x + x^2/2! + x^3/3! + x^4/4! + \dots \qquad (1.22)$$

which provides an alternative definition of the exponential function.

We may differentiate the infinite series in equation (1.22) term by term. (Such term-by-term procedures are not always legal; they are in this case; see Apostol (1974, chapters 8 and 9), for a rigorous statement of the validating conditions.) Thus we have

$$\frac{d}{dx}(e^x) = 0 + 1 + \frac{2x}{2!} + \frac{3x^2}{3!} + \frac{4x^3}{4!} + \dots$$

or,

$$\frac{d}{dx}[e^x] = e^x. \qquad (1.23)$$

As the *value* of the function $y = e^x$ increases, so does the *rate* at which it increases, and the two measures are equal. See figure 1.8, where the ordinate at A equals the slope at A equals e^a.

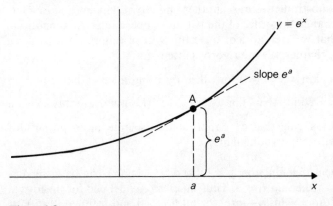

Figure 1.8

By the chain rule, we have

$$\frac{d}{dx}[e^{f(x)}] = f'(x)e^{f(x)} \qquad (1.24)$$

for any differentiable function $f(x)$.

The exponential function is infinitely differentiable: by repeatedly applying equation (1.23) we see that $f^{(n)}(x) = e^x$ for all x. Therefore we may apply Taylor's theorem. Put $f(x) = \exp(x)$ and $a = 0$ in equation (1.11). Since $f^{(n)}(0) = 1$ for all n, the Taylor formula says:

$$e^x = 1 + x + \frac{x^2}{2!} + \frac{x^3}{3!} + \ldots + \frac{x^{n-1}}{(n-1)!} + R_n$$

where $R_n = x^n \, e^{\theta x}/n!$. This remainder term can be shown to approach zero as $n \to \infty$ for any x and θ; thus the infinite series for $y = e^x$ given in equation (1.22) is in fact its Taylor series expansion.

1.4.1 Exercises

(a) Show from the definition in equation (1.1) that

$$\frac{d}{dx}(e^x) = e^x \cdot \lim_{\Delta x \to 0} \left[\frac{(e^{\Delta x} - 1)}{\Delta x} \right].$$

Now substitute on the right-hand side for $e^{\Delta x}$ from equation (1.22) and show that $\lim_{\Delta x \to 0} [(e^{\Delta x} - 1)/\Delta x] = 1$. (This is another generally dubious mathematical operation: equation (1.22) expresses $e^{\Delta x}$ as the *limit of a series*, and we substitute this into another limit, to obtain an *iterated limit*; we then interchange the order of the two limit operations. As economists we may feel that we are entitled to do this sort of thing: but, again, see Apostol (1974, chapter 8), for a rigorous discussion).

(b) Show that $\lim_{x \to \infty} x^n e^{-x} = 0$ for all n, by using a series like equation (1.22) for e^{-x}. Deduce that $\lim_{x \to \infty} x^{-n} e^x = \infty$. (Loosely, we may explain these results by saying that $e^{\pm x}$ approaches its limit 'more powerfully' than any power of x/polynomial in x).

The *natural logarithm* function, $y = \ln(x)$ or $y = \log(x)$, can be defined as follows: if $e^a = b$ then $\ln(b) = a$. Thus $\ln(x)$ is only defined for positive x. In particular $\ln(bc) = \ln(b) + \ln(c)$ for all $b, c > 0$ and $\ln(b^c) = c \ln(b)$ for all c and all $b > 0$. The property

$$\ln[\exp(x)] = x = \exp[\ln(x)]$$

shows that the exponential and natural logarithm functions are inverses: recall the discussion preceding equation (1.7). From equation (1.7),

$$\exp'[\ln(x)] = \frac{1}{\ln'(x)} \quad \text{and} \quad \ln'[\exp(x)] = \frac{1}{\exp'(x)}.$$

Since exp' = exp, we have

$$\frac{d}{dx}[\ln(x)] = \frac{1}{x} \tag{1.25}$$

for all x. A different application of the chain rule gives us

$$\frac{d}{dx}\{\ln[f(x)]\} = \frac{f'(x)}{f(x)} \tag{1.26}$$

for any differentiable $f(x) > 0$.

Since for any $a > 0$ we may write

$$a^x = \exp[\ln(a^x)] = \exp[x\ln(a)]$$

an easy application of equation (1.26) yields the very useful rule of differentiation:

$$\frac{d}{dx}[a^x] = a^x \cdot \ln(a). \tag{1.27}$$

This generalizes equation (1.23).

1.4.2 Exercises

(a) If $f(x) = \ln(x)$ what is $f^{(n)}(x)$? Show that $\ln(1+x)$ can be written as a convergent series $\ln(1+x) = x - x^2/2 + x^3/3 - x^4/4 + \ldots$ provided $\lim[x/(1+\theta x)]^n/n = 0$ for all $\theta \in (0, 1)$. Differentiate this series term by term: do you recognize the binomial expansion of $(1+x)^{-1}$?

(b) Satisfy yourself, by differentiating the continuous function

$$f(x) = \begin{cases} \exp(-1/x^2) & x \neq 0 \\ 0 & x = 0 \end{cases}$$

a few times, that for $a \neq 0$ each derivative $f^{(n)}(a)$ is a sum of terms of the form $c_m \exp(-1/a^2)/a^m$ for certain constants c_m and integers m. Use Exercise 1.4.1(b) to conclude that as $a \to 0$, $f^{(n)}(a) \to 0$. What happens to the series

$$f(a) + xf'(a) + x^2 f''(a)/2! + \ldots + x^n f^{(n)}(a)/n! + \ldots$$

as $a \to 0$? Does it converge to the same value as does $f(x+a)$? If not, why not?

1.5 SOME ECONOMIC APPLICATIONS OF DIFFERENTIATION

In this section we sketch some simple applications of differentiation, looking at topics which range from the conditions for profit maximization to properties of income tax revenue.

1.5.1 Example   Total and marginal cost and revenue

Let $C(Q)$ be the total cost of producing an output of Q units of a good. Suppose that the unit of measure is small enough relative to the magnitude of Q that we can represent $C(Q)$ as a smooth function, as in figure 1.9. For example, Q may be measured in millions. Then the marginal cost of producing the $(Q+1)^{st}$ unit is

$$C(Q+1)-C(Q) = BC = BC/AB \doteq \text{slope at } A = C'(Q) \qquad (1.28)$$

since $AB = 1$. If the good in question is *infinitely divisible*, for example it could be lengths of cloth or lead for propelling pencils, then we define the marginal cost, not as the cost of producing an extra inch, or foot, etc., which would be arbitrary, but as the *rate* of increase of cost $[C(Q+\Delta Q)-C(Q)]/\Delta Q$ for a 'marginal' increase in output. Again the derivative $C'(Q) = dC/dQ$ is the measure of marginal cost.

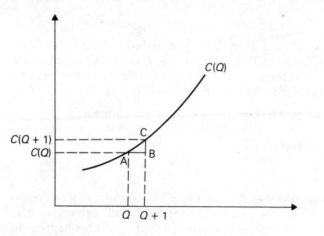

Figure 1.9

Similarly if $R(Q)$ is the total revenue accruing to the firm from the sale of Q units of output, and if $R(Q)$ can be assumed smooth, then marginal revenue is $R'(Q)$. Total profit is $\pi(Q) = R(Q)-C(Q)$ and for profit to be maximized at $Q = Q_0$ we require $\pi'(Q_0) = 0$, i.e. $R'(Q_0) = C'(Q_0)$, a familiar condition. A sufficient condition that $Q = Q_0$ represents profit *maximization*, and not profit minimization or an inflection of the function $\pi(Q)$, is that $\pi''(Q_0) < 0$ (see condition (1.9)) equivalently $R''(Q_0) < C''(Q_0)$. This is guaranteed if the marginal cost curve cuts the marginal revenue curve *from below* at $Q = Q_0$, e.g. if marginal cost slopes upwards $(C''(Q) > 0)$ and marginal revenue downwards $(R''(Q) < 0)$ at $Q = Q_0$.

1.5.2 Example   Growth through time

Another use of the derivative to approximate an increment to a function is in the dynamic context. For example, let $K(t)$ denote the economy's (or a firm's) capital stock in period t. In the next period it is $K(t+1)$. The increment equals investment during period t net of depreciation, which we might assume to take place at a constant proportionate rate b:

$$K(t+1) - K(t) = I(t) - bK(t). \tag{1.29}$$

If we are prepared to model time periods at very short (fleeting, even, so that time becomes *continuous* rather than *discrete*) then we can bring the differential (and integral) calculus to bear by assuming $K(t)$ is differentiable and writing equation (1.29) as

$$K'(t) = I(t) - bK(t) \tag{1.30}$$

(in some books this would be $\dot{K} = I - bK$). This is a *differential equation* whereas equation (1.29) is a *difference equation*. The mathematics is generally simpler if time is continuous, but continuous-time models do not proceed step by step. In particular we lose the notion of a time period *per se*, and can no longer distinguish at what points within a time period things happen (investment may take place at the beginning of each time period, depreciation at the end; expectations may get formed at one point, and markets clear at another, etc.). See Buiter (1980) for an interesting discussion of aspects of this issue.

1.5.3 Exercises

(a) Show that the differential equation (1.30) can be written in the form

$$\frac{d}{dt}[e^{bt}K(t)] = e^{bt}I(t).$$

(b) If $I(t) = I_0$ for all t, show that for every constant a, $K(t) = a(1-b)^t + I_0/b$ is a solution to equation (1.29) and $K(t) = ae^{-bt} + I_0/b$ is a solution to equation (1.30).

(c) In a discrete time model a variable $X(t)$ grows at a *constant proportionate rate* g if $[X(t+1)-X(t)]/X(t) = g$ for all $t = 0, 1, 2, \ldots$. Show that this implies $X(t) = X_0(1+g)^t$. If time is continuous the equivalent statement is $X'(t)/X(t) = g$ for all t. Show that $X(t) = X_0 e^{gt}$ is a solution to this differential equation (such an $X(t)$ is said to be *growing exponentially*, and g is the (constant) *exponential growth rate*).

(d) If $K(t)$ has exponential growth rate g and equation (1.30) holds, deduce that investment must satisfy $I(t) = (g+b)K(t)$. Can you interpret this?

1.5.4 Example   Elasticities

Let the quantity demanded of a good at price P be $Q = Q(P)$. Assuming differentiability, the condition for the demand curve to be downward-sloping is $Q'(P) < 0$. The *price elasticity of demand* measures the responsiveness of Q to changes in P. Suppose that $P \rightarrow P+\Delta P$, $Q \rightarrow Q+\Delta Q$. Since these changes are in opposite directions we define the elasticity, which is the percentage effect on quantity demanded for each 1% change in price, *with a minus sign*, as

$$\frac{-(100\Delta Q/Q)}{(100\Delta P/P)} = \frac{-(P/Q)\Delta Q}{\Delta P} \geqslant 0. \tag{1.31}$$

This is an *arc elasticity*, being dependent upon the particular change ΔP that provoked the change in demand. The *point measure* of elasticity, or *instantaneous elasticity* is the limit of equation (1.31) as $\Delta P \rightarrow 0$:

$$e_{Q,P} = \frac{-(P/Q)\,dQ}{dP} = \frac{-PQ'(P)}{Q(P)} \geqslant 0. \tag{1.32}$$

Generally, if Y is a differentiable function of X, we may define

$$e_{Y,X} = (X/Y)\left|\frac{dY}{dX}\right| \geqslant 0 \tag{1.33}$$

as the instantaneous elasticity of Y with respect to X.

A useful result for the estimation of price elasticities of demand (and indeed for other elasticities too, see on) is the following:

$$e_{Q,P} = \frac{-d[\ln(Q)]}{d[\ln(P)]}. \tag{1.34}$$

The proof is easy using the chain rule:

$$\frac{d[\ln(Q)]}{d[\ln(P)]} = \frac{d[\ln(Q)]}{dQ} \times \frac{dQ}{dP} \times \frac{dP}{d[\ln(P)]}$$

$$= \left(\frac{d[\ln(Q)]}{dQ} \times \frac{dQ}{dP}\right) \div \left(\frac{d[\ln(P)]}{dP}\right)$$

$$= \left(\frac{P}{Q}\right)\frac{dQ}{dP}. \tag{1.35}$$

Thus if $\ln(Q) = a + b.\ln(P)$ then the price elasticity of demand is constant and equal to b. Assuming constancy, elasticity can be estimated from a given set of prices and quantities by regressing $\ln(Q)$ on $\ln(P)$.

The total revenue function of Example 1.5.1 is $R(Q) = PQ$, so that marginal revenue is

$$MR = R'(Q) = P + Q(dP/dQ) = P + Q/(dQ/dP)$$

i.e.

$$MR = P\left(1 - \frac{1}{e_{Q,P}}\right). \tag{1.36}$$

This is a useful formula. Revenue is maximized where $R'(Q) = MR = 0$ (i.e. by equation (1.36)), where price elasticity of demand is unity, $e_{Q,P} = 1$. A price-discriminating monopolist, who determines the quantities of his product to be transacted in a number of demand-differentiated markets to equate his marginal revenues, sets a high price where demand is very inelastic and the lowest price where demand is most elastic: again, this is evident from equation (1.36).

Elasticity is a valuable measure of responsiveness for many other functional relationships of economic interest. Consider for example the income tax. Let total personal income be X and let total income tax revenue be T. Suppose that people's incomes are growing equiproportionately through time, and that there are no changes taking place in the tax schedule. Then there is a well-defined relationship $T = T(X)$ between total revenue and total income. In view of the discussion above, the elasticity $e_{T,X}$ could be estimated by log-linear regression (assuming it is constant). This elasticity (about 1.7 for the UK) estimates by what percentage tax revenue will grow for each 1 % increase in people's incomes; it is a useful ready-reckoner for the effects on tax revenue of inflation, for example. An approach to measuring $e_{T,X}$ that avoids the constancy assumption and some of the statistical problems of the regression exercise, and which uses results in the *multivariate calculus*, is outlined in chapter 3 (see the discussion around equation (3.48), p. 97). See also a strikingly simple result, that uses *integration*, in Exercise 1.8.4(b), p. 31.

1.6 THE INTEGRAL

Let $y = f(x)$ be a function defined at each value of x in an interval $[a, b]$. We denote by

$$\int_a^b f(x)\,dx \qquad\qquad (1.37)$$

the area bounded by the curve $y = f(x)$, the x-axis and the lines $x = a$ and $x = b$ (see figure 1.10). This is the *integral of* f(x) *between* x = a *and* x = b.

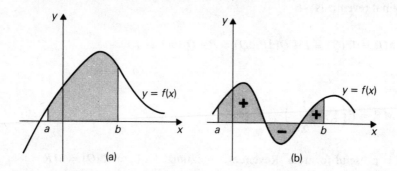

Figure 1.10

Area above the x-axis counts positively, and area below counts negatively. Thus in figure 1.10(b) the net value of $\int_a^b f(x)\,dx$ could be positive, zero or negative depending on the relative magnitudes of the offsetting areas marked.

A function $y = f(x)$ need not be continuous for its integral to exist. If there were a vertical step within the range $[a, b]$, the area could still be defined. But some functions cannot be integrated. For example, it is hard to envisage what we could mean by the integral of the function

$$f(x) = \begin{cases} 1 & \text{if } x \text{ is rational} \\ 0 & \text{if } x \text{ is irrational} \end{cases}$$

over *any* range $[a, b]$. (A rational number is a fraction p/q where p, q are both integers; the graph of this function consists of two parallel dotted lines $y = 0$ and $y = 1$, the dots on one line being vertically aligned with the gaps on the other. All the dots and gaps are infinitesimal in length!)

Roughly, for a function $y = f(x)$ to be *Riemann integrable* (or, simply, *integrable*) over an interval $[a, b]$, a common limit must exist of all summations

$$\sum_{i=1}^{n-1} f(z_i)(x_{i+1}-x_i) \tag{1.38}$$

for all *partitions*

$$a = x_1 < x_2 < \ldots < x_{n-1} < x_n = b \tag{1.39}$$

of the interval $[a,b]$ into n sub-intervals $[x_i, x_{i+1}]$, and for all $z_i \in [x_i, x_{i+1}]$, as $n \to \infty$ and each sub-interval becomes vanishingly small (see Apostol (1974, chapter 7) for a formal treatment). We note that all continuous functions are integrable (this includes all differentiable functions), and that if $f(x)$ and $g(x)$ are integrable over $[a,b]$ then so are $f(x)+g(x)$ and $f(x)g(x)$.

There are other types of integral. Two which are generalizations of the Riemann integral, and are of interest to economists in some specialized contexts, are the *Riemann–Stieltjes* and *Lebesque* integrals. These do not measure area as the Riemann integral does. For a simplified treatment of these integrals, see Lambert and Poskitt (1983, chapter 3).

Two rules of Riemann integration that stem from the formal definition, and are intuitively appealing, are as follows:

$$\int_a^b [f(x)+g(x)]\,\mathrm{d}x = \int_a^b f(x)\,\mathrm{d}x + \int_a^b g(x)\,\mathrm{d}x \tag{1.40}$$

for all integrable $f(x)$ and $g(x)$, and

$$\int_a^b f(x)\,\mathrm{d}x = \int_a^c f(x)\,\mathrm{d}x + \int_c^b f(x)\,\mathrm{d}x \tag{1.41}$$

for any integrable $f(x)$ and for each $c \in (a,b)$.

In fact result (1.41) holds for *all* c, if we adopt the general convention that for

$$d > e \qquad \int_d^e f(x)\,\mathrm{d}x = -\int_e^d f(x)\,\mathrm{d}x. \tag{1.42}$$

The summand $f(z_i)(x_{i+1}-x_i)$ in expression (1.38) is the area of the rectangle with base $[x_i, x_{i+1}]$ and height $f(z_i)$. The summation clearly approximates the area we require: see figure 1.11. The notation $\int_a^b f(x)\,\mathrm{d}x$ becomes more understandable if we imagine that in the limit each sub-interval $[x_i, x_{i+1}]$ becomes infinitesimal, of the form $[x, x+\mathrm{d}x]$ for some $x \in [a,b]$, and if we regard the integral sign $\int_a^b$ as performing an infinite summation of the resultant infinitesimal areas $f(x)\,dx$ over the continuum of x-values from $x = a$ to $x = b$.

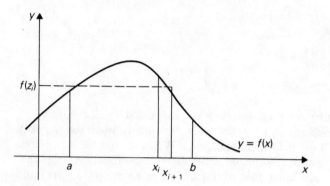

Figure 1.11

This interpretation of the integral as the summation over a continuum is central to many economic applications, as we shall see.

As a matter of notation we could as well write $\int_a^b f(t)\,dt$ as $\int_a^b f(x)\,dx$, for the integral of $y = f(.)$ over the interval $[a, b]$: the t serves the same purpose as the x.

An important theorem, which connects integration with differentiation, is the following:

1.6.1 Theorem

If $f(x)$ is integrable over $[a, b]$ and $A(x) = \int_a^x f(t)\,dt$, then $A(x)$ is differentiable and $A'(x) = f(x)$ for every $x \in (a, b)$.

Proof   It is immediate from the definition of the function $A(x)$ and from equation (1.41) that $A(x + \Delta x) - A(x) = \int_x^{x+\Delta x} f(t)\,dt$ whenever Δx is small enough that $x + \Delta x \in (a, b)$. That is, $A(x + \Delta x) - A(x)$ is the area under $y = f(t)$ between $t = x$ and $t = x + \Delta x$. The area of this thin strip is approximately $f(x)\Delta x$, the approximation getting better as $x \to 0$. Thus $[A(x + \Delta x) - A(x)]/\Delta x \doteq f(x)$. Letting $\Delta x \to 0$ we obtain the result, $A'(x) = f(x)$.

This result has several implications. Note first that we could write it as:

$$A(x) = \int_a^x A'(t)\,dt \tag{1.43}$$

or as:

$$\frac{d}{dx}\int_a^x f(t)\,dt = f(x). \tag{1.44}$$

This shows differentiation and integration to be *inverses* of each other; if we *differentiate* the function $A(t)$ and then *integrate* up to $t = x$, we recover the value $A(x)$ – and if we *integrate* the function $f(t)$ up to $t = x$ and then *differentiate*, we recover the value $f(x)$. Whilst the first of these statements is specific to the function $A(x)$, the second is quite general, and provides a guide as to how we might carry out integration in practice: the value of an integral $\int_a^b f(t)\,dt$ is the value at $x = b$ of some function of x whose derivative is $f(x)$.

1.6.2 Definition

An *indefinite integral* of a function $y = f(x)$ is any function $F(x)$ such that $F'(x) = f(x)$.

For example e^x is an indefinite integral of e^x for all x (as is, equally, $e^x + c$ for any constant c), and $\ln(x)$ is an indefinite integral of $1/x$ for all $x > 0$: see equations (1.23) and (1.25). Indefinite integrals can be difficult to find, and for some functions they do not exist. But they *do* exist for integrable functions, as Theorem 1.6.1 showed.

1.6.3 Theorem

If $F(x)$ is any indefinite integral for an integrable function $f(x)$ then $\int_a^b f(x)\,dx = F(b) - F(a)$.

Proof If two functions $u(x)$ and $v(x)$ have the same derivative everywhere then they differ by a constant. This is virtually self-evident, but also follows directly from the intermediate value theorem (see Exercise 1.3.1(a)). Now by Theorem 1.6.1, $A(x) = \int_a^x f(t)\,dt$ is an indefinite integral for $f(x)$ on the interval (a, b), as is $F(x)$ by supposition. Both have derivative $f(x)$. Thus

$$\int_a^x f(t)\,dt = F(x) + c \tag{1.45}$$

for some c and for all $x \in (a, b)$. By continuity (1.45) holds at $x = a$ and $x = b$. Thus $c = -F(a)$ and the result follows.

1.6.4 Exercises

(a) Verify that an indefinite integral for $f(x) = \ln(x)$ is $F(x) = x \ln(x) - x$.

(b) Show that if $f(x)$ is integrable over an interval $[b, c]$ then $\int_b^c f(t)\,dt = (c - b)f(d)$ for some $d \in (b, c)$. (*Hint:* apply the intermediate value theorem of Exercise 1.3.1(a) to any indefinite integral $F(x)$ of $f(x)$.) This result is known as the *intermediate value theorem for integration*: it says that the area beneath $y = f(x)$ between $x = b$ and $x = c$ is the same as the area of a rectangle with base $[b, c]$ and height equal to some value of the function between $x = b$ and $x = c$.

(c) Suppose that $f(x)$ is continuous and that $\int_a^b f(x)g(x)\,dx = 0$ for *every* continuous function $g(x)$ defined on $[a,b]$. Show that $f(x)$ must be equal to zero for all $x \in [a,b]$. (*Hint*: suppose for a contradiction that there is a sub-interval $[c,d]$ on which $f(x)$ is either strictly positive or strictly negative. If this is not so, $f(x)$ must be identically zero. Now show that $\int_c^d f(x)h(x)\,dx = 0$ for every continuous function $h(x)$ defined on the interval $[c,d]$, and apply the intermediate value theorem for integration.)

1.7 EVALUATING INTEGRALS

We sketch briefly here, mainly by means of examples, some of the techniques most widely used in evaluating integrals. The basic result is, of course, that of Theorem 1.6.3, which may be written in the form:

$$\int_a^b f(x)\,dx = \int_a^b F'(x)\,dx = F(b) - F(a) = F(x)\Big|_a^b. \tag{1.46}$$

To integrate any function $f(x)$ between $x = a$ and $x = b$, it is simply a matter of determining an indefinite integral $F(x)$ and evaluating this at the two end-points $x = a$ and $x = b$.

For example, if $a, b > 0$ then

$$\int_a^b \left[\frac{1}{x}\right] dx = \ln(x)\Big|_a^b = \ln\left(\frac{b}{a}\right),$$

because an indefinite integral for $1/x$ is $\ln(x)$.

Some seemingly intractable integrals become more transparent after a change of variables. For example consider the integral

$$I = \int_a^b x^2 (1 - x^3)^{\frac{2}{3}}\,dx \tag{1.47}$$

whose value may not be clear at first sight. Let $t = 1 - x^3$, so that $dt/dx = -3x^2$. Regarding this derivative as a ratio of infinitesimals, we may write $dt = -3x^2\,dx$. Now replace the terms $x^2\,dx$ and $(1-x^3)^{\frac{2}{3}}$ in equation (1.47) by corresponding terms involving t, and change the limits of integration:

$$I = \int_{1-a}^{1-b} (-t^{\frac{2}{3}}/3)\,dt = -t^{\frac{5}{3}}/5\Big|_{1-a}^{1-b}. \tag{1.48}$$

The value of I is immediately obvious. This is an example of *integration by substitution*. The formal rule that underpins this technique is as follows: if

$x = g(t)$ is a *function whose derivative* g'(t) *does not change sign* then:

$$\int_{g(u)}^{g(v)} f(x)\,dx = \int_{u}^{v} f[g(t)]g'(t)\,dt. \tag{1.49}$$

An integral of the form

$$\int_{a}^{b} f'(x)g(x)\,dx \tag{1.50}$$

where one factor in the integrand, $f'(x)$, is recognizable as a derivative but there is also another factor $g(x)$, can sometimes be manipulated to advantage using *integration by parts*. Specifically, we may integrate the recognizable term $f'(x)$ and differentiate the other term, provided we change the sign of the resulting new integral and make another adjustment, as follows.

1.7.1 Theorem   Integration by parts

For any differentiable functions $f(x), g(x)$ we have

$$\int_{a}^{b} f'(x)g(x)\,dx = - \int_{a}^{b} f(x)g'(x)\,dx + f(x)g(x)\Big|_{a}^{b}.$$

Proof   Integrate from $x = a$ to $x = b$ the equation

$$\frac{d}{dx}[f(x)g(x)] = f'(x)g(x) + f(x)g'(x),$$

and re-arrange.

Integration by parts does not provide a recipe for *calculating* $\int_{a}^{b} f'(x)g(x)\,dx$; but it does enable the integral to be *expressed differently*, and this can result in a more tractable form. As will be seen, integration by parts is a particularly fruitful device for re-formulating certain economic problems.

As an example, consider $\int_{1}^{10} x \ln(x)\,dx$. We recognize, within the integrand, the factor x as a derivative (of $x^2/2$). Integrating by parts, we have

$$\int_{1}^{10} x \ln(x)\,dx = - \int_{1}^{10} \left(\frac{x^2}{2}\right)\cdot\left(\frac{1}{x}\right) dx + \left[\frac{x^2 \ln(x)}{2}\right]_{1}^{10}$$

$$= \left[\frac{-x^2}{4} + \frac{x^2 \ln(x)}{2}\right]_{1}^{10}.$$

Now consider $\int_{a}^{b} \ln(x)\,dx$ where $a, b > 0$. We may write this as $\int_{a}^{b} 1 \cdot \ln(x)\,dx$

and integrate the 1, differentiate the $\ln(x)$. Thus:

$$\int_a^b 1 \cdot \ln(x)\,dx = -\int_a^b x \cdot (1/x)\,dx + [x\ln(x)]_a^b = [-x + x\ln(x)]_a^b.$$

This result is confirmed by Exercise 1.6.4(a).

Finally, although we have throughout confined our attention to integrating *bounded* functions $y = f(x)$ over *finite* intervals $[a,b]$, we can extend the definition of the integral, using limits, to unbounded functions and infinite ranges of integration. Such integrals are known as *improper integrals*: they measure areas which may be infinite. For example, an infinite range of integration *may* result in an infinite area:

$$\int_a^\infty e^t\,dt = \lim_{X \to \infty} \int_a^X e^t\,dt = \lim_{X \to \infty} [e^X - e^a] = \infty \tag{1.51}$$

but this need not be the case:

$$\int_a^\infty e^{-t}\,dt = \lim_{X \to \infty} \int_a^X e^{-t}\,dt = \lim_{X \to \infty} [-e^{-X} + e^{-a}] = e^{-a}. \tag{1.52}$$

The first of these is a *divergent* improper integral, the second a *convergent* improper integral. We deal in a similar way with integrals in which the integrand becomes infinite in the range of integration. Such improper integrals may also be convergent:

$$\int_0^1 t^{-\frac{1}{2}}\,dt = \lim_{X \downarrow 0} \int_X^1 t^{-\frac{1}{2}}\,dt = \lim_{X \downarrow 0} [2t^{\frac{1}{2}}]_X^1 = 2 \tag{1.53}$$

or divergent:

$$\int_0^1 t^{-2}\,dt = \lim_{X \downarrow 0} \int_X^1 t^{-2}\,dt = \lim_{X \downarrow 0} [-t^{-1}]_X^1 = \infty. \tag{1.54}$$

1.7.2 Exercises

(a) Evaluate $\int_a^b [1/x]\,dx$ when $a < 0$ and $b < 0$ (what is the derivative of $\ln(-x)$ if $x < 0$?). What can you say if $a < 0$ and $b > 0$?

(b) Use integration by substitution to calculate $\int_0^1 [x^3/(x^4 + 1)]\,dx$ and $\int_0^1 (2x + 3)(x^2 + 3x - 4)^{122}\,dx$. (Make the substitutions $t = x^4 + 1$ and $t = x^2 + 3x - 4$ respectively.) Could you calculate

$$\int_{-4}^1 (2x + 3)(x^2 + 3x - 4)^{122}\,dx$$

using this latter substitution? Try it.

(c) Evaluate $\int_0^1 x\,e^x\,dx$ and $\int_0^1 x(1+x)^{\frac{1}{2}}\,dx$ using integration by parts. (In each case choose a factor to integrate and one to differentiate: try to simplify, not complicate, the integral.)

(d) Show that the 'doubly improper' integral $\int_0^\infty x^{-\frac{1}{3}}\,dx$ diverges by splitting it into two parts, and evaluating each as the limit of an integral of a bounded function over a finite range.

(e) Assuming that $I(s) = \int_0^\infty x^s e^{-x}$ is finite for all s, use integration by parts to prove that $I(s) = sI(s-1)$ (you will need to use Exercise 1.4.1(b)).

1.8 SOME ECONOMIC APPLICATIONS OF INTEGRATION

In this section we look at some of the ways in which integrals are used in economics.

1.8.1 Example   Marginal cost and total variable cost

If the good being produced is infinitely divisible, and the total cost function is $C(Q)$, the marginal cost function is $C'(Q)$ (see Example 1.5.1). This expresses the *rate* at which total cost increases: we interpret $C'(Q)\,dQ$ as the increment to costs when output is increased from Q to $Q+dQ$. Then $\int_0^{\bar{Q}} C'(Q)\,dQ$ is the aggregated cost of producing output $\bar{Q}$. In fact

$$\int_0^{\bar{Q}} C'(Q)\,dQ = C(\bar{Q}) - C(0) \tag{1.55}$$

by Theorem 1.6.3 (see also equation (1.46)). Thus *the integral of the marginal cost function is the total variable cost function*: fixed costs $C(0)$ get netted out.

1.8.2 Example   Problems in continuous time

In chapter 7 we shall encounter dynamic economic models in which the evolution of variables through continuous time is described by differential equations. Recall the capital stock example, in Exercise 1.5.2 and equation (1.30). If $K(t)$ is a firm's capital stock at moment t, let $P[K(t)]$ be the *rate of profit* earnable. By 'rate of profit' we mean that profits accruing in the time interval $[t, t+dt]$ are $P[K(t)]\,dt$. Similarly, let $C[I(t)]\,dt$ be the cost of undertaking investment at rate $I(t)$ in the time interval $[t, t+dt]$. The firm's objective, when planning its activities at time $t = 0$, for the period from $t = 0$ to $t = T$, say, could be to maximize the *discounted present value* of its net profit stream. In discrete time this would involve applying discount factors $1/(1+r), 1/(1+r)^2, 1/(1+r)^3 \ldots$ to net profits in periods $1, 2, 3 \ldots$; in continuous time the equivalent operation is to discount net profit in time interval $[t, t+dt]$ by the factor e^{-rt} (look again at Exercise 1.5.3(c)). Then the firm maximizes

$$\int_0^T e^{-rt}\{P[K(t)] - C[I(t)]\}\, dt \tag{1.56}$$

subject to differential equation (1.30) being satisfied. We address this quite sophisticated problem, and others like it which invoke integration to compute the present value of a utility stream in chapter 7.

1.8.3 Example   Aggregating across an income distribution

Consider a population of P income recipients. If P is very large we could model the P incomes along the continuum $[0, \infty)$ by specifying a *frequency density function* $f(x)$ for income. This is defined in such a way that for any infinitesimal number dx, the proportion of the population whose incomes lie in the interval $[x, x+dx]$ is $f(x)\, dx$ (and the number of such incomes is $Pf(x)\, dx$). The function $f(x)$ would normally be continuous, and it behaves rather like a probability density function. Thus if $u(x)$ is any attribute of income x (e.g. $u(x) = x$ itself, or $u(x) =$ utility of income x, etc.), then the average value of $u(x)$ across the population is

$$\bar{u} = \int_0^\infty u(x) f(x)\, dx \tag{1.57}$$

and the total value is $P\bar{u}$. The integral sign is performing an infinite summation of infinitesimals.

In particular, total income is

$$X = P \int_0^\infty x f(x)\, dx \tag{1.58}$$

and if $t(x)$ is the tax liability of an income x then total income tax revenue is

$$T = T(X) = P \int_0^\infty t(x) f(x)\, dx. \tag{1.59}$$

Supposing that all incomes grow equiproportionately, in fact that $x \to kx$ for all x, tax revenue becomes:

$$T(kX) = P \int_0^\infty t(kx) f(x)\, dx \tag{1.60}$$

The $Pf(x)dx$ incomes that were in the interval $[x, x+dx]$ each pay tax $t(kx)$ instead of $t(x)$. Now treat the left- and right-hand sides of equation (1.60) as functions of k, and differentiate. This involves differentiating 'under the integral sign' on the right-hand side, an operation that is not always valid; see Apostol (1974, p. 167). It is valid in this case if $t(x)$ is differentiable and $t'(x)$ is continuous. Then we have:

$$XT'(kX) = P \int_0^\infty xt'(kx)f(x)dx. \tag{1.61}$$

Now set $k = 1$ and divide equation (1.61) by equation (1.58):

$$e_{T,X} = XT'(X)/T(X) = \int_0^\infty xt'(x)f(x)dx \bigg/ \int_0^\infty t(x)f(x)dx. \tag{1.62}$$

This is an expression for income tax revenue elasticity which may readily be calculated, given mathematical forms for the income distribution and tax schedule (see Exercise 1.8.4(b), p. 31).

Now let $F(x)$ be the *distribution function* for income,

$$F(x) = \int_0^x f(t)dt. \tag{1.63}$$

This defines the proportion of income recipients with incomes not exceeding x. For each $0 \leqslant p \leqslant 1$ let

$$p = F(y). \tag{1.64}$$

Then an individual with income y is ranked $100p\%$ of the way up the income distribution. The total income of the bottom $100p\%$ of income recipients is:

$$X(p) = P \int_0^y xf(x)dx. \tag{1.65}$$

The *Lorenz curve* for the distribution, $\theta(p)$, is defined for each p as the proportion of total income accruing to the bottom $100p\%$ of income recipients:

$$\theta(p) = X(p)/X = \int_0^y xf(x)dx/\mu \tag{1.66}$$

where μ is mean income.

Clearly $\theta(0) = 0$ and $\theta(1) = 1$. We may differentiate equation (1.66) to determine the slope of the Lorenz curve:

$$\theta'(p) = \frac{d}{dy}\left[\int_0^y xf(x)\,dx/\mu\right]\cdot\frac{dy}{dp} = \frac{d}{dy}\left[\int_0^y xf(x)\,dx\right]\bigg/\mu\frac{dp}{dy}$$

$$= yf(y)/\mu F'(y)$$

$$= y/\mu \tag{1.67}$$

using the chain rule as in equations (1.6) and (1.7), the definition in equation (1.64) and Theorem 1.6.1.

At each point $p = p_0$ on the Lorenz curve, the slope $\theta'(p_0)$ measures the income of an individual of rank p_0 relative to mean income. Clearly the slope increases with p, unless all incomes are equal. Thus $\theta(p)$ is convex, as in figure 1.12 – again, unless all incomes are equal, in which case $\theta(p) = p$ defines the 45°-line or *line of complete equality*.

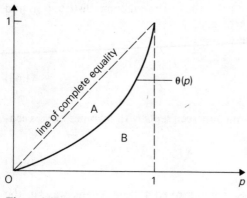

Figure 1.12

We have shown the following: whatever the distribution of income, if it is not perfectly equal then the bottom $100p\,\%$ of the population receive less than $100p\,\%$ of total income *for all* p.

One way to quantify the *inequality* present in an income distribution is by means of its *Gini coefficient* (G). This can be defined as the area between the Lorenz curve $\theta(p)$ and the line of complete equality, relative to the total area below the line of complete equality:

$$G = A/(A+B) = 2A = 2(\tfrac{1}{2} - B) = 1 - 2B$$

$$= 1 - 2\int_0^1 \theta(p)\,dp \tag{1.68}$$

(since $A + B = \tfrac{1}{2}$). The Gini coefficient is a widely quoted index of inequality and can easily be calculated from actual data (see Cowell, 1977, p. 116 *et seq.*; Exercise 1.8.4(e), below). Its value for the *pre-tax* income distribution may be compared with that for the *post-tax* income distribution, to gauge the redistributive effect of an income tax.

1.8.4 Exercises

(a) The *Pareto distribution*, defined on $[b, \infty)$, has density function $f(x) = ab^a x^{-a-1}$. Verify that $\int_b^\infty f(x)\,dx = 1$; that the distribution function is $F(x) = 1 - [b/x]^a$; that the Lorenz curve is $\theta(p) = 1 - (1-p)^{(a-1)/a}$; and that the Gini coefficient is $G = 1/(2a-1)$.

(b) Suppose that the incomes in a population are distributed on the interval $[0, \infty)$; that the income tax liability $t(x)$ on an income x is zero below a threshold b and twice differentiable for all $x > b$; and that incomes above b are distributed as Pareto, i.e. $f(x \mid x > b) = ab^a x^{-a-1}$. Use equation (1.62) and integration by parts to prove that

$$e_{T,X} = \int_b^\infty t'(x)x^{-a}\,dx \Big/ \int_b^\infty t(x)x^{-a-1}\,dx = a. \tag{1.69}$$

(This remarkable result says that revenue elasticity is quite independent of the form of the tax schedule above the tax threshold – indeed, is invariant to changes in tax rates – provided that the incomes of taxpayers are distributed as Pareto. See Hutton and Lambert (1979, 1982) for further discussion and applications of this result.)

(c) Evaluate the second derivative $\theta''(p)$ along the Lorenz curve $\theta(p)$ by differentiating equation (1.67).

(d) Integrate by parts formula (1.68) for the Gini coefficient, to show that

$$G = -1 + 2\int_0^1 p\theta'(p)\,dp.$$

Now use integration by substitution to prove that

$$G = -1 + 2\int_0^\infty yF(y)f(y)\,dy/\mu. \tag{1.70}$$

(e) The integral in equation (1.70) is the mean of $yF(y)$, i.e. it is an average of incomes weighted by their ranks. Show that this expression for the Gini coefficient is equivalent to the formula

$$G = 1 + \frac{1}{n} - 2[x_1 + 2x_2 + 3x_3 + \ldots + nx_n]/n^2\bar{x} \tag{1.71}$$

for a discrete income distribution with incomes

$$x_1 \geqslant x_2 \geqslant x_3 \geqslant \ldots \geqslant x_n$$

(given in Cowell, 1977, p. 116) *when* n *is large.* (*Hint*: the rank of x_i is $p_i = (n+1-i)/n$, and the integral $\int_0^\infty yF(y)f(y)\mathrm{d}y$ is the continuous analogue of $\Sigma_{i=1}^n p_i x_i/n$.)

1.9 DIFFERENTIAL AND DIFFERENCE EQUATIONS

In equations (1.30) and (1.29) we have already encountered examples of first-order linear differential and difference equations:

$$K' = I - bK \tag{1.30}$$

$$K_{t+1} = I_t - (1+b)K_t. \tag{1.29}$$

The simplest general form for a first-order linear differential equation is

$$x' + px = c \tag{1.72}$$

where $x = x(t)$ and p, c are constants.

(An example of a first-order *non-linear* differential equation is $(x')^2 + px^3 = c$. We do not deal with such equations, nor with non-linear difference equations, in this book: see Gandolpho (1980) for treatments of these.)

We may assume $p \neq 0$ in equation (1.72) since otherwise equation (1.72) may be integrated readily to give $x(t) = ct + d$ for some constant d. More generally p and c may be functions of t. An nth-order linear differential equation with constant coefficients takes the form

$$x^{(n)} + p_1 x^{(n-1)} + \ldots + p_n x = c \tag{1.73}$$

where $x^{(i)} = \mathrm{d}^i x/\mathrm{d}t^i$ is the notation we use for the ith derivative of x with respect to t. By defining new variables

$$y_1 = x \qquad y_{i+1} = x^{(i)} \qquad 1 \leqslant i \leqslant n-1 \tag{1.74}$$

we may *replace the* n*th-order linear differential equation in equation (1.73) by an equivalent system of* n *first-order linear differential equations in* n *variables*:

$$y_i' = y_{i+1} \qquad 1 \leqslant i \leqslant n-1$$

$$y_n' = -p_1 y_n - p_2 y_{n-1} - \ldots - p_{n-1} y_1 + c. \tag{1.75}$$

This is a particular instance of a more general formulation

$$y_i' = \sum_{j=1}^{n} a_{ij} y_j + k_i \tag{1.76}$$

$(1 \leqslant i \leqslant n)$ for a system of first-order linear differential equations, involving variables and their first derivatives, which can be addressed using matrix algebra.

Thus we need never go beyond *first*-order linear differential equations – provided we can deal with systems of them. We shall see in this chapter how to solve first-order linear differential equations. In addition we shall examine second-order linear differential equations, though not very rigorously. Systems of first-order linear differential equations are dealt with in detail in chapter 2, section 2.9. Systems of *two* first-order differential equations (not necessarily linear) can be studied by means of *diagrammatic analysis*: this is dealt with in chapter 7, section 7.8.

For first-order linear *difference* equations, a general form is

$$x_{t+1} + px_t = c. \tag{1.77}$$

An nth-order linear difference equation, say

$$x_{t+n} + p_1 x_{t+n-1} + \ldots + p_n x_t = c, \tag{1.78}$$

can be written as a system of n first-order linear difference equations in n variables, the general form for which is

$$y_{i,\,t+1} = \sum_{j=1}^{n} a_{ij} y_{j,\,t} + k_i \tag{1.79}$$

$(1 \leqslant i \leqslant n)$. We return to first-order linear difference equations later; and to systems of first-order linear difference equations in chapter 2, section 2.9.

Let us consider now a first-order linear differential equation with constant coefficients p and c:

$$x' + px = c. \tag{1.72}$$

Since $(\mathrm{d}/\mathrm{d}t)[x \cdot e^{pt}] = (x' + px)e^{pt}$, we may fruitfully multiply through equation (1.72) by e^{pt}:

$$\frac{\mathrm{d}}{\mathrm{d}t}[x \cdot e^{pt}] = (x' + px)e^{pt} = ce^{pt} \tag{1.80}$$

and then integrate, using Theorem 1.6.3:

$$x \cdot e^{pt} \Big|_{t=0}^{t=s} = c \int_0^s e^{pt} \, dt = c(e^{ps}-1)/p, \tag{1.81}$$

Since $x(0)$ has not been specified in equation (1.72), it is arbitrary. That is, the *general solution* of equation (1.72) takes the form

$$x(s) e^{ps} = c e^{ps}/p + d \tag{1.82}$$

where d is arbitrary, any particular value specifying the initial point as $x(0) = c/p + d$. Multiplying equation (1.82) through by e^{-ps}, and changing the s into a t, we arrive at the explicit general solution to the first-order linear difference equation (1.72):

$$x(t) = c/p + de^{-pt}. \tag{1.83}$$

We may conveniently represent equation (1.83) in the form

$$GS = PS + CF \tag{1.84}$$

where GS = the general solution;
   PS = a *particular solution* = c/p = an obvious solution, obtained from equation (1.72) by setting $x(t) = x^* =$ constant, i.e. $x' = 0$;
   CF = the *complementary function* = de^{-pt} = the general solution to the *reduced form equation* $x' + px = 0$, which is obtained from equation (1.72) by setting the constant term to zero. (It is clear that the general solution to the reduced form differential equation $x' + px = 0$ is in this form, since we may write that equation as $(d/dt)[\ln(x)] = (1/x) \cdot (dx/dt) = -p$: now integrate.)

If p is positive then the solution in equation (1.83) converges to $x^* = c/p$. This can be interpreted as the *steady-state value* in the case that t is time. It is given by the constant particular solution, when in the limit the complementary function is zero.

The formula $GS = PS + CF$ provides a useful approach to solving higher-order linear differential equations also. It is quite general. If $x_1(t)$ and $x_2(t)$ are two solutions to the nth-order linear differential equation

$$x^{(n)} + p_1 x^{(n-1)} + \ldots + p_{n-1} x = c, \tag{1.73}$$

then their difference $u(t) = x_1(t) - x_2(t)$ satisfies the reduced form equation:

$$u^{(n)} + p_1 u^{(n-1)} + \ldots + p_{n-1} u = (x_1 - x_2)^{(n)} + p_1 (x_1 - x_2)^{(n-1)}$$
$$+ \ldots + p_{n-1}(x_1 - x_2)$$

$$= [x_1^{(n)} + p_1 x_1^{(n-1)} + \ldots + p_{n-1} x_1]$$
$$- [x_2^{(n)} + p_1 x_2^{(n-1)} + \ldots + p_{n-1} x_2]$$
$$= c - c = 0.$$

So, letting $x_1(t)$ vary across all solutions to equation (1.73), and keeping $x_2(t)$ fixed, the equation $x_1(t) = x_2(t) + u(t)$ becomes $GS = x_2(t) + CF$: proving that $GS = PS + CF$ in the general case.

We shall apply this useful algorithm to second-order linear differential equations. Let us first observe that the approach used to solve

$$x' + px = c \tag{1.72}$$

readily adapts to cases in which c and/or p are not constants but functions of t. With p and c constant, we made the differential equation integrable by multiplying through e^{pt}; for this reason e^{pt} is called the *integrating factor* for equation (1.72). If c is a function of t, $c = c(t)$, and p is constant, this approach still works: equation (1.80) remains true but equation (1.81) gets replaced by

$$x \cdot e^{pt} \Big|_{t=0}^{t=s} = \int_0^s c(t) e^{pt} \, dt \tag{1.81a}$$

and the solution (1.83) by

$$x(t) = e^{-pt} \int_0^t c(u) e^{pu} \, du/p + d e^{-pt}. \tag{1.83a}$$

However, if p is a function of t, $p = p(t)$, then we need to use a different integrating factor. Let $P(t)$ be an indefinite integral of $p(t)$. We may use $e^{P(t)}$ as the integrating factor, replacing equation (1.80) by the equation

$$\frac{d}{dt}[x \cdot e^{P(t)}] = (x' + P'x) e^{P(t)} = (x' + px) e^{P(t)} = c e^{P(t)} \tag{1.80b}$$

and arriving at the general solution in much the same way as before. We shall use this more general type of integrating factor again in chapter 7.

1.9.1 Exercises

(a) Verify that equation (1.83a) is in the form $GS = PS + CF$.

(b) Obtain the general solution to equation (1.72) when $p = p(t)$, $c = c(t)$ using equation (1.80b).

1.9.2 Example

Consider the second-order linear differential equation with constant coefficients

$$x'' + px' + qx = c \tag{1.85}$$

and assume $q \neq 0$ (otherwise we have a first-order linear differential equation in $y = x'$). Following the GS = PS + CF approach, we first seek an obvious value for the particular solution. The simplest possibility is to try $x(t) = x^* = $ constant. This requires $x^{*\prime\prime} + px^{*\prime} + qx^* = c$, i.e. $qx^* = c$ or $x^* = c/q$. The complementary function is the general solution to $x'' + px' + qx = 0$. Guided by our experience in solving the first-order linear differential equation in (1.72), we might expect solutions of the form $x(t) = d\,e^{rt}$ for some d and r. This would require $d\,e^{rt}(r^2 + pr + q) = 0$, which is true for any d if r is one of the roots of the quadratic equation

$$r^2 + pr + q = 0. \tag{1.86}$$

If this equation has two real and distinct roots $r = r_1, r_2$ (which happens if $p^2 > 4q$) then it is easy to see that $x = d_1 \exp(r_1 t) + d_2 \exp(r_2 t)$ is a solution of the reduced-form equation whatever the values of d_1 and d_2. We *assert* that this is in fact the general solution of the reduced-form equation, i.e. the complementary function for the original differential equation (1.85). A proof will emerge in the next chapter: see Exercise 2.9.1, p. 64. Then the overall solution to equation (1.85) is

$$GS = c/q + d_1 \exp(r_1 t) + d_2 \exp(r_2 t) \tag{1.87}$$

in the case that $p^2 > 4q$. If r_1 and r_2 are both negative then, as $t \to \infty$, $x(t)$ converges to $x^* = c/q$: the constant PS is the steady-state value. If either or both of r_1 and r_2 is positive, then equation (1.87) diverges. Neither of r_1 and r_2 can be zero since $q \neq 0$ by assumption.

If $p^2 = 4q$ there is just one root of equation (1.86), given by $r = -p/2$. In this case, we assert, the complementary function is CF $= (d_1 + d_2 t)e^{rt}$ and the general solution is

$$GS = c/q + (d_1 + d_2 t)e^{rt}. \tag{1.88}$$

Convergence requires only that $r < 0$, i.e. $p > 0$.

If $p^2 < 4q$ then equation (1.86) has two complex roots. We put aside any examination of the solution in this case, simply stating that convergence again requires $p > 0$, and that the general solution approaches the steady state through damped oscillations.

We now turn to first-order linear difference equations. The general form is

$$x_{t+1} + px_t = c \tag{1.77}$$

and the solution can be obtained quite readily using iteration.

1.9.3 Exercises

(a) If $x_{t+1} - x_t = c$, show by iteration that the general solution is of the form $x_t = ct + d$ for some d. (Express x_1 in terms of x_0; x_2 in terms of x_1; x_3 in terms of x_2; etc. The initial value x_0 is arbitrary.)

(b) If $x_t + px_t = 0$, show by iteration that the general solution is of the form $x_t = d(-p)^t$ for some d.

The GS = PS + CF approach is still valid. For a particular solution to equation (1.77) we try $x_{t+1} = x_t = x^*$, a constant value. This implies $x^* = c/(1+p)$, which is fine provided that $p \neq -1$. If $p = -1$ then we may be guided by Exercise 1.9.3(a) above; a particular solution is $x(t) = ct$. The complementary function is the general solution to the reduced form $x_{t+1} + px_t = 0$, and here we may be guided by the solution to Exercise 1.9.3(b); thus CF $= d(-p)^t$. The general solution is therefore

$$\text{GS} = \begin{cases} c/(1+p) + d(-p)^t & p \neq -1 \\ ct + d & p = -1. \end{cases} \tag{1.89}$$

If $c \neq 0$, then for convergence we require $|p| < 1$; if $-1 < p < 0$ the solution converges monotonically to $x^* = c/(1+p)$ and if $0 < p < 1$ there are damped oscillations. If $p = -1$ there is a linear trend and if $p = 1$ the solution oscillates indefinitely between $c/2 + d$ and $c/2 - d$. If $|p| > 1$, the solution is divergent.

In the case of a second-order linear difference equation, say

$$x_{t+2} + px_{t+1} + qx_t = c \tag{1.90}$$

we may follow the GS = PS + CF approach. We note that PS $= c/(1+p+q)$ is a particular solution if $1 + p + q \neq 0$, and, trying the function $x_t = d \cdot r^t$ as a solution to the reduced form equation $x_{t+2} + px_{t+1} + qx_t = 0$, we obtain an identical requirement on r to that which arose for the equivalent second-order differential equation: $r^2 + pr + q = 0$. The reasoning from this point parallels the earlier case, and the general solution is

$$\text{GS} = \begin{cases} c/(1+p+q) + d_1 r_1^t + d_2 r_2^t \\ c/(1+p+q) + (d_1 + d_2 t)r^t \end{cases} \tag{1.91}$$

according as $p^2 \geqq 4q$ (assuming $1 + p + q \neq 0$). For convergence we require $|r_1| < 1$ and $|r_2| < 1$ (or just $|r| < 1$ in the equal roots case).

This concludes chapter 1. Differential equations bring together the two main strands of the calculus, differentiation and integration, and they will be encountered again later in the book. Although difference equations are strictly not part of the differential and integral calculus, their treatment is so similar that it was worth introducing them here. They re-appear in chapter 7, section 7.9.

2 Matrix Algebra

In this chapter we survey the basic matrix algebra which will be needed for the treatment of static and dynamic optimization in the rest of the book. We give some examples of the use of matrices in economics; we also extend our coverage of differential and difference equations, using matrix algebra. But perhaps the most powerful and useful application of matrix algebra is to systems of simultaneous linear equations.

2.1 SYSTEMS OF LINEAR EQUATIONS

Consider a system of m simultaneous linear equations in n unknowns. They could be written in full, as

$$\left.\begin{array}{l} a_{11}x_1 + a_{12}x_2 + a_{13}x_3 + \ldots + a_{1n}x_n = b_1 \\ a_{21}x_1 + a_{22}x_2 + a_{23}x_3 + \ldots + a_{2n}x_n = b_2 \\ a_{31}x_1 + a_{32}x_2 + a_{33}x_3 + \ldots + a_{3n}x_n = b_3 \\ \vdots \\ a_{m1}x_1 + a_{m2}x_2 + a_{m3}x_3 + \ldots + a_{mn}x_n = b_m \end{array}\right\} \tag{2.1}$$

or we could put the coefficients a_{ij} $(1 \leqslant i \leqslant m, 1 \leqslant j \leqslant n)$ into an array, and similarly the unknowns and the constants on the right-hand side, and then represent equations (2.1) as:

$$\begin{bmatrix} a_{11} & a_{12} & a_{13} & \cdots & a_{1n} \\ a_{21} & a_{22} & a_{23} & \cdots & a_{2n} \\ a_{31} & a_{32} & a_{33} & \cdots & a_{3n} \\ \vdots & \vdots & \vdots & & \vdots \\ a_{m1} & a_{m2} & a_{m3} & \cdots & a_{mn} \end{bmatrix} \begin{bmatrix} x_1 \\ x_2 \\ x_3 \\ \vdots \\ x_n \end{bmatrix} = \begin{bmatrix} b_1 \\ b_2 \\ b_3 \\ \vdots \\ b_m \end{bmatrix}$$

which can be summarized very compactly as

$$A\underline{x} = \underline{b}. \tag{2.2}$$

A is called an $m \times n$ *matrix*. Similarly $\underline{x}$ is an $n \times 1$ matrix, or *column vector*, and $\underline{b}$ is an $m \times 1$ matrix or column vector. We may also use the notation

$$A = (a_{ij})_{1 \leqslant i \leqslant m, 1 \leqslant j \leqslant n} \tag{2.3}$$

for the array which forms the matrix A.

The representation of the equation system (2.1) as a single *matrix equation* (2.2) makes for a significant saving in the use of symbols, if nothing else. But it also leads us into a large body of theory and technique, broadly called linear algebra, that permits penetrating analysis of linear equation systems.

In economics, linear modelling, leading to equation systems like (2.1), is pervasive. From the simplest and most familiar text-book macroeconomic models, to the most sophisticated systems of forecasting equations for real-world economies, linearity in the variables is found. (Indeed non-linear models tend to get 'linearized': see chapter 3.) This is largely because linear equation systems are so well understood.

In building a predictive model of the economy, one starts with a number of key endogenous variables, and builds up a system of identities, technical equations and behavioural equations on the basis of assumed linear (sometimes log-linear) relations, using coefficients estimated from regression analysis of past data. In the UK the larger models have upwards of 100 behavioural equations (mainly linear in logarithms) and in all as many as 600–700 (see Keating, 1985 for an excellent survey).

A model with too few equations (or, what is the same thing, too many variables) cannot lead to a determinate solution. Borrowing an illuminative term from econometrics, we might call such a system *under-identified*. With too many equations relative to the number of variables, the system may be over-identified or *inconsistent*. A major question is how to 'close' the model, i.e. at what stage in the building process the equation system becomes identified, guaranteeing a unique solution.

2.1.1 Theorem

If $m < n$ the $m \times n$ equation system $A\underline{x} = \underline{b}$ has 0 or ∞ solutions.

For a proof of this, see any good mathematics text covering linear algebra. A particularly clear treatment is in O'Nan (1977). A forthcoming exercise (Exercise 2.2.1(b), p. 42), goes some way towards a proof: see also section 2.6.

Hence we need at least as many equations as variables for a unique solution to a simultaneous linear-equation system. Having exactly as many equations as variables may do the trick: but this is not guaranteed. Exact conditions will emerge in section 2.6, but first we need to establish the basic matrix manipulations.

2.1.2 Exercise

By selecting appropriate pairs of equations from the following three, demonstrate that having the same number of equations as unknowns does not guarantee the existence of a solution to a simultaneous equation system, nor indeed, if one exists, of a unique solution:

1. $2x_1 + 3x_2 = 1$

2. $4x_1 + 6x_2 = 2$

3. $4x_1 + 6x_2 = 3.$

2.2 BASIC MATRIX MANIPULATIONS

We summarize quite briefly some definitions.

Matrix addition If $A = (a_{ij})$ and $B = (b_{ij})$ are two $m \times n$ matrices, then $A + B$ is defined as $A + B = (a_{ij} + b_{ij})$. Thus we add, element by element, the two arrays. Clearly $A + B = B + A$.

Null matrix Denote by $0_{m,n}$, or simply by 0, the $m \times n$ matrix with zeros everywhere. An alternative notation for $0_{m,1}$ is $\underline{0}$ (the zero column vector). Clearly $A + 0_{m,n} = 0_{m,n} + A = A$ for all $m \times n$ matrices A.

Scalar multiplication If $A = (a_{ij})$ then for any k define $kA = (ka_{ij})$; thus we multiply each element in A by k.

Matrix multiplication If A is $m \times n$, and B is $n \times p$, then the $m \times p$ matrix AB or $A.B$ is

$$AB = \left(\sum_{k=1}^{n} a_{ik} b_{kj} \right)_{1 \leqslant i \leqslant m, 1 \leqslant j \leqslant p}.$$

The rule for dimensions is $(m \times n)(n \times p) \rightarrow (m \times p)$. A must have the same number of columns as B has rows. Then A and B are said to be *conformable*. The (i,j)th element of AB is obtained by 'going along' the ith row of A, and down the jth column of B, multiplying and adding as you go. For example

$$\begin{bmatrix} 1 & 2 \\ 4 & 0 \end{bmatrix} \begin{bmatrix} 3 & -1 \\ 4 & 3 \end{bmatrix} = \begin{bmatrix} 11 & 5 \\ 12 & -4 \end{bmatrix}$$

and clearly if A is $m \times n$ then $A.0_{n,p} = 0_{m,p}$ and $0_{p,m}.A = 0_{p,n}$. We may write this as $A.0 = 0$ and $0.A = 0$ (but not, of course, as $A.0 = 0.A = 0$ unless $m = n = p$). AB and BA are not both defined unless A and B are both $n \times n$, i.e. *square*, and then they may differ (consider the example above). Denote by A^2, A^3, etc., the matrix products AA, AAA, etc. It can be shown, by routine, but fairly tedious, manipulations that (conformable) matrices follow the same sort of rules of composition as real numbers; namely that

$$A(B+C) = AB + AC \quad \text{and} \quad A(BC) = (AB)C. \tag{2.4}$$

Matrices also have a rather satisfying property, when decomposed into 'blocks'. Let A be $m \times n$ and let B be $n \times p$ and write

$$A = \begin{bmatrix} A_1 & A_2 \\ \hline A_3 & A_4 \end{bmatrix} \qquad B = \begin{bmatrix} B_1 & B_2 \\ \hline B_3 & B_4 \end{bmatrix}$$

where A_1 is $m_1 \times n_1$, A_2 is $m_1 \times (n-n_1)$, A_3 is $(m-m_1) \times n_1$, A_4 is $(m-m_1) \times (n-n_1)$ and B_1 is $n_1 \times p_1$, etc., then

$$AB = \begin{bmatrix} A_1B_1 + A_2B_3 & A_1B_2 + A_2B_4 \\ \hline A_3B_1 + A_4B_3 & A_3B_2 + A_4B_4 \end{bmatrix}.$$

The blocks compose just like elements in 2×2 matrices. Note finally that in the matrix equation (2.2), $A\underline{x} = \underline{b}$, for the linear system (2.1), the left-hand side is in fact a matrix product: the kth equation in equations (2.1) is $\sum_{j=1}^{n} a_{kj}x_j = b_k$, and the left-hand side of this expression is also by definition the kth element in the $m \times 1$ column vector $A\underline{x}$.

2.2.1 Exercises

(a) Consider the matrix equation $A\underline{x} = \underline{0}$ where A is $m \times n$ and $m < n$. Show that there are an infinite number of solutions (use Theorem 2.1.1).

(b) Suppose that the matrix equation $A\underline{x} = \underline{b}$ has a solution $(x_1, x_2, \ldots, x_n) = (h_1, h_2, \ldots, h_n)$, i.e. $\underline{x} = \underline{h}$. Suppose also that the system $A\underline{x} = \underline{0}$ has a *non-zero* solution $\underline{x} = \underline{g} \neq 0$. Show that $\underline{x} = \underline{h} + k\underline{g}$ is a solution to $A\underline{x} = \underline{b}$ for every real number k. (Hence if $A\underline{x} = \underline{0}$ has a non-zero solution, $A\underline{x} = \underline{b}$ has 0 or ∞ solutions. Proving Theorem 2.1.1 reduces to proving that if $m < n$ then $A\underline{x} = 0$ has a non-zero solution.)

(c) Show that if $A\underline{h} = \underline{b}$ then *every* solution to $A\underline{x} = \underline{b}$ is of the form $\underline{x} = \underline{h} + \underline{g}$ where $\underline{g}$ is a vector satisfying $A\underline{g} = \underline{0}$.

These exercises explore the links between solutions to the equation system $A\underline{x} = \underline{b}$ and solutions to the system $A\underline{x} = \underline{0}$. The latter is known as a *homogeneous* system of equations: it has only zeros on the right-hand side. One obvious solution is $\underline{x} = \underline{0}$.

We return to matrix definitions.

Diagonal matrix A square $(n \times n)$ matrix A is diagonal if all entries off the 'main diagonal' are zero: thus

$$A = \begin{bmatrix} a_{11} & 0 & 0 & \cdots & 0 \\ 0 & a_{22} & 0 & \cdots & 0 \\ \vdots & \vdots & \vdots & \vdots & \vdots \\ 0 & 0 & 0 & \cdots & a_{nn} \end{bmatrix}.$$

Trace of a square matrix If A is square, the trace of A, denoted tr A, is the sum of the elements on the main diagonal of A. Thus, tr $A = \Sigma_{i=1}^{n} a_{ii}$.

Identity matrix Denote by I_n the $n \times n$ diagonal matrix with $a_{ii} = 1$ for all i. This may be written

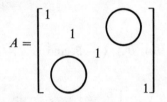

$$A = \begin{bmatrix} 1 & & & \\ & 1 & & \\ & & 1 & \\ & & & 1 \end{bmatrix}$$

the large $\bigcirc$s denoting triangular blocks of zeros. If A is $m \times n$ it is easy to see that $A \cdot I_n = A = I_m \cdot A$.

Inverse of a square matrix Given an $n \times n$ matrix A, if there exists an $n \times n$ matrix B such that $AB = BA = I_n$ then B is called the inverse of A, and is written $B = A^{-1}$. We are justified in calling B *the* inverse of A, since there could not be two such matrices B_1 and B_2: otherwise consider the following string of equations:

$$B_1 = B_1 I = B_1(AB_2) = (B_1 A)B_2 = IB_2 = B_2.$$

A matrix with an inverse is *invertible*. Clearly $I_n = I_n^{-1}$. If A and B are invertible, so is AB and $(AB)^{-1} = B^{-1}A^{-1}$.

Transpose of a matrix If A is $m \times n$ denote by A^t the $n \times m$ matrix whose rows are the columns of A. So $A^t = (a_{ji})$. For example

$$\begin{bmatrix} 1 & -3 \\ -6 & 4 \end{bmatrix}^t = \begin{bmatrix} 1 & -6 \\ -3 & 4 \end{bmatrix}.$$

In many books A' is used to denote the transpose of A. It is straightforward to transpose the sum of two matrices: $(A+B)^t = A^t + B^t$; but for a product of conformable matrices one needs to be more careful: $(AB)^t = B^t A^t$. The transpose of a column vector $\underline{x}$ is a row vector (or $n \times 1$ matrix) $\underline{x}^t = (x_1, x_2, \ldots, x_n)$. If A is $n \times n$ then $\underline{x}^t A \underline{x}$ is a 1×1 matrix, which is just a number: $\underline{x}^t A \underline{x} = \Sigma_{i=1}^n \Sigma_{j=1}^n a_{ij} x_i x_j$. This is known as a *quadratic form*: see section 2.10.

Symmetric matrix   A square matrix A is symmetric if $A = A^t$. The identity matrix I and square null matrix 0 are symmetric.

2.2.2 Exercises

(a) If $A^2 = 0$ show that $A + I$ has an inverse. (*Hint*: try $B = I - A$.)

(b) Show that

$$A = \begin{bmatrix} 1 & 3 \\ 2 & 6 \end{bmatrix}$$

has no inverse.

(c) Calculate, where possible, AB, $A^t B$, BA, $B^t A$, $C^t - B$, and $C^t - AC^t B^t$ when

$$A = \begin{bmatrix} 3 & 5 \\ 1 & 1 \end{bmatrix}, \qquad B = \begin{bmatrix} 6 & 7 & 2 \\ 0 & 3 & 0 \end{bmatrix}, \qquad C = \begin{bmatrix} 9 & 2 \\ 1 & 7 \\ 0 & 0 \end{bmatrix}.$$

(d) Evaluate $\underline{x}^t A \underline{x}$ when $n = 2$ and A is as in (b) above. Express $x_1^2 + 2x_2^2 - 3x_1 x_2 + x_2 x_3$ in the form $\underline{x}^t A \underline{x}$ where A is 3×3. Can you make A symmetric?

(e) If $\underline{x}$ is $m \times 1$, A is $m \times n$ and $\underline{y}$ is $n \times 1$, evaluate $\underline{x}^t A \underline{y}$. What is the transpose of a 1×1 matrix? Prove $\underline{x}^t A \underline{y} = \underline{y}^t A^t \underline{x}$.

(f) If A is invertible and $AB = I$ prove $BA = I$.

(g) If A and $A + B$ are invertible prove $I + A^{-1} B$ is invertible.

(h) If A and $I + A^{-1} B$ are invertible prove $A + B$ is invertible. Let $C = (I + A^{-1} B)^{-1}$. Show $(A + B)^{-1} = CA^{-1}$.

(i) If A and B are invertible, is $A + B$ necessarily invertible?

We will shortly establish criteria which determine whether a matrix is invertible. To do this, we need the notions of *determinant* and *rank*.

2.3 DETERMINANTS OF SQUARE MATRICES

We shall define the determinant $\det A$ of an $n \times n$ matrix A inductively.

For $n = 2$ we define

$$\det \begin{bmatrix} a & b \\ c & d \end{bmatrix} = ad - bc.$$

Now let A be $n \times n$ $(n \geqslant 3)$ and suppose that $(n-1) \times (n-1)$ determinants have been defined. Let M_{ij} be the sub-matrix obtained from A by *striking out* the ith row and jth column of A $(1 \leqslant i, j \leqslant n)$.
For example if

$$A = \begin{bmatrix} 1 & 2 & 1 \\ 0 & 1 & 2 \\ -3 & 4 & 1 \end{bmatrix} \tag{2.5}$$

then

$$M_{11} = \begin{bmatrix} 1 & 2 \\ 4 & 1 \end{bmatrix}, \qquad M_{23} = \begin{bmatrix} 1 & 2 \\ -3 & 4 \end{bmatrix} \text{etc.}$$

Because M_{ij} is an $(n-1) \times (n-1)$ matrix its determinant is defined. (In fact $\det M_{ij}$ is called the (i,j)th *minor* of A.) Let

$$A_{ij} = (-1)^{i+j} \det M_{ij}. \tag{2.6}$$

This is the (i,j)th *cofactor of* A. For example with A as in equation (2.5), we have $A_{11} = -7$, $A_{23} = -10$ etc. We are now ready to give the definition of $\det A$.

2.3.1 Definition

$$\det A = a_{11}A_{11} + a_{12}A_{12} + \ldots + a_{1n}A_{1n}.$$

This says that to calculate $\det A$ we 'go along' the first row of A, multiplying the elements by their cofactors and adding as we go. This is called the *cofactor expansion* of A along the first row. There is nothing special about the first row of a matrix: the following theorem says that we could use any row, or indeed any column, to calculate $\det A$ as a cofactor expansion.

2.3.2 Theorem

$$\det A = \sum_{i=1}^{n} a_{ij}A_{ij} = \sum_{j=1}^{n} a_{ij}A_{ij} \qquad \text{for all } i, j.$$

Taking A as in equation (2.5) again, and using the first row cofactor expansion, we find $\det A = [1 \times (-7)] + [2 \times (-6)] + [1 \times 3] = -16$. Using instead the second-column cofactor expansion, for example, we have $\det A = [2 \times (-6)] + [1 \times 4] + [4 \times (-2)] = -16$; etc.

Determinants satisfy certain very useful properties. In particular we have

1. $\det A = \det A^t$
2. $\det A \cdot B = \det A \cdot \det B$
3. $\det I_n = 1$ for all n
4. $\det kA = k^n \det A$
5. if A has a row/column of zeros, $\det A = 0$
6. if we multiply a row/column of A by k, and A^* is the result, then $\det A^* = k \cdot \det A$.

(Parts 1 and 4–6 are quite obvious: Why?) A very important property of cofactors is known as the *alien cofactor expansion theorem*.

2.3.3 Theorem

$$\sum_{i=1}^{n} a_{ij} A_{ik} = 0 \qquad \text{if } k \neq j$$

$$\sum_{j=1}^{n} a_{ij} A_{kj} = 0 \qquad \text{if } k \neq i.$$

If we go along any row/column of A taking products of elements and cofactors, adding as we go, we know from Theorem 2.3.2 that the result is $\det A$. But if we go along any row/column of A taking products of elements with the cofactors of *another* (=alien) row/column, adding as we go, this theorem tells us we will always get *zero*.

For example, with A as in equation (2.5) again, we have

| elements of last row: | -3 | 4 | 1 |
| cofactors of first row: | -7 | -6 | 3. |

Multiplying and adding, we get zero.

For proofs of Theorem 2.3.2, properties 2 and 3 for determinants and Theorem 2.3.3 see O'Nan (1977, chapter 3).

As a consequence of the alien cofactor expansion theorem we have the following additional, useful property of the determinant:

7. if we add a multiple of one row/column of A to another row/column, and A^* is the result, then $\det A = \det A^*$.

For example

$$\det \begin{bmatrix} 1 & 2 & 1 \\ 0 & 1 & 2 \\ -3 & 4 & 1 \end{bmatrix} = \det \begin{bmatrix} 1 & 2+k & 1+2k \\ 0 & 1 & 2 \\ -3 & 4 & 1 \end{bmatrix}$$

(we have added k times the second row to the first). In general if A^* is obtained by adding k times the sth row of A to the ith row of A, then evaluating $\det A^*$ as the cofactor expansion along the ith row we have

$$\det A^* = \sum_{j=1}^{n} a_{ij}^* A_{ij}^* = \sum_{j=1}^{n} (a_{ij}+ka_{sj})A_{ij} = \det A.$$

This comes from Theorem 2.3.3 and the observation that the cofactors of A^* and A *along the ith row* are identical: A and A^* only differ in the ith row, and we delete that to obtain cofactors.

We also have, as a direct corollary of 7 above:

8. a matrix with two identical rows/columns, or one row/column equal to a multiple of another, has zero determinant.

Property 7 is very useful for manipulating large determinants. By modifying A to create as many zeros as possible in the resultant A^*, we do not change the determinant, but we can then choose to evaluate it using a cofactor expansion along a row/column with a lot of zeros. This obviates the need to calculate a lot of cofactors.

2.3.4 Exercises

(a) Identify the manipulations that justify the following:

$$\det \begin{bmatrix} 6 & 2 & 2 & 2 \\ 6 & 3 & 3 & 3 \\ -12 & -2 & 3 & 0 \\ 6 & 1 & 1 & 5 \end{bmatrix} = \det \begin{bmatrix} 0 & 1 & 1 & -3 \\ 6 & 3 & 3 & 3 \\ -12 & -2 & 3 & 0 \\ 6 & 1 & 1 & 5 \end{bmatrix}$$

$$= \det \begin{bmatrix} 0 & 1 & 1 & -3 \\ 0 & 2 & 2 & -2 \\ -12 & -2 & 3 & 0 \\ 6 & 1 & 1 & 5 \end{bmatrix} = \det \begin{bmatrix} 0 & 1 & 1 & -3 \\ 0 & 2 & 2 & -2 \\ 0 & 0 & 5 & 10 \\ 6 & 1 & 1 & 5 \end{bmatrix}$$

$$= -6 . \det \begin{bmatrix} 1 & 1 & -3 \\ 2 & 2 & -2 \\ 0 & 5 & 10 \end{bmatrix} = -6 . \det \begin{bmatrix} 1 & 1 & -3 \\ 0 & 0 & 4 \\ 0 & 5 & 10 \end{bmatrix}$$

$$= (-6) . (-4) . \det \begin{bmatrix} 1 & 1 \\ 0 & 5 \end{bmatrix} = 120.$$

(b) Find

$$\det \begin{bmatrix} 3 & 2 & 7 \\ 0 & 1 & -3 \\ 3 & 4 & 1 \end{bmatrix}.$$

(c) Find

$$\det \begin{bmatrix} 4 & 3 & 1 & 9 & 2 \\ 0 & 3 & 2 & 4 & 2 \\ 0 & 3 & 4 & 6 & 4 \\ 1 & -1 & 2 & 2 & 2 \\ 0 & 0 & 3 & 3 & 3 \end{bmatrix}.$$

(d) Let A be a square matrix and let A^* be the matrix formed from A by replacing the elements $a_{1j}, j \neq 1$, in the first row by their negatives, and the elements $a_{i1}, i \neq 1$, in the first column by their negatives. Show that $\det A = \det A^*$ (use property 6 of determinants).

It should be clear from (a)–(c) above that we can often avoid actually calculating the determinant of anything bigger than 2×2, by judicious choice and manipulation of rows/columns to create zeros.

2.4 THE INVERSE OF A SQUARE MATRIX

We define the *adjoint* of an $n \times n$ matrix A as

$$\text{adj } A = (\text{matrix of cofactors})^t = (A_{ji}). \tag{2.7}$$

Then Theorems 2.3.2 and 2.3.3 together imply

$$A \cdot \text{adj } A = (\text{adj } A) \cdot A = \begin{bmatrix} \det A & & & \\ & \det A & & \bigcirc \\ & & \ddots & \\ \bigcirc & & & \det A \end{bmatrix} = (\det A)I_n. \tag{2.8}$$

2.4.1 Theorem

(a) A has an inverse if and only if $\det A \neq 0$, and (b) the inverse equals $\text{adj } A / \det A$.

Proof If $\det A \neq 0$ then from equation (2.8) $B = \text{adj } A / \det A$ satisfies the conditions to be the inverse of A. Suppose $\det A = 0$ and nevertheless the inverse B of A exists. Since $AB = I$, $\det A . \det B = \det I = 1$. This is a contradiction.

2.4.2 Exercises

(a) Is the matrix

$$\begin{bmatrix} 3 & 2 & 7 \\ 0 & 1 & -3 \\ 3 & 4 & 1 \end{bmatrix}$$

invertible? (Recall Exercise 2.3.4(b).)

(b) If $A^2 = A$, show that either $A = I$ or $\det A = 0$.

(c) If $AB = I$ show that A is invertible.

(d) Suppose $AB = 0$. If neither A nor B is the null matrix, show that $\det A = \det B = 0$.

2.5 THE RANK OF A MATRIX

The matrix

$$A = \begin{bmatrix} 3 & 2 & 7 \\ 0 & 1 & -3 \\ 3 & 4 & 1 \end{bmatrix}$$

in Exercise 2.4.2(a) is not invertible because it has zero determinant. Note that in this matrix

$$3 \times (\text{third column}) = [13 \times (\text{first column})] - [9 \times (\text{second column})].$$
$$(2.9)$$

By multiplying the third column of A by 3 (and thereby multiplying the determinant by 3: see property 6 above) and adding/subtracting the right multiples of the other two columns, we could have created a column of zeros in a matrix A^* whose determinant equals $3 . \det A$. This is a contrived way to show $\det A = 0$, but it illustrates a new concept: because of equation (2.9), the columns of A are said to be *linearly dependent*. Had we been unable to find such a linear relationship, the columns of A would have been *linearly independent*. Linear dependence ensures a zero determinant, i.e. non-invertibility.

2.5.1 Definition

Non-zero row/column vectors $\underline{e}_1, \underline{e}_2, \ldots, \underline{e}_n$ are linearly independent if $\Sigma_{i=1}^{n} a_i \underline{e}_i = \underline{0}$ implies $a_1 = a_2 = \ldots = a_n = 0$. Otherwise $\underline{e}_1, \underline{e}_2, \ldots, \underline{e}_n$ are linearly dependent.

Linear dependence means that there exists an equation $\Sigma_{i=1}^{n} a_i \underline{e}_i = \underline{0}$ in which not all of the a_i are zero. Suppose $a_j \neq 0$. Then

$$\underline{e}_j = - \sum_{i \neq j} (a_i/a_j) \underline{e}_i, \tag{2.10}$$

i.e. one vector can be expressed as a linear combination of the others. Thus a pair of non-zero row/column vectors are linearly dependent if and only if one is a multiple of the other.

2.5.2 Definition

The *rank* of an $m \times n$ matrix A, denoted rk A, equals the maximum number of linearly independent columns.

It follows that the rank of the matrix A in Exercise 2.4.2(a) above is 2. In fact, we may use rows, instead of columns, to evaluate the rank of a matrix, because of the following theorem.

2.5.3 Theorem

For any matrix the maximum number of linearly independent columns equals the maximum number of linearly independent rows.

2.5.4 Exercises

(a) Find a linear relation between the rows of the matrix A in Exercise 2.4.2(a) above.

(b) Show that the identity matrix I_n has rank n (let $\underline{e}_i$ be the ith column: What is $\Sigma_{i=1}^{n} a_i \underline{e}_i$?).

It is clear from the interchangeability of rows and columns in determining rank that if A is $m \times n$ then

$$\text{rk } A \leqslant \min[m, n]. \tag{2.11}$$

An $n \times n$ (square) matrix has *full rank* if rk $A = n$.

Evaluating rank offers an alternative criterion for invertibility of a matrix.

2.5.5 Theorem

An $n \times n$ matrix A is invertible if and only if it is of full rank, i.e. rk $A = n$.

Unless A has full rank we can manipulate its rows/columns by multiplying them by constants, and adding and subtracting multiples of them to each other, until we arrive at a row/column of zeros. Then det $A = 0$. If A has full rank, then such an operation is impossible and det A cannot be zero. A more formal discussion than this would take us into the realms of vector space theory and linear transformations: see O'Nan (1977, chapter 5).

2.5.6 Exercise

Identify a linear dependence between the second, third and fifth rows of the matrix

$$\begin{bmatrix} 4 & 3 & 1 & 9 & 2 \\ 0 & 3 & 2 & 4 & 2 \\ 0 & 3 & 4 & 6 & 4 \\ 1 & -1 & 2 & 2 & 2 \\ 0 & 0 & 3 & 3 & 3 \end{bmatrix}$$

whose determinant you found to be zero in Exercise 2.3.4(c).

2.6 SOLVING SYSTEMS OF LINEAR EQUATIONS

We now return to systems of linear equations. Specifically, we seek explicit conditions under which the system

$$A\underline{x} = \underline{b} \tag{2.2}$$

has a unique solution, and the means of finding that solution.

If A is $m \times n$ and $m < n$ we have asserted in Theorem 2.1.1 that there are 0 or ∞ solutions. We can now prove this (given Theorem 2.5.3). From equation (2.11) rk $A < n$, i.e. there is a linear dependence among the columns of A. If $\underline{e}_1, \underline{e}_2, \ldots, \underline{e}_n$ are the columns of A then there is an equation $\Sigma_{i=1}^n a_i\underline{e}_i = \underline{0}$ whose coefficients are not all zero. Writing $\underline{a} = (a_1, a_2, \ldots, a_n)$, this says

$$\sum_{i=1}^n a_i\underline{e}_i = A\underline{a} = \underline{0} \quad \text{and} \quad \underline{a} \neq \underline{0}. \tag{2.12}$$

Therefore $A\underline{x} = \underline{0}$ has a non-zero solution. Therefore, by Exercise 2.2.1(b), $A\underline{x} = \underline{b}$ has 0 or ∞ solutions.

If $m = n$, i.e. if the equation system has the same number of equations as variables, the necessary and sufficient condition for a unique solution is simply the invertibility of A. We can see this as follows.

Suppose A does have an inverse. By pre-multiplying by A^{-1} in equation (2.2) we find

$$A^{-1}(A\underline{x}) = (A^{-1}A)\underline{x} = I\underline{x} = \underline{x} = A^{-1}\underline{b}. \tag{2.13}$$

Hence invertibility is sufficient for a unique solution.

Suppose A has no inverse. Then by Theorem 2.5.5 rk $A < n$, and an argument just like the one that led to condition (2.12) shows $A\underline{x} = \underline{0}$ has a non-zero solution. Then by Exercise 2.2.1(b), $A\underline{x} = \underline{b}$ has 0 or ∞ solutions: certainly not a unique solution. Hence invertibility is necessary.

Because of the rk $A = n$ criterion, building a closed linear model, based upon a given set of endogenous variables, is simply a matter of adding new equations which are not linearly related to the existing ones until there are the same number of non-related equations as variables.

2.6.1 Exercises

(a) Suppose that A is $m \times n$ with $m > n$. Show, (i) if rk $A = n$ then $A\underline{x} = \underline{b}$ has at most one solution, and (ii) if $A\underline{x} = \underline{b}$ has a unique solution then rk $A = n$. Use equation (2.11) to deduce that if the system has a unique solution, there are $(m-n)$ redundant equations.

(b) Find a system $A\underline{x} = \underline{b}$ of three equations in two unknowns for which, (i) rk $A = 2$ and there is no solution, and (ii) rk $A = 2$ and there is a unique solution. In case (ii), show that one equation could be discarded.

If in $A\underline{x} = \underline{b}$ we have the same number of (non-related) equations as variables, we have seen that the solution involves inverting A:

$$\underline{x} = A^{-1}\underline{b}. \tag{2.13}$$

This involves calculating n^2 cofactors, each an $(n-1) \times (n-1)$ determinant. This is obviously a daunting task (see Glaister, 1984, chapters 6–7, for computer programs for the case $n = 3$).

However, we do not actually need to know A^{-1} to solve the system, only $A^{-1}\underline{b}$. By equation (2.13) the solution is

$$\underline{x} = (\text{adj } A).\underline{b}/\det A \tag{2.14}$$

or, in full,

$$x_i = (A_{1i}b_1 + A_{2i}b_2 + \ldots + A_{ni}b_n)/\det A \tag{2.15}$$

(recall that adj A is the *transpose* of the matrix of cofactors).

The numerator on the right-hand side of equation (2.15) is rather like a cofactor expansion along the ith column of A – except that the elements are not those of the ith column of A, they are those of $\underline{b}$. Define A_i as matrix obtained from A by replacing the ith column by $\underline{b}$. This matrix has the 'correct' elements in its ith column – and the same cofactors along its ith column as does A! (We *strike out* the ith column to obtain these cofactors: the only difference between A_i and A disappears.) Hence the numerator on the right-hand side of equation (2.15) is indeed a cofactor expansion, not of A but of A_i. Therefore

$$x_i = \det A_i / \det A. \tag{2.16}$$

This result is known as *Cramer's rule*.

Cramer's rule reduces significantly the amount of computation, only $(n+1)$ determinants, each $n \times n$, being needed to solve the system. Moreover, if we are interested in only *some* of the variables x_i then even less computation is required.

For example, when $n = 3$ Cramer's rule says that

$$x_1 = \det \begin{bmatrix} b_1 & a_{12} & a_{13} \\ b_2 & a_{22} & a_{23} \\ b_3 & a_{32} & a_{33} \end{bmatrix} \Bigg/ \det \begin{bmatrix} a_{11} & a_{12} & a_{13} \\ a_{21} & a_{22} & a_{23} \\ a_{31} & a_{32} & a_{33} \end{bmatrix}$$

and

$$x_2 = \det \begin{bmatrix} a_{11} & b_1 & a_{13} \\ a_{21} & b_2 & a_{23} \\ a_{31} & b_3 & a_{33} \end{bmatrix} \Bigg/ \det \begin{bmatrix} a_{11} & a_{12} & a_{13} \\ a_{21} & a_{22} & a_{23} \\ a_{31} & a_{32} & a_{33} \end{bmatrix}$$

and similarly for x_3; but if x_3 is a variable we are not interested in we need go no further.

Note finally (and obviously) that if $\underline{b}$ equals one of the columns of A, say the ith column of A, and if $\det A \neq 0$, so that Cramer's rule applies, then the solution to $A\underline{x} = \underline{b}$ is simply $x_i = 1, x_j = 0, j \neq i$.

2.6.2 Exercise

Solve for x_2 the equation system

$$x_1 + x_2 + x_3 + x_4 = 2$$
$$x_1 + x_2 + x_3 - x_4 = 4$$
$$x_1 + x_2 - x_3 + x_4 = 6$$
$$x_1 - x_2 + x_3 + x_4 = 8.$$

2.7 SOME USES OF MATRIX ALGEBRA

There are of course a great many uses for matrix notation, and applications of matrix algebra, in economics. We mention two here: see Casson (1973) for many others. We also set up the matrix formulations for systems of first-order linear differential and difference equations, as promised in chapter 1.

2.7.1 Example   A multi-product firm

A multi-product firm faces inter-related but *linear* demand schedules for the n goods it produces:

$$q_i = \sum_{j=1}^{n} a_{ij}p_j + b_i \qquad (1 \leqslant i \leqslant n).$$

We may write this

$$\underline{q} = A\underline{p} + \underline{b} \tag{2.17}$$

and if A is invertible, say $B = A^{-1}$, then we can obtain the inverse demand functions in matrix form as

$$\underline{p} = B(\underline{q} - \underline{b}). \tag{2.18}$$

Total revenue is $R = \sum_{i=1}^{n} p_i q_i = \underline{p}^t \underline{q}$. Thus from equation (2.18) we have

$$R = (\underline{q} - \underline{b})^t B^t \underline{q} = \underline{q}^t B^t \underline{q} - \underline{b}^t B^t \underline{q} \tag{2.19}$$

which involves a quadratic form. If the joint cost function is also a quadratic form, say $C = \sum_{i=1}^{n} \sum_{j=1}^{n} c_{ij} q_i q_j = \underline{q}^t C \underline{q}$ then total profit $\pi = R - C$ can readily be expressed in the form

$$\pi = \underline{q}^t D\underline{q} - \underline{e}^t \underline{q} \tag{2.20}$$

where $D = B^t - C$ and $\underline{e} = B\underline{b}$. We will use this formulation to examine the conditions for profit maximization in chapter 3 (see Exercise 3.6.2(e)).

2.7.2 Example   A linear programming problem

A company manufactures two products X_1 and X_2. Each X_1 requires 6 hours on the company's machines and each X_2 requires 5 hours, and there is a maximum of 6000 machine hours available every month. There are two basic raw materials, A and B, used in manufacture. To make each X_1,

3 lb of A and 1 lb of B are used, and to make each X_2, 1 lb of A and 2 lb of B are used. In this particular month, the company has available 2400 lb of A and 2000 lb of B. The profit on each X_1 is £3 and the profit on each X_2 is £2: the problem is to determine how many of each product the company should manufacture this month to maximize profit.

In mathematical terms the problem is to maximize $3x_1 + 2x_2$ by choice of non-negative values of x_1 and x_2, subject to the production constraints

$$6x_1 + 5x_2 \leqslant 6000$$

$$3x_1 + x_2 \leqslant 2400$$

$$x_1 + 2x_2 \leqslant 2000.$$

This is a typical *linear programming problem* and it will be solved in chapter 5. We may express it in matrix form as

$$\max \underline{c}^t \underline{x}$$

$$\text{s.t. } A\underline{x} \leqslant \underline{b}$$

$$\underline{x} \geqslant \underline{0}$$

where

$$\underline{c} = \begin{bmatrix} 3 \\ 2 \end{bmatrix} \qquad A = \begin{bmatrix} 6 & 5 \\ 3 & 1 \\ 1 & 2 \end{bmatrix} \quad \text{and} \quad \underline{b} = \begin{bmatrix} 6000 \\ 2400 \\ 2000 \end{bmatrix}.$$

Here we encounter *vector inequalities*. They conveniently summarize the situation. Throughout this book, if we write $\underline{u} \leqslant \underline{v}$ then we shall allow some or all components of $\underline{u}$ and $\underline{v}$ to be equal (i.e. $u_i \leqslant v_i$ for all i); but if we write $\underline{u} < \underline{v}$ then all inequalities will be strict ($u_i < v_i$ for all i).

The particular problem outlined above has, in fact, an easy graphical solution (see Example 5.5.1, p. 134). But as we shall see in section 5.5, simple matrix manipulations can lead to a very helpful solution technique for similar problems with more than two variables.

2.7.3 Example First-order linear differential and difference equations

We saw in chapter 1 that an nth-order linear differential equation with constant coefficients could be expressed as a simultaneous system of n first-order linear differential equations with constant coefficients:

$$y_i' = \sum_{j=1}^{n} a_{ij} y_j + k_i. \tag{1.76}$$

In matrix form this could be written

$$\underline{y}' = A\underline{y} + \underline{k} \tag{2.21}$$

where $\underline{y}'$ is the vector of derivatives of $\underline{y}$ (not the transpose). Similarly the difference equation system

$$y_{i,t+1} = \sum_{j=1}^{n} a_{ij} y_{j,t} + k_i \tag{1.79}$$

is, in matrix form,

$$\underline{y}_{t+1} = A\underline{y}_t + \underline{k}. \tag{2.22}$$

Let us explore briefly the solution of equation (2.21) using the approach enunciated in chapter 1, of finding a 'particular solution' and 'complementary function' (see equation (1.84)): rigorous treatments of equations (2.21) and (2.22) will be given in section 2.9.

For the particular solution we try setting $\underline{y}' = \underline{0}$; this yields the steady-state solution, if such exists. Then $A\underline{y} + \underline{k} = \underline{0}$, i.e. *if* A *is invertible* we have

$$\underline{y} = \underline{y}^p = -A^{-1}\underline{k}. \tag{2.23}$$

A well-defined steady-state solution cannot exist if A is not invertible: there will be 0 or ∞ solutions to $A\underline{y} + \underline{k} = \underline{0}$.

For the complementary function we solve

$$\underline{y}' = A\underline{y}. \tag{2.24}$$

Following a familiar line, try $y_i = d_i e^{rt}$ (with $d_i \neq 0$). That is,

$$\underline{y} = e^{rt}.\underline{d}. \tag{2.25}$$

Differentiating, we require $\underline{y}' = r e^{rt}.\underline{d} = A\underline{y} = A(e^{rt}.\underline{d}) = e^{rt}.A\underline{d}$, or that

$$(A - rI)\underline{d} = \underline{0}. \tag{2.26}$$

There exists a $\underline{d} \neq \underline{0}$ satisfying equation (2.26) if and only if $\operatorname{rk}(A - rI) < n$ or, equivalently, if and only if

$$\det(A - rI) = 0. \tag{2.27}$$

To proceed further with the complementary function, we need to find the value(s) of r for which equation (2.27) holds.

2.8 EIGENVALUES AND EIGENVECTORS

Let A be any $n \times n$ square matrix. The equation

$$\det(A - rI) = 0 \tag{2.28}$$

is called the *characteristic equation* of A. The left-hand side is called the *characteristic polynomial* of A.

2.8.1 Exercise

Consider the matrix

$$A = \begin{bmatrix} -2 & 3 & 1 \\ 0 & 1 & 1 \\ -3 & 4 & 1 \end{bmatrix}.$$

Show that its characteristic polynomial is

$$\det(A - rI) = \det \begin{bmatrix} -2-r & 3 & 1 \\ 0 & 1-r & 1 \\ -3 & 4 & 1-r \end{bmatrix} = -r^3 + 4r.$$

The solutions to the characteristic equation are called the *characteristic roots* or, more commonly, *eigenvalues* of A. The characteristic polynomial of an $n \times n$ matrix has degree n, and there are therefore n eigenvalues, not necessarily all real or all distinct. The eigenvalues of the matrix in Exercise 2.8.1 above *are* all real and distinct: they are $r = 0, 2, -2$.

To proceed further with the differential equation system $\underline{y}' = A\underline{y} + \underline{k}$ along the line just indicated in Example 2.7.3, we would need to calculate the eigenvalues of the coefficient matrix A.

If $r = r_0$ is an eigenvalue of the matrix A then $\det(A - r_0 I) = 0$, i.e. the matrix $A - r_0 I$ is not invertible and $\text{rk}(A - r_0 I) < n$. Following the argument that led to equation (2.13) this means there exists an $\underline{x} \neq \underline{0}$ such that $(A - r_0)\underline{x} = \underline{0}$, i.e.

$$A\underline{x} = r_0\underline{x} \qquad (\underline{x} \neq \underline{0}). \tag{2.29}$$

Such an $\underline{x}$, non-zero and satisfying equation (2.29), is called an *eigenvector* for the eigenvalue $r = r_0$.

2.8.2 Example

To find the eigenvectors of the matrix

$$A = \begin{bmatrix} -2 & 3 & 1 \\ 0 & 1 & 1 \\ -3 & 4 & 1 \end{bmatrix}$$

in Exercise 2.8.1 requires us to solve $(A - rI)\underline{x} = 0$ for $r = 0, 2, -2$. This matrix equation may be written

$$\begin{bmatrix} -2-r & 3 & 1 \\ 0 & 1-r & 1 \\ -3 & 4 & 1-r \end{bmatrix} \begin{bmatrix} x \\ y \\ z \end{bmatrix} = \begin{bmatrix} 0 \\ 0 \\ 0 \end{bmatrix}$$

and solved for $r = 0, 2, -2$ by elementary simultaneous equation methods. We find that the eigenvectors for $r = 0$ have $x = y = -z$, i.e. they are of the form

$$\begin{bmatrix} a \\ a \\ -a \end{bmatrix} = a \begin{bmatrix} 1 \\ 1 \\ -1 \end{bmatrix}$$

whilst for $r = 2, -2$ they are

$$\begin{bmatrix} b \\ b \\ b \end{bmatrix} = b \begin{bmatrix} 1 \\ 1 \\ 1 \end{bmatrix} \quad \text{and} \quad \begin{bmatrix} 5c \\ -3c \\ 9c \end{bmatrix} = c \begin{bmatrix} 5 \\ -3 \\ 9 \end{bmatrix}$$

respectively. Notice that the three 'underlying' eigenvectors above are linearly independent: if

$$a_1 \begin{bmatrix} 1 \\ 1 \\ -1 \end{bmatrix} + a_2 \begin{bmatrix} 1 \\ 1 \\ 1 \end{bmatrix} + a_3 \begin{bmatrix} 5 \\ -3 \\ 9 \end{bmatrix} = \begin{bmatrix} 0 \\ 0 \\ 0 \end{bmatrix}$$

then $a_1 = a_2 = a_3 = 0$.

2.8.3 Exercises

(a) Let A be the matrix

$$\begin{bmatrix} 1 & 2 & 1 \\ 0 & 1 & 2 \\ -3 & 4 & 1 \end{bmatrix}$$

as in equation (2.5). Show that the characteristic polynomial of A is $-r^3 + 3r^2 + 2r - 16$. (Notice that $\det A = -16$ emerges as the constant term in this polynomial: a useful check of accuracy.) One eigenvalue is $r = -2$; are there any other real eigenvalues? Find the general form for the eigenvectors corresponding to the eigenvalue $r = -2$.

(b) Find the characteristic equation of the 2×2 matrix

$$\begin{bmatrix} a & b \\ c & d \end{bmatrix}.$$

Let the two eigenvalues be r_1 and r_2 (not necessarily distinct). Show that $r_1 + r_2 = \text{tr } A$ and $r_1 r_2 = \det A$.

(c) Suppose that an $n \times n$ matrix A has n distinct real eigenvalues $r_1, r_2, \ldots, r_n$ and let $\underline{e}_1, \underline{e}_2, \ldots, \underline{e}_n$ be respective eigenvectors. Show that $\underline{e}_1, \underline{e}_2, \ldots, \underline{e}_n$ are linearly independent, by, (i) supposing that they are not, (ii) choosing from the set of all possible linear equations $\sum_{i=1}^{n} a_i \underline{e}_i = \underline{0}$ in which not all of the coefficients are zero, one, say

$$\sum_i b_i \underline{e}_i = \underline{0} \tag{A}$$

with the *fewest* non-zero coefficients, (iii) pre-multiplying this equation by A, to obtain

$$\sum_i b_i r_i \underline{e}_i = \underline{0}, \tag{B}$$

and (iv) eliminating one of the $\underline{e}_i$ from (A) and (B).

(d) Show that the matrix

$$A = \begin{bmatrix} 1 & 0 \\ 1 & 1 \end{bmatrix}$$

does not have two distinct eigenvalues, nor does it have two linearly independent eigenvectors.

Let $r_1, r_2, \ldots, r_n$ (not necessarily all distinct) be the n eigenvalues of an $n \times n$ matrix A. Further, let $\underline{x}_1, \underline{x}_2, \ldots, \underline{x}_n$ be eigenvectors for these eigenvalues. If P is the $n \times n$ matrix whose columns are these eigenvectors of A, thus

$$P = [\underline{x}_1, \underline{x}_2, \ldots, \underline{x}_n] \tag{2.30}$$

then it is easy to see that

$$AP = (A\underline{x}_1, A\underline{x}_2, \ldots, A\underline{x}_n) = (r_1 \underline{x}_1, r_2 \underline{x}_2, \ldots, r_n \underline{x}_n) = PD \tag{2.31}$$

where D is the diagonal matrix containing the eigenvalues of A:

$$D = \begin{bmatrix} r_1 & 0 & . & . & . & 0 \\ 0 & r_2 & . & . & . & 0 \\ . & . & . & & & . \\ . & . & & . & & . \\ . & . & & & . & . \\ 0 & 0 & . & . & . & r_n \end{bmatrix}. \tag{2.32}$$

The equation

$$AP = PD \tag{2.33}$$

is a compact, matrix version of the set of equations

$$A\underline{x}_i = r_i \underline{x}_i \qquad (1 \leqslant i \leqslant n) \tag{2.34}$$

which summarizes all of the eigenvalue/eigenvector information about the matrix A.

If the eigenvectors $\underline{x}_1, \underline{x}_2, \ldots, \underline{x}_n$ which form the columns of P are linearly independent (as is the case if $r_1, r_2, \ldots, r_n$ are all distinct, see Exercise 2.8.3(c)) then rk $P = n$, i.e. P is invertible and we can write equation (2.33) as

$$P^{-1}AP = D. \tag{2.35}$$

Of course, the matrix P is not uniquely defined: to form P, we *chose* eigenvectors corresponding to the eigenvalues of A. If we had chosen differently, P would have been different. How, then, might we settle upon eigenvectors in a well-defined way? If A is *symmetric*, and its eigenvalues are *distinct*, then we can easily prove a result, as below, which turns out to be crucial for our treatment of quadratic forms in section 2.10.

2.8.4 Theorem

If A is $n \times n$ symmetric and has n distinct eigenvalues, then a matrix P can be chosen to satisfy equations (2.33) and (2.35) for which $P^{-1} = P^t$.

Proof In general if the columns of P are the eigenvectors $\underline{x}_1, \underline{x}_2, \ldots, \underline{x}_n$ then the (i,j)th element of P^tP is $\underline{x}_i^t \underline{x}_j$. We can always choose each $\underline{x}_i$ such that $\underline{x}_i^t \underline{x}_i = 1$. For if $1 \neq \underline{x}_i^t \underline{x}_i = k_i > 0$, we could replace $\underline{x}_i$ by $\underline{x}_i^* = \underline{x}_i/k_i$ and then $\underline{x}_i^{*t} \underline{x}_i^* = 1$ (e.g. replace

$$\begin{bmatrix} 1 \\ 1 \\ 1 \end{bmatrix}, \text{ for which } \begin{bmatrix} 1 \\ 1 \\ 1 \end{bmatrix}^t \begin{bmatrix} 1 \\ 1 \\ 1 \end{bmatrix} = 3 \text{ by } \begin{bmatrix} 1/\sqrt{3} \\ 1/\sqrt{3} \\ 1/\sqrt{3} \end{bmatrix},$$

which has the desired property). However we may choose $\underline{x}_1, \underline{x}_2, \ldots, \underline{x}_n$, the off-diagonal terms $\underline{x}_i^t \underline{x}_j$ ($i \neq j$) in $P^t P$ are zero. For consider:

$$r_i \underline{x}_i^t \underline{x}_j = (r_i \underline{x}_i)^t \underline{x}_j = (A\underline{x}_i)^t \underline{x}_j = \underline{x}_i^t A^t \underline{x}_j = \underline{x}_i^t A \underline{x}_j = \underline{x}_i^t (r_j \underline{x}_j) = r_j \underline{x}_i^t \underline{x}_j.$$

By assumption $r_i \neq r_j$, and so (comparing first and last terms in this equation string) $\underline{x}_i^t \underline{x}_j = 0$. Therefore we can choose P such that $P^t P = I$. This is enough to prove the result.

A matrix P satisfying $P^{-1} = P^t$ is called *orthogonal*. If we can choose P in this way, then A is said to be *orthogonally diagonalizable* and equation (2.35) becomes

$$P^t A P = D. \tag{2.36}$$

In fact an $n \times n$ symmetric matrix does not need to have n distinct eigenvalues to be orthogonally diagonalizable.

2.8.5 Theorem

If A is $n \times n$ symmetric, then A has n real eigenvalues and there exists an orthogonal matrix P such that equation (2.36) holds.

Proof See O'Nan (1977, chapter 7).

2.8.6 Exercises

(a) Show that

$$A = \begin{bmatrix} 0 & 0 & 1 \\ 0 & 0 & 0 \\ 1 & 0 & 0 \end{bmatrix}$$

has eigenvalues $r = 0, 1, -1$. Find the eigenvectors $\underline{x}$ for each eigenvalue which satisfy $\underline{x}^t \underline{x} = 1$. Show that

$$P = \begin{bmatrix} 0 & 1/\sqrt{2} & 1/\sqrt{2} \\ 1 & 0 & 0 \\ 0 & 1/\sqrt{2} & -1/\sqrt{2} \end{bmatrix}$$

satisfies $PP^t = P^t P$ and evaluate $P^t A P$.

(b) Verify that

$$A = \begin{bmatrix} 1 & 0 & -2 \\ 0 & 0 & 0 \\ -2 & 0 & 4 \end{bmatrix}$$

has eigenvalues $r = 0$ (repeated) and $r = 5$. Find the eigenvectors of A. Show that you can choose two for $r = 0$, call them $\underline{x}_1$ and $\underline{x}_2$, and one for $r = 5$, call it $\underline{x}_3$, such that $P = (\underline{x}_1, \underline{x}_2, \underline{x}_3)$ satisfies $P^{-1} = P^t$ and

$$P^t A P = \begin{bmatrix} 0 & 0 & 0 \\ 0 & 0 & 0 \\ 0 & 0 & 5 \end{bmatrix}.$$

(*Hint*: ensure that each $\underline{x}_i$ satisfies $\underline{x}_i^t \underline{x}_i = 1$.)

(c) Show that for any $n \times n$ matrix A with eigenvalues $r_1, r_2, \ldots, r_n$, $\det A = r_1 r_2 \ldots r_n$. (*Hint*: what is the constant term in the characteristic polynomial of A? Recall Exercise 2.8.3(a).)

2.9 SYSTEMS OF DIFFERENTIAL AND DIFFERENCE EQUATIONS

We consider first the system of first-order linear differential equations

$$\underline{y}' = A\underline{y} + \underline{k} \tag{2.21}$$

with constant coefficients.

In section 2.7 we adopted the particular solution/complementary function approach to solving this system. We found a particular solution $\underline{y}^p = -A^{-1}\underline{k}$ (assuming A to be invertible) and, guided by our experience with single equations in chapter 1, a complementary function involving exponentials e^{rt} for which r had to be an eigenvalue of A.

Here, we shall *prove* that the solution is of this form, thereby justifying the choice of exponential functions, *under the assumption that* A *is invertible and has* n *linearly independent eigenvectors*. By Exercise 2.8.6(c), the assumption of invertibility of A is equivalent to an assumption of *non-zero eigenvalues*.

Let the eigenvalues of A be $r_1, r_2, \ldots, r_n$. Then because of the linear independence in the corresponding eigenvectors, we know that there exists a matrix P such that

$$P^{-1} A P = D \tag{2.35}$$

with D as in equation (2.32). Now let

$$\underline{w} = P^{-1}\underline{y}'. \tag{2.37}$$

Then

$$P\underline{w} = \underline{y}' \tag{2.38}$$

and it is easily seen that

$$\underline{w}' = P^{-1}\underline{y}'' = P^{-1}(A\underline{y}+\underline{k})' = P^{-1}A\underline{y}' = P^{-1}AP\underline{w} = D\underline{w}$$

i.e.

$$w_i' = r_i w_i. \tag{2.39}$$

This is a simple first-order differential equation for w_i and it implies

$$w_i = k_i \exp(r_i t) \tag{2.40}$$

where k_i is constant $(1 \leqslant i \leqslant n)$ (see equation (1.83)).
    Therefore we may write

$$\underline{w} = K\underline{e} \tag{2.41}$$

where

$$K = \begin{bmatrix} k_1 & & & \\ & k_2 & & \bigcirc \\ & & \ddots & \\ & \bigcirc & & \\ & & & k_n \end{bmatrix} \quad \text{and} \quad \underline{e} = \begin{bmatrix} \exp(r_1 t) \\ \exp(r_2 t) \\ \exp(r_n t) \end{bmatrix}.$$

Then

$$\underline{y} = A^{-1}(\underline{y}'-\underline{k}) = A^{-1}(P\underline{w}-\underline{k}) = A^{-1}P\underline{w} - A^{-1}\underline{k} = C\underline{e} - A^{-1}\underline{k} \tag{2.42}$$

where $C = A^{-1}PK$. This is in the form

$$\underline{y} = \underline{y}^c + \underline{y}^p \tag{2.43}$$

where

$$y_i^c = \sum_{j=1}^{n} c_{ij} \exp(r_j t) \tag{2.44}$$

and

$$y^p = -A^{-1}\underline{k} \tag{2.45}$$

as in equation (2.23).

Thus we validate the choice of exponentials e^{rt} for the complementary function. But recall our initial assumption, that A must have n linearly independent eigenvectors. If this is not so, the solution cannot be established in the form of equations (2.43)–(2.45).

2.9.1 Exercise

Consider the second-order linear differential equation with constant coefficients $x'' + px' + qx = c$. Verify that, as a matrix system of two first-order equations, this can be written

$$\begin{bmatrix} y' \\ x' \end{bmatrix} = \begin{bmatrix} -p & -q \\ 1 & 0 \end{bmatrix} \begin{bmatrix} y \\ x \end{bmatrix} + \begin{bmatrix} c \\ 0 \end{bmatrix}.$$

Prove that if $p^2 > 4q$ the general solution is of the form

$$x = d_1 \exp(r_1 t) + d_2 \exp(r_2 t) + c/q$$

(this was *asserted* in equation (1.87)). If $p^2 = 4q$ show that the coefficient matrix

$$\begin{bmatrix} -p & -q \\ 1 & 0 \end{bmatrix}$$

does not have two linearly independent eigenvectors and hence the matrix approach does not work. (This is the case of Example 1.9.2, where the general solution was asserted in equation (1.88) to be $x = (d_1 + d_2 t)e^{rt} + c/q$ with $r = -p/2$.)

Before turning to the difference equation system, we note that the condition for convergence of the complementary function, i.e. of the general solution to the steady state $y^p = -A^{-1}\underline{k}$, is that *all eigenvalues of A be negative*. If any are positive, the relevant exponentials $\exp(r_i t)$ go to infinity as $t \to \infty$ (recall no eigenvalue is zero by assumption).

For $n = 2$ this condition is equivalent to a simple condition on the matrix A that is easily checked:

$$\det A > 0 \quad \text{and} \quad \operatorname{tr} A < 0 \tag{2.46}$$

(recall Exercise 2.8.3(b)). For $n > 2$ the *Routh conditions* on the coefficients of the characteristic polynomial of A guarantee negative eigenvalues (see, for example, Chiang, 1984). See also Theorem 2.10.7.

The reader is also referred to chapter 7, section 7.8, where diagrammatic analysis is used to illustrate the steady-state properties of a *pair* of first-order differential equations: the differential equations do not need to be linear for this approach.

We turn now to the first-order linear difference equation system

$$\underline{y}_{t+1} = A\underline{y}_t + \underline{k}. \tag{2.22}$$

A steady-state solution, if such exists, is given by putting $\underline{y}_{t+1} = \underline{y}_t = \underline{y}^*$, say, in equation (2.21). Thus if $I - A$ *is invertible*, equivalently *if* A *does not have an eigenvalue of* $r = 1$ a steady state exists and is given by

$$\underline{y}^* = (I - A)^{-1}\underline{k}. \tag{2.47}$$

As in the case of the differential equation system, we shall also assume *that* A *has* n *linearly independent eigenvectors*. Then we can write

$$P^{-1}AP = D \tag{2.35}$$

with D as before. Now define

$$\underline{z}_t = \underline{y}_t - \underline{y}^* \tag{2.48}$$

so that

$$\underline{z}_{t+1} = A\underline{z}_t \tag{2.49}$$

and let

$$\underline{w}_t = P^{-1}\underline{z}_t \tag{2.50}$$

so that

$$\underline{z}_t = P\underline{w}_t. \tag{2.51}$$

Then

$$\underline{w}_{t+1} = P^{-1}\underline{z}_{t+1} = P^{-1}(A\underline{z}_t) = P^{-1}A(P\underline{w}_t) = D\underline{w}_t,$$

i.e.

$$w_{i,t+1} = r_i w_{i,t}. \tag{2.52}$$

This is a simple first-order linear difference equation in a single variable, whose solution we know to be in the form

$$w_{i,t} = k_i r_i^t \tag{2.53}$$

where k_i is constant $(1 \leqslant i \leqslant n)$ (see Exercise 1.9.3(b)).
   Therefore we may write

$$\underline{w}_t = K\underline{f}_t \tag{2.54}$$

where

$$\underline{f}_t = \begin{bmatrix} r_1^t \\ r_2^t \\ \vdots \\ r_n^t \end{bmatrix}. \tag{2.55}$$

Thus

$$\underline{y}_t = \underline{z}_t + \underline{y}^* = P\underline{w}_t + \underline{y}^* = PK\underline{f}_t + \underline{y}^*, \tag{2.56}$$

i.e. the solution to the system is in the form

$$\underline{y}_t = \underline{y}_t^c + \underline{y}^* \tag{2.57}$$

where

$$y_{i,t}^c = \sum_{j=1}^{n} c_{ij} r_j^t. \tag{2.58}$$

   This is precisely in the form advanced for certain single difference equations in chapter 1. As in the case of the differential equation system, we cannot, however, establish the general solution in this form if the coefficient matrix A violates the linear independence of eigenvectors assumption.

2.9.2 Exercise

Write the second-order difference equation $x_{t+2} + px_{t+1} + qx_t = c$ in the form $\underline{y}_{t+1} = A\underline{y}_t + \underline{k}$. Verify that the condition $\det(I - A) \neq 0$ is equivalent to $1 + p + q \neq 0$, and prove that if $p^2 > 4q$ then the general solution is of the form $x_t = d_1 r_1^t + d_2 r_2^t + c/(1 + p + q)$, using the matrix approach (this was asserted in equation (1.91)).

Finally, for convergence of equation (2.58) it is necessary and sufficient that $-1 < r_i < 1, 1 \leqslant i \leqslant n$. That is, *all eigenvalues of* A *must be less than unity in absolute value* (we have already assumed $r = 1$ is not an eigenvalue).

The conditions which guarantee this are the *Schur conditions* (see Chiang, 1984). For $n = 2$ they reduce to

$$1 + \det A + \operatorname{tr} A > 0$$
$$1 + \det A - \operatorname{tr} A > 0$$
$$1 - \det A > 0. \tag{2.59}$$

2.10 QUADRATIC FORMS

A *quadratic form* in n variables is an expression of the form

$$\sum_{i=1}^{n} \sum_{j=1}^{n} a_{ij} x_i x_j. \tag{2.60}$$

It is an important example of a *multi-variate function*, and may be written in matrix form as

$$q(\underline{x}) = \underline{x}^t A \underline{x} \tag{2.61}$$

where $A = (a_{ij})$. In Example 2.7.1 we saw that a firm's profit function, when facing linear demand schedules for n jointly produced and marketed goods, involved a quadratic form with output quantities q_i $(1 \leqslant i \leqslant n)$ as the variables. Multivariate functions will be studied further in the next chapter. Here, we record some of the properties of quadratic forms that are derivable using simple matrix algebra.

Quadratic forms involve variables to the second power, and cross-products of variables.

2.10.1 Examples

(a) $q(x_1, x_2) = x_1^2 + x_1 x_2 + x_2^2$ is a quadratic form. It may be written as

$$[x_1 \quad x_2] \begin{bmatrix} 1 & 1 \\ 0 & 1 \end{bmatrix} \begin{bmatrix} x_1 \\ x_2 \end{bmatrix} \quad \text{or as} \quad [x_1 \quad x_2] \begin{bmatrix} 1 & 0 \\ 1 & 1 \end{bmatrix} \begin{bmatrix} x_1 \\ x_2 \end{bmatrix}$$

or, indeed as

$$[x_1 \quad x_2] \begin{bmatrix} 1 & \frac{1}{2} \\ \frac{1}{2} & 1 \end{bmatrix} \begin{bmatrix} x_1 \\ x_2 \end{bmatrix}$$

etc.

(b) $q(x, y, z) = 2x^2 + 3y^2 + 10z^2 + 2xy - 6xz$ is a quadratic form in x, y and z. It may be written as, for example,

$$[x \quad y \quad z] \begin{bmatrix} 2 & 1 & -3 \\ 1 & 3 & 0 \\ -3 & 0 & 10 \end{bmatrix} \begin{bmatrix} x \\ y \\ z \end{bmatrix} \quad \text{or} \quad [x \quad y \quad z] \begin{bmatrix} 2 & 2 & 0 \\ 0 & 3 & 1 \\ -6 & -1 & 10 \end{bmatrix} \begin{bmatrix} x \\ y \\ z \end{bmatrix}.$$

Unfortunately there is no unique way to write a given quadratic form in matrix terms. The ambiguity arises because of the cross-product terms $x_i x_j$, $i \neq j$. For example, in (a) above we wrote

$$x_1 x_2 = 1 . x_1 x_2 + 0 . x_2 x_1 = 0 . x_1 x_2 + 1 . x_2 x_1 = (\tfrac{1}{2}) x_1 x_2 + (\tfrac{1}{2}) x_2 x_1,$$

arriving at a different matrix representation in each case. Indeed, where a cross-product term does not exist (e.g. yz in case (b) above), we could even put it in (as $+yz$) and then take it out again (as $-zy$). For each choice of how to write cross-product terms, a different matrix A arises in representing the given form as $q(\underline{x}) = \underline{x}^t A \underline{x}$.

We may resolve this situation by always choosing A to be *symmetric*. In doing this we treat all cross-product terms $x_i x_j$ systematically as $(\tfrac{1}{2}) x_i x_j + (\tfrac{1}{2}) x_j x_i$, and thereby eliminate all but one of the matrix possibilities.

2.10.2 Exercises

(a) Write each of the following quadratic forms in the form $\underline{x}^t A \underline{x}$ where A is symmetric:

(i) $q(x_1, x_2, x_3) = 2x_1 x_3$,

(ii) $q(x_1, x_2, x_3) = x_1^2 + 4x_3^2 - 4x_1 x_3$,

(iii) $q(x_1, x_2, x_3) = 4(x_1^2 + x_2^2 + x_3^2 + x_1 x_2 + x_2 x_3 + x_1 x_3)$,

(iv) $q(x_1, x_2, x_3, x_4, x_5) = 3x_1^2 + 3x_2^2 + 2x_3^2 + 2x_4^2 + 2x_5^2 + 2x_1 x_2 + 2x_3 x_4 \\ + 2x_3 x_5 + 2x_4 x_5.$

(b) Let $q(\underline{x}) = \underline{x}^t B \underline{x}$ where B is *not* symmetric. Let $A = (B + B^t)/2$ and $C = (B - B^t)/2$. Show that A is symmetric and evaluate both $\underline{x}^t A \underline{x}$ and $\underline{x}^t C \underline{x}$ (recall Exercise 2.2.2(e)).

Our main interest in quadratic forms will be in *signing* them. Could either of the quadratic forms in Examples 2.10.1 above be negative, for example? Are there non-zero values of the variables that make them zero?

2.10.3 Examples

(a) The quadratic form $q(x_1, x_2) = x_1^2 + x_1 x_2 + x_2^2$ of Exercise 2.10.1(a) can be written as $q(x_1, x_2) = (x_1 + x_2/2)^2 + 3x_2^2/4$. As a sum of squares, it cannot be negative and can only be zero when $(x_1 + x_2/2) = x_2 = 0$, i.e. when $x_1 = x_2 = 0$. We call this a *positive definite* quadratic form.

(b) The quadratic form $q(x, y, z) = 2x^2 + 3y^2 + 10z^2 + 2xy - 6xz$ of Exercise 2.10.1(b) can be written as $(x + y)^2 + 2y^2 + (x - 3z)^2 + z^2$. (There are also other ways of representing it as a sum of squares.) Thus $q(x, y, z) \geqslant 0$ for all x, y, z and $= 0$ only when $x = y = z = 0$. This is also a positive definite quadratic form.

(c) The quadratic form $x_1^2 + 2x_1 x_2 + x_2^2 = (x_1 + x_2)^2$ is always non-negative, but is zero whenever $x_1 = -x_2$; i.e. it is zero for non-zero values of the variables. We call this a *positive semi-definite* quadratic form.

(d) The quadratic form $x_1^2 - 6x_1 x_2 = (x_1 - 3x_2)^2 - 9x_2^2$ can be positive or negative: it is an *indefinite* quadratic form.

2.10.4 Definition

A quadratic form $q(\underline{x}) = \underline{x}^t A \underline{x}$ is

positive definite if $q(\underline{x}) \geqslant 0$ for all $\underline{x}$, and $= 0$ only if $\underline{x} = \underline{0}$;
positive semi-definite if $q(\underline{x}) \geqslant 0$ for all $\underline{x}$, and $= 0$ for some $\underline{x} \neq \underline{0}$;
negative definite if $q(\underline{x}) \leqslant 0$ for all $\underline{x}$, and $= 0$ only if $\underline{x} = \underline{0}$;
negative semi-definite if $q(\underline{x}) \leqslant 0$ for all $\underline{x}$, and $= 0$ for some $\underline{x} \neq \underline{0}$;
indefinite if there exist $\underline{x}_1, \underline{x}_2$ such that $q(\underline{x}_1) > 0$ and $q(\underline{x}_2) < 0$.

The technique used in Examples 2.10.3 to examine the sign of the quadratic forms is known as *completing the square*. It amounts to choosing linear combinations of the variables in such a way that the entire quadratic form is expressed as a sum/difference of squares.

Let is examine the problem of signing a quadratic form $q(\underline{x}) = \underline{x}^t A \underline{x}$ using the eigenvalue/eigenvector information about the symmetric matrix A. By Theorem 2.8.5 we can choose a matrix P of eigenvectors of A such that

$$P^{-1} = P^t \quad \text{and} \quad P^t A P = D = \begin{bmatrix} r_1 & 0 & . & . & . & 0 \\ 0 & r_2 & . & . & . & 0 \\ . & . & . & & & . \\ . & . & & . & & . \\ . & . & & & . & . \\ 0 & 0 & . & . & . & r_n \end{bmatrix}. \tag{2.62}$$

Now let $\underline{y} = P^t \underline{x}$. This defines new variables $y_1, y_2, \ldots, y_n$ as linear combinations of the old ones:

$$y_i = \sum_{j=1}^{n} p_{ji} x_j. \tag{2.63}$$

Further, since $PP^t = I$ we have $\underline{x} = P\underline{y}$ and

$$q(\underline{x}) = \underline{x}^t A \underline{x} = (P\underline{y})^t A P \underline{y} = \underline{y}^t (P^t A P) \underline{y} = \sum_{i=1}^{n} r_i y_i^2. \tag{2.64}$$

Thus we 'complete the square': the quadratic form is expressed in terms of the new variables as a sum/difference of squared terms. To determine the sign that $q(\underline{x})$ takes, we simply inspect the signs of the coefficients in equation (2.64), i.e. *the signs of the eigenvalues of* A. Note that $\underline{y} = \underline{0}$ if and only if $\underline{x} = \underline{0}$.

2.10.5 Theorem

If A is symmetric then the quadratic form $q(\underline{x}) = \underline{x}^t A \underline{x}$ is:

positive definite if all eigenvalues of A are positive;
positive semi-definite if all eigenvalues are non-negative, and at least one is zero;
negative definite if all eigenvalues of A are negative;
negative semi-definite if all eigenvalues are non-positive, and at least one is zero;
indefinite if there are positive *and* negative eigenvalues.

(For example, suppose that $r_1 = 0$ and $r_2, \ldots, r_n$ are all positive. Then $q(\underline{x}) = \sum_{i=2}^{n} r_i y_i^2 \geqslant 0$ for all $\underline{y}$, i.e. for all $\underline{x} = P\underline{y}$, and is zero when $y_1 = 1$, $y_2 = y_3 = \ldots = y_n = 0$, i.e. when $\underline{x} = P(1, 0, 0, \ldots, 0)^t \neq \underline{0}$.)

2.10.6 Exercise

For each quadratic form in Exercise 2.10.2(a) find the eigenvalues of the associated matrix A, and thereby classify the form as definite/indefinite.

Checking eigenvalues can be tedious. There is a convenient condition on the matrix A, in terms of certain sub-determinants, which can be used to identify positive definite and negative definite quadratic forms; this criterion will be particularly useful in the next chapter.

2.10.7 Theorem

The quadratic form $\underline{x}^t A \underline{x}$, A symmetric, is positive definite if and only if:

$$a_{11} > 0 \quad \det \begin{bmatrix} a_{11} & a_{12} \\ a_{21} & a_{22} \end{bmatrix} > 0 \quad \det \begin{bmatrix} a_{11} & a_{12} & a_{13} \\ a_{21} & a_{22} & a_{23} \\ a_{31} & a_{32} & a_{33} \end{bmatrix} > 0 \quad \ldots$$

i.e. if and only if all of these sub-determinants are positive.

The quadratic form is negative definite if and only if the signs alternate:

$$a_{11} < 0 \quad \det\begin{bmatrix} a_{11} & a_{12} \\ a_{21} & a_{22} \end{bmatrix} > 0 \quad \det\begin{bmatrix} a_{11} & a_{12} & a_{13} \\ a_{21} & a_{22} & a_{23} \\ a_{31} & a_{32} & a_{33} \end{bmatrix} < 0 \quad \ldots$$

The negative definiteness condition in Theorem 2.10.7 may also be used to check for convergence in the solution of a differential equation system $\underline{y}' = A\underline{y} + \underline{k}$ *if* A *is symmetric*: as we have seen, this requires negative eigenvalues.

These conditions on a symmetric matrix A, in Theorems 2.10.5 and 2.10.7, permit the signing of the quadratic form $\underline{x}^t A\underline{x}$. We may say that the matrix A is itself positive definite if $\underline{x}^t A\underline{x}$ is positive definite; negative definite if $\underline{x}^t A\underline{x}$ is negative definite; etc. Then the conditions on eigenvalues in Theorem 2.10.5 and on sub-determinants in Theorem 2.10.7 are conditions which determine the definiteness/indefiniteness of the matrix A. We meet these conditions again in the next chapter.

2.10.8 Exercise

Complete the square for the quadratic form

$$[x \quad y]\begin{bmatrix} a & b \\ c & d \end{bmatrix}\begin{bmatrix} x \\ y \end{bmatrix}.$$

Hence find conditions on a, b, c and d which are necessary and sufficient for positive definiteness/negative definiteness of the matrix

$$\begin{bmatrix} a & b \\ c & d \end{bmatrix}.$$

Confirm that they are as in Theorems 2.10.5 and 2.10.7 above.

3 Multivariate Calculus

In this chapter we review the calculus of functions of several variables. Let $x_1, \ldots, x_n$ be n variables and let $y = f(x_1, \ldots, x_n)$ be a function of $x_1, \ldots, x_n$. We may write $(x_1, \ldots, x_n)$ as a $1 \times n$ row vector, $\underline{x} = (x_1, \ldots, x_n)$, and then $y = f(\underline{x})$.

In economics, functions of several variables abound. For example: the conventional production function $Q = F(K, L)$ where K is capital stock, L is labour and Q is output (here $n = 2$); the consumption function suggested by the work of Patinkin (1965) and others, $C = C(Y_d, r, A)$, where Y_d is total disposable income, r the interest rate and A total real cash balances (here $n = 3$); and an extension $T = T(X, \underline{b})$ of the income tax revenue function $T(X)$ discussed in chapter 1, in which explicit account is taken of the effect on revenue of (changes in) a vector $\underline{b}$ of tax parameters, e.g. allowances, thresholds and marginal rates (here n may be very large).

3.1 PARTIAL DIFFERENTIATION

Given a function $y = f(x_1, \ldots, x_n) = f(\underline{x})$, we shall be interested in the effect upon y of (small) changes in the variables $x_1, \ldots, x_n$. If we are seeking to maximize y, for example, then much as in the univariate case in chapter 1 we need to find values of $\underline{x}$ at which $f(\underline{x})$ is stationary: very small changes in the x_i ($1 \leqslant i \leqslant n$) should produce no change in y.

If only *one* of the x_i ($1 \leqslant i \leqslant n$), say x_j, is allowed to change, to $x_j + \Delta x_j$ (e.g. for the consumption function above consider a *ceteris paribus* change in the interest rate), then we may measure the rate of response of $y = f(x_1, \ldots, x_n)$ by the *partial derivative*, holding the other x_i ($i \neq j$) constant. This is denoted variously by

$$\frac{\partial f}{\partial x_j} \quad \text{or} \quad f_j(x_1, \ldots, x_n) \quad \text{or} \quad \frac{\partial y}{\partial x_j}$$

and is defined formally as

$$\frac{\partial f}{\partial x_j} = \lim_{\Delta x_j \to 0} [f(x_1, \ldots, x_{j-1}, x_j + \Delta x_j, x_{j+1}, \ldots, x_n) - f(x_1, \ldots, x_n)] / \Delta x_j$$

if this limit exists.

$$(3.1)$$

The discussion of non-differentiability in chapter 1 is applicable here too: if the above limit does not exist we may nevertheless be able to define *left and right partial derivatives*, denoted

$$\left(\frac{\partial f}{\partial x_j}\right)^{-} \quad \text{and} \quad \left(\frac{\partial f}{\partial x_j}\right)^{+}$$

where, in the limit in the definition above, $\Delta x_j \nearrow 0$ or $\searrow 0$ respectively. We shall encounter left and right partial derivatives again in chapter 5.

Partial differentiation is very much like univariate differentiation; in holding the other x_i constant, we treat $y = f(x_1, \ldots, x_n)$ as a function of the single variable x_j only.

3.1.1 Example

Let us obtain $\partial y/\partial x_1$, $\partial y/\partial x_2$ and $\partial y/\partial x_3$ when $y = x_1^2 + x_1 x_3 - x_2 \exp(x_3)$. For each of the partial derivatives, we treat the irrelevant variables as constants. Thus

$$\frac{\partial y}{\partial x_1} = 2x_1 + x_3$$

$$\frac{\partial y}{\partial x_2} = -\exp(x_3)$$

$$\frac{\partial y}{\partial x_3} = x_1 - x_2 \exp(x_3).$$

3.1.2 Exercises

Find all partial derivatives, in the following cases:

(a) $y = 3x_1^2 + x_2^3 - 3x_1 x_2$.

(b) $y = x_1 x_2 x_3$.

(c) $y = x_2 + \ln(x_1 x_3)$.

(d) $y = x_1^{x_2}$ (care: see equation (1.27)).

(e) $Q = K^a L^b$ (the Cobb–Douglas production function).

(f) $Q = (K^{-r} + aL^{-r})^{(-1/r)}$ (the CES production function).

We may also differentiate repeatedly with respect to the same variable, or, equally, first with respect to one variable and then another. Thus

$$\frac{\partial^2 f}{\partial x_i \partial x_j} = \frac{\partial(\partial f/\partial x_j)}{\partial x_i}$$

is the partial derivative with respect to x_i of $f_j(x_1, \ldots, x_n)$, and may alternatively be denoted $(\partial/\partial x_i)(\partial f/\partial x_j)$ or $f_{ij}(x_1, \ldots, x_n)$ or $\partial^2 y/\partial x_i \partial x_j$. It is called the *second partial derivative*; if $i \neq j$ it may be called the *cross-partial derivative*.

Young's theorem says that if $f(x_1, \ldots, x_n)$, $f_i(x_1, \ldots, x_n)$ and $f_{ij}(x_1, \ldots, x_n)$ are all *continuous* functions of $(x_1, \ldots, x_n)$ then

$$f_{ij}(x_1, \ldots, x_n) = f_{ji}(x_1, \ldots, x_n) \tag{3.2}$$

$(1 \leq i,j \leq n)$. Thus it does not matter in which order you differentiate, if the function and its partial derivatives are 'well-behaved'. (Economists often tend to assume that their functions are well-behaved: exploring non-well-behavedness is more the province of the pure mathematician.) Young's theorem has some strikingly surprising economic consequences, as we shall see in chapter 6. A rigorous proof may be found in Widder (1961, p. 52); this makes clear the exact mathematical nature of the continuity assumptions.

3.1.3 Exercise

(a) Verify that $\partial^2 f/\partial x_1 \partial x_2 = \partial^2 f/\partial x_2 \partial x_1$ for the functions in Exercise 3.1.2(a), (b), (c) and (d).

(b) Find $\partial^2 Q/\partial K^2$, $\partial^2 Q/\partial L^2$ and $\partial^2 Q/\partial K \partial L$ for the production function in Exercise 3.1.2(e).

Let us now consider the usefulness of partial derivatives to the economist.

For example, consider the production function $Q = F(K, L)$. The definition of $\partial Q/\partial K$ is

$$\partial Q/\partial K = \lim_{\Delta K \to 0} [F(K+\Delta K, L) - F(K, L)]/\Delta K \tag{3.3}$$

assuming that this exists (i.e. that the production function is well-behaved). If K is very large, say it is measured in millions, then putting $\Delta K = 1$ is an extremely small change; and we may approximate

$$\partial Q/\partial K \doteq F(K+1, L) - F(K, L),$$

i.e. $\partial Q/\partial K$ is the marginal product of one more unit of capital. More generally, if $K \to K + \Delta K$, then from equation (3.3) $\Delta Q = F(K+\Delta K, L) - F(K, L)$ may be approximated as

$$\Delta Q \doteq \left(\frac{\partial Q}{\partial K}\right) \Delta K \tag{3.4}$$

i.e. we may use the marginal product of capital as a multiplier to determine the output effect of small changes in K. The second partial derivative $\partial^2 Q/\partial K \partial L$ represents, in a similar manner, the effect upon the marginal product of capital of one more unit of labour (or *vice versa*, by Young's theorem).

Similarly, for the consumption function $C(Y_d, r, A)$, the partial derivative $\partial C/\partial Y_d$ is the marginal propensity to consume; and for the tax function $T(X, \underline{b})$, $\partial T/\partial X$ is the *effective marginal rate*, or the increase in revenue following a unit increase in total income. If in $T(X, \underline{b})$, b_1 is the basic tax allowance, then $\partial T/\partial b_1$ measures the effect on tax revenue of an increase of £1 in the allowance (and is therefore *negative*). Thus the partial derivatives convey useful information about the tax.

3.2 GRAPHICAL REPRESENTATIONS

It is worth examining more closely the general formulation $y = f(x_1, \ldots, x_n)$, when $n = 2$. For in this case we can 'graph' the function, rather as we did for the univariate case (where, of course, $n = 1$). However, we need three dimensions to do it. Imagine, therefore, that the axes in figure 3.1 are

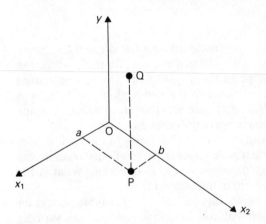

Figure 3.1

mutually perpendicular. The x_1-axis and x_2-axis are drawn (coming out of the page, if you like) for *positive* values of x_1 and x_2 only (for negative values, go back into the page). P denotes the point in the (x_1, x_2)-*plane* whose co-ordinates are (a, b); and by raising a vertical line from P whose height is $f(a, b)$ we reach the point Q – whose co-ordinates in three-dimensional space are therefore $[a, b, f(a, b)]$. Now let a and b vary freely; Q traces out a *surface* in three dimensions. Just as a function of one variable can be graphed as a curve in two dimensions, a function of two variables can be graphed as a surface in three dimensions. Functions of three or more variables are hard to envisage graphically.

Figure 3.2 shows the graph of the function $y = 3x_1^2 + x_2^3 - 3x_1x_2$ of Exercise 3.1.2(a), drawn by computer for $-3 \leqslant x_1 \leqslant 3$ and $-3 \leqslant x_2 \leqslant 3$. We are looking at the surface from an angle, seeing some of it from above and some of it from below (turned up, as it were).

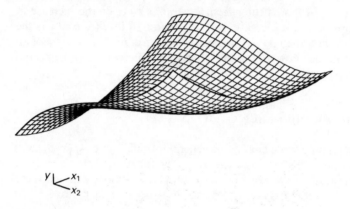

Figure 3.2

It is clear from the way we constructed the partial derivatives that in general $\partial f/\partial x_1$ represents the slope along the surface in the x_1-direction and $\partial f/\partial x_2$ represents the slope in the x_2-direction. The second partial derivatives $\partial^2 f/\partial x_i^2$ measure curvature in the x_i-direction ($i = 1, 2$), as in the univariate case, whilst $\partial^2 f/\partial x_1 \partial x_2$ measures the rate at which the slope in one direction changes as you move in the other direction.

(Imagine standing on the surface in figure 3.2, facing in the x_1-direction, recording the slope, and then side-stepping a small distance in the x_2-direction and re-recording the slope in the x_1-direction. What is the interpretation of Young's theorem in this context?)

Surfaces $y = f(x_1, x_2)$ in three dimensions can resemble mountain ranges, valleys, cliffs, etc. Differentiable functions yield *smooth* surfaces (with no cliffs, precipices, spikes).

3.3 TURNING POINTS

Given a differentiable function $y = f(x_1, x_2)$, we may look for turning points. We will recognize a local maximum as a mountain top; a minimum as a valley bottom. There will also be inflections (in fact one is pictured in figure 3.2, in addition to a minimum) and *saddle points*: see figure 3.3, which portrays a minimum in one direction and a maximum in the other.

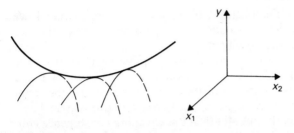

Figure 3.3

A common feature of all turning points is that they are stationary points. In other words they satisfy

$$\frac{\partial f}{\partial x_1} = 0 \quad \text{and} \quad \frac{\partial f}{\partial x_2} = 0.$$

3.3.1 Exercise

For the function in Exercise 3.1.2(a), graphed in figure 3.2, verify that the turning points are at $(x_1, x_2) = (0, 0)$ and $(\frac{1}{4}, \frac{1}{2})$.

For $n > 2$, we may define the turning points of $f(x_1, \ldots, x_n)$ similarly. They must satisfy

$$\frac{\partial f}{\partial x_1} = \frac{\partial f}{\partial x_2} = \ldots = \frac{\partial f}{\partial x_n} = 0. \tag{3.5}$$

These are necessary conditions and do not, of course, tell us what type of turning points the function has.

3.3.2 Exercises

Find the turning points, if any, of the following functions.

(a) $y = 3x_1 + 2x_2 - x_3 + 6$.

(b) $y = x_1 x_2 x_3 - x_1 x_2 + 2x_3 - x_3^2$ (care: there are infinitely many).

(c) $y = 3x_1^2 + 2x_2^2 - 4x_2 + 1$. What is the stationary value of y?

3.4 THE TAYLOR SERIES EXPANSION

Suppose we start at a point $f(\underline{a}) = f(a_1, \ldots, a_n)$, not necessarily a turning point, and move away slightly. Namely, let $a_i \rightarrow a_i + \Delta a_i$ for each i. What happens to the value of the function? In the $n = 1$ case, in chapter 1, we used Taylor's theorem and the Taylor series expansion to answer this; we need a generalization of that result here.

Recall the univariate case. We were able in equation (1.14) to write $f(x+a) = f(a) + xf'(a) + x^2 f''(a)/2! + \ldots$ assuming smoothness of f and convergence of a remainder term. For the several-variable case the result is similar. Using vector notation, the similarity becomes transparent.

Provided f is 'sufficiently smooth' then under certain convergence conditions we may write

$$f(\underline{x}+\underline{a}) = f(\underline{a}) + \sum_{i=1}^{n} x_i f_i(\underline{a}) + \sum_{i=1}^{n} \sum_{j=1}^{n} x_i x_j f_{ij}(\underline{a})/2! + \ldots \tag{3.6}$$

with higher-order terms involving third, fourth,... partial derivatives, extra summations and quotients $3!, 4!, \ldots$ etc. See Apostol (1974, p. 361), for a detailed statement of the actual mathematical requirements.

Using matrix notation, we may conveniently represent the first few terms of equation (3.6) as

$$f(\underline{x}+\underline{a}) = f(\underline{a}) + \underline{x}^t \nabla f(\underline{a}) + \underline{x}^t H(\underline{a})\underline{x}/2! + \ldots \tag{3.7}$$

where

$$\nabla f(\underline{a}) = \begin{bmatrix} f_1(\underline{a}) \\ \vdots \\ f_n(\underline{a}) \end{bmatrix} \tag{3.8}$$

is called (naturally enough) the *gradient vector* of f at $\underline{a}$, and

$$H(\underline{a}) = \begin{bmatrix} f_{11}(\underline{a}) & f_{12}(\underline{a}) & f_{13}(\underline{a}) & \cdots & f_{1n}(\underline{a}) \\ f_{21}(\underline{a}) & f_{22}(\underline{a}) & f_{23}(\underline{a}) & \cdots & f_{2n}(\underline{a}) \\ f_{31}(\underline{a}) & f_{32}(\underline{a}) & f_{33}(\underline{a}) & \cdots & f_{3n}(\underline{a}) \\ \vdots & \vdots & \vdots & \ddots & \vdots \\ f_{n1}(\underline{a}) & f_{n2}(\underline{a}) & f_{n3}(\underline{a}) & \cdots & f_{nn}(\underline{a}) \end{bmatrix} \tag{3.9}$$

is the *Hessian matrix* of f at $\underline{a}$, which is symmetric by Young's theorem. Notice the *quadratic form* in equation (3.7).

In the Appendix we show how the gradient vector can be extended to certain non-differentiable functions (e.g, functions which have left and right partial derivatives).

3.4.1 Exercise

Given that, for any function $f(\underline{x})$, $\nabla f(\underline{x})$ is the column vector of partial derivatives of $f(\underline{x})$, show that, (i) $\nabla(\underline{x}^t A \underline{x}) = 2A\underline{x}$, and (ii) $\nabla(\underline{b}^t \underline{x}) = \underline{b}$.

3.5 TAYLOR SERIES: FIRST- AND SECOND-ORDER APPROXIMATIONS

If in the Taylor expansion equation (3.6) each x_i is small enough then we could ignore terms involving products $x_i x_j$. Let $x_i = \Delta a_i$, a suitably small change in the value a_i. The first-order approximation for $f(\underline{a} + \Delta \underline{a})$ is then

$$f(\underline{a} + \Delta \underline{a}) \doteqdot f(\underline{a}) + \sum_i \Delta a_i f_i(\underline{a}). \tag{3.10}$$

Writing $f(\underline{a} + \Delta \underline{a}) - f(\underline{a}) = \Delta f$, and re-arranging, we obtain

$$\Delta f \doteqdot \frac{\partial f}{\partial x_1} \cdot \Delta a_1 + \frac{\partial f}{\partial x_2} \cdot \Delta a_2 + \ldots + \frac{\partial f}{\partial x_n} \cdot \Delta a_n. \tag{3.11}$$

The effect on f of changes in all variables is, to a first-order approximation, the sum of the partial effects of *ceteris paribus* changes in each variable taken separately.

Let us consider the production function $Q = F(K, L)$ again. If K and L change, to $K + \Delta K$ and $L + \Delta L$, where ΔK and ΔL are small enough that $(\Delta K)^2$, $(\Delta L)^2$ and $\Delta K . \Delta L$ can be ignored, then

$$\Delta Q \doteqdot \frac{\partial Q}{\partial K} \cdot \Delta K + \frac{\partial Q}{\partial L} \cdot \Delta L. \tag{3.12}$$

Compare with approximation (3.4).

As a further example, consider figure 3.1 again. The height of the function at $(a + \Delta a, b + \Delta b)$, very close to (a, b), can be obtained as $PQ + h$ where

$$h \doteqdot \frac{\partial f}{\partial x_1} \cdot \Delta a + \frac{\partial f}{\partial x_2} \cdot \Delta b. \tag{3.13}$$

It is determined to a first-degree approximation by the movements $\Delta a, \Delta b$ in the x_1- and x_2-directions, and the slopes of the surface in the x_1- and x_2-directions. To the extent that there is significant curvature of the surface in the x_1- and x_2-directions, and $(\Delta a)^2$, $(\Delta b)^2$ and $\Delta a . \Delta b$ are not negligible, formula (3.13) for h clearly needs adjustment. Going to a second-order approximation, which is correspondingly more accurate in that it ignores only third-order terms and beyond in the Taylor series expansion, we may write (in a slightly more compact notation):

$$h \doteqdot f_1(a, b)\Delta a + f_2(a, b)\Delta b$$
$$+ [f_{11}(a, b)(\Delta a)^2 + f_{22}(a, b)(\Delta b)^2 + 2f_{12}(a, b)\Delta a . \Delta b]/2. \tag{3.14}$$

The second and cross-partial derivatives convey information about the curvature of the surface, making the approximation that much better.

3.5.1 Exercise

For the function $y = 3x_1^2 + 2x_2^2 - 4x_2 + 1$ of Exercise 3.3.2(c) you will have found a turning point at $(0, 1)$, and that $f(0, 1) = -1$. Evaluate $f(\frac{1}{8}, \frac{10}{9})$ using a second-order Taylor series approximation. What kind of turning point do you think this function has?

3.6 IDENTIFYING TURNING POINTS: SECOND-ORDER CONDITIONS

Let $\underline{a} = (a_1, \ldots, a_n)$ be a turning point of the function $f(\underline{x})$. By examining the second-order Taylor series approximation of f about $f(\underline{a})$ we can, as in the univariate case dealt with in chapter 1, derive conditions which determine if the turning point is a maximum or a minimum. Saddle points and inflections are more difficult to identify in general, but we can make some progress here too.

Consider the matrix equation (3.7). At the turning point we have $\nabla f(\underline{a}) = \underline{0}$ using the necessary conditions (3.5). Then, for small $\underline{x}$, we may write

$$\Delta f = f(\underline{x} + \underline{a}) - f(\underline{a}) \doteqdot \underline{x}^t H(\underline{a})\underline{x}/2 \qquad (3.15)$$

as a second-order approximation for the change in 'height' as we move from the turning point $\underline{a}$ to the nearby $\underline{x} + \underline{a}$. This is a quadratic form in $\underline{x}$! It gives us an immediate means of identifying the nature of the turning point.

If $H(\underline{a})$ is positive definite/negative definite then Δf is strictly positive/negative for all non-zero (and small) $\underline{x}$; thus $\underline{a} = (a_1, \ldots, a_n)$ is a unique minimum/maximum point. If $H(\underline{a})$ is positive *semi*-definite/negative *semi*-definite, then still the sign of Δf cannot change: but *semi*-definiteness means there is a non-zero (and, without loss of generality, small) $\underline{x}$ such that $\Delta f = \underline{x}^t H(\underline{a})\underline{x}$ is zero. Moving from the turning point at $\underline{a}$ to the nearby $\underline{x} + \underline{a}$ does not affect the (stationary) value. In the easily envisaged $n = 2$ case, we identify the crest of a ridge, or the floor of a valley. Thus $\underline{a}$ is not the *unique* minimum/maximum point, in this case, but the turning point *is* a minimum/maximum. If $H(\underline{a})$ is indefinite, the turning point could be an inflection or a saddle point; only if $H(\underline{a}) = 0$ (the null matrix) need we go to a third-order Taylor series expansion, or beyond.

Let us summarize this situation. The condition:

$$\nabla f(\underline{a}) = \underline{0} \qquad (3.16)$$

is necessary for a turning point at $\underline{a}$; it is known as the *first-order condition* for a turning point. It picks out maxima and minima, but also inflections, saddle points and other forms of stationary value. However, the further condition on the Hessian:

$$H(\underline{a}) \text{ positive (semi-)definite/negative (semi-)definite} \tag{3.17}$$

is sufficient for a minimum/maximum at $f(\underline{a})$. This is known as the *second-order condition* for a minimum/maximum.

It is worth stating the second-order sufficient condition using the determinant criterion given in chapter 2 for positive/negative definiteness of a symmetric matrix. Let H_i be the sub-determinant of the Hessian $H(\underline{a})$ formed by the i^2 elements in the top left-hand corner. Thus

$$H_1 = f_{11}(\underline{a}) \tag{3.18}$$

$$H_2 = \det \begin{bmatrix} f_{11}(\underline{a}) & f_{12}(\underline{a}) \\ f_{21}(\underline{a}) & f_{22}(\underline{a}) \end{bmatrix} \tag{3.19}$$

etc. Then, using Theorem 2.10.7, condition (3.16) and the definiteness part of condition (3.17) may be re-stated as follows:

Nec. for TP: $\nabla f(\underline{a}) = \underline{0}$ or $f_1(\underline{a}) = f_2(\underline{a}) = \ldots = f_n(\underline{a}) = 0$

Suff. for max: $H_1 < 0, H_2 > 0, \ldots$ signs alternating

Suff. for min: $H_1 > 0, H_2 > 0, \ldots$ signs all positive. $\tag{3.20}$

For the case $n = 2$ these sufficient conditions amount to:

Suff. for max: $f_{11} < 0$ and $f_{11}f_{22} > f_{12}^2$

Suff. for min: $f_{11} > 0$ and $f_{11}f_{22} > f_{12}^2$. $\tag{3.21}$

Notice that the inequality implies f_{11} and f_{22} have the same sign, evaluated at the turning point: negative for a maximum, positive for a minimum. Thus the signs of the second partial derivatives in the x_1- and x_2-directions correspond with what obtains for the sign of the second derivative of a univariate function, at a maximum/minimum: recall conditions (1.9) and (1.10).

3.6.1 Example

Consider the function $y = 3x_1^2 + x_2^3 - 3x_1x_2$ of Exercise 3.1.2(a), graphed in figure 3.2. The first-order conditions for a turning point yield the two values $(0,0)$ and $(\frac{1}{4}, \frac{1}{2})$. At an arbitrary point (x_1, x_2), we have

$$f_{11} = 6 \qquad f_{22} = 6x_2 \qquad f_{12} = -3.$$

Using second-order conditions (3.21) we can identify $(\frac{1}{4}, \frac{1}{2})$ as a *minimum*. But at $(0,0)$ the conditions fail; this point is neither a minimum nor a maximum.

In fact the point $(0,0)$ in this example is an inflection. Since $f_{11}(0,0) > 0$ the function is convex in the x_1-direction (figure 3.2 shows this). It is hard to infer anything from a zero second derivative in general (in this case $f_{22}(0,0) = 0$: examine the graph). But if, in a particular problem, we should find that f_{11} and f_{22} have opposite signs at a turning point, then we may identify a saddle point – the function being convex in one direction, and concave in the other, at the stationary value (see figure 3.3).

3.6.2 Exercise

(a) Verify that the function $y = 3x_1^2 + 2x_2^2 - 4x_2 + 1$ has a minimum at $(0, 1)$ (see Exercise 3.5.1).

(b) Verify that none of the infinitely many turning points of the function $y = x_1 x_2 x_3 - x_1 x_2 + 2x_3 - x_3^2$ are maxima or minima (see Exercise 3.3.2(b)).

(c) Find the turning point, and identify it, when $y = 6x_1^2 - 9x_1 - 3x_1 x_2 - 7x_2 + 5x_2^2$.

(d) A firm producing two goods x and y has profit function $\pi = 32x - x^2 + 2xy - 2y^2 + 16y - 8$. Find the profit-maximizing output levels, checking carefully the second-order conditions.

(e) In the case of a producer offering n related products, facing linear demand functions and quadratic costs, and having profit function $\pi(q) = q^t D q - e^t q$ as shown in Example 2.7.1, verify that the first-order conditions for maximum profit can be written in the form $2Dq = e$. Show that the second-order conditions are satisfied if D is negative definite. What is maximum profit?

3.7 PARTIAL DERIVATIVES AND CONCAVITY

We have alluded to the concepts of concavity and convexity for functions of two variables, by referring to curvature in the x_1-direction and in the x_2-direction in terms of the signs of the second partial derivatives $\partial^2 f / \partial x_1^2$ and $\partial^2 f / \partial x_2^2$.

However, for a general definition of concavity and convexity for functions of two or more variables we turn to a characterization suggested by Definitions 1.2.1 and 1.2.2:

3.7.1 Definition

$y = f(\underline{x})$ is concave if and only if

$$f[k\underline{x}+(1-k)\underline{x}'] \geqslant kf(\underline{x})+(1-k)f(\underline{x}')$$

for all $\underline{x}, \underline{x}'$ and for all k such that $0 < k < 1$.

3.7.2 Definition

$y = f(\underline{x})$ is convex if and only if

$$f[k\underline{x}+(1-k)\underline{x}'] \leqslant kf(\underline{x})+(1-k)f(\underline{x}')$$

for all $\underline{x}, \underline{x}'$ and for all k such that $0 < k < 1$.

Consider the easily-imagined $n = 2$ case. Just as it did in chapter 1, $k\underline{x}+(1-k)\underline{x}'$ represents a 'roving point' between $\underline{x}$ and $\underline{x}'$; $f[k\underline{x}+(1-k)\underline{x}']$ is the height of the surface $y = f(\underline{x})$ at this point, and $kf(\underline{x})+(1-k)f(\underline{x}')$ is the height of the corresponding point on the chord. We are saying that *for a concave/convex function, chords joining two points on the surface lie beneath/above the surface itself.* Thus we describe, respectively, a mound-like or dish-like surface.

3.7.3 Example

(a) The function $y = 3x_1^2+x_2^3-3x_1x_2$ of Exercise 3.1.2(a), graphed in figure 3.2, is not concave or convex. Although regions of the surface look mound-like/dish-like, clearly there are chords that violate Definitions 3.7.1 and 3.7.2. To see this, let $\underline{x} = (0,3)$, $\underline{x}' = (3,0)$, $\underline{x}'' = (-3,-3)$, $\underline{x}''' = (0,0)$ and $k = \frac{1}{2}$. Then

$$f(k\underline{x}+(1-k)\underline{x}') = 3.375 < 27 = kf(\underline{x})+(1-k)f(\underline{x}'),$$

whilst

$$f(k\underline{x}''+(1-k)\underline{x}''') = -3.375 > -13.5 = kf(\underline{x}'')+(1-k)f(\underline{x}''').$$

(b) The function $y = ax_1+bx_2+x_1^2$ is convex for all a, b. To see this, verify by direct computation that:

$$kf(x_1,x_2)+(1-k)f(x_1',x_2')-f[kx_1+(1-k)x_1', kx_2+(1-k)x_2']$$
$$= k(1-k)(x_1-x_1')^2 \geqslant 0.$$

3.7.4 Exercises

(a) Show that $y = x_1 x_2$ is not concave or convex.

(b) Show that if $y = f(\underline{x})$ is concave then $y = -f(\underline{x})$ is convex.

(c) Deduce that $y = ax_1 + bx_2 - x_1^2$ is concave for all a, b.

What is the relationship between concavity/convexity thus defined and partial derivatives? The second partial derivatives $\partial^2 f/\partial x_1^2, \partial^2 f/\partial x_2^2 \ldots$ measure curvature along sections through the function, holding all but one variable constant. It turns out that the Hessian $H(\underline{x})$ of the function embodies all the information needed to determine concavity/convexity:

3.7.5 Theorem

$y = f(\underline{x})$ is concave/convex if and only if $H(\underline{x})$ is negative semi-definite/positive semi-definite for all $\underline{x}$.

A consequence of this result and conditions (3.17) is that if $\underline{x} = \underline{a}$ satisfies the first-order conditions for a turning point of $f(\underline{x})$, and $f(\underline{x})$ is concave/convex, then the turning point is a maximum/minimum. Concavity/convexity implies negative/positive second partial derivatives of $f(\underline{x})$, but requires much more than that in general.

Definitions 3.7.1 and 3.7.2 do not preclude equality between $f[k\underline{x} + (1-k)\underline{x}']$ and $kf(\underline{x}) + (1-k)f(\underline{x}')$ for any $\underline{x}$. See Exercise 3.7.13, p. 88. If we insist that the inequalities in Definitions 3.7.1 and 3.7.2 be *strict*, this defines the more restrictive concepts *strict concavity* and *strict convexity*. The Hessian can be used to identify strict concavity/convexity:

3.7.6 Theorem

If $H(\underline{x})$ is negative definite/positive definite for all $\underline{x}$, then $y = f(\underline{x})$ is strictly concave/strictly convex.

As we might anticipate, these results linking Hessians and concavity/convexity are obtained using second order Taylor series expansions of $f(\underline{x})$: the proofs are beyond the scope of this book (requiring in particular *exact* Taylor series expansions), but detailed expositions may be found in Karlin (1959, Appendix), and in Lancaster (1968); see also Madden (1985).

3.7.7 Exercises

(a) Confirm that the function $y = 3x_1^2 + x_2^3 - 3x_1 x_2$, graphed in figure 3.2, is neither concave nor convex, by examining the Hessian $H(x_1, x_2)$.

(b) Suppose that the *univariate* functions $y = f(x)$ and $y = g(x)$ are concave and differentiable (i.e. $f''(x) \leqslant 0$ and $g''(\underline{x}) \leqslant 0$). Show that $y = f(x_1) + g(x_2)$ is concave as a function of two variables. Is it strictly concave? Can you generalize this to n variables?

(c) Suppose that $f(x, y)$ is concave in x and y and that for each fixed y, $f(x, y)$ has a maximum at $x = x_0 = x_0(y)$. Let $g(y) = f(x_0, y)$. Prove that $g(y)$ is concave in y.

We now return to the (perhaps rather vague) description of concave/convex functions in the two variable case as 'mound-like/dish-like'. We can of course represent any three-dimensional surface, i.e. any function of two variables, as geographers do by the familiar device of a *contour map*. This consists of a set of contour lines representing various heights $y_1, y_2, \ldots$ of the function, in the (x_1, x_2)-plane.

Figure 3.4 shows another view of the function $y = 3x_1^2 + x_2^3 - 3x_1 x_2$, drawn this time for $-1 \leqslant x_1 \leqslant 2$, $-1 \leqslant x_2 \leqslant 2$, with the contour map shown below it. The minimum at $(\frac{1}{4}, \frac{1}{2})$ is identified by the closed contour around that point.

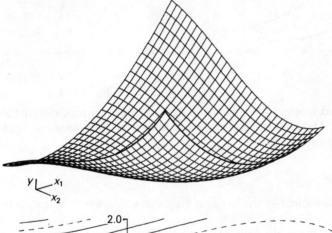

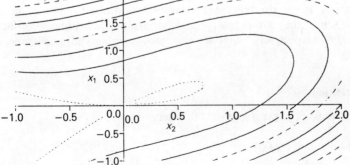

Figure 3.4

Contour maps are familiar in economics. Contours of a production function $Q = F(K, L)$ are *isoquants*; contours of a utility function $u(x_1, x_2)$ defined over two goods are *indifference curves*.

Now consider the contour maps (a) and (b) in figure 3.5. They seem to describe, respectively, mound-like and dish-like surfaces. The underlying functions are increasing away from the origin. Are these functions, respectively, concave and convex? The answer is 'not necessarily': examples can

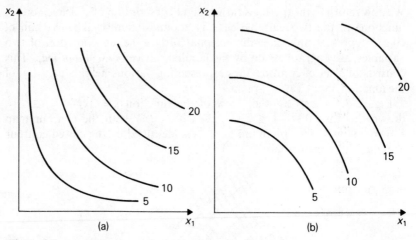

Figure 3.5

be constructed whose contour maps look like this but which violate the conditions in Definitions 3.7.1 and 3.7.2. Indeed we have seen one such function already.

3.7.8 Exercise

Draw the contour map of the function $f(x_1, x_2) = x_1 x_2$ for $x_1 > 0, x_2 > 0$.

Such contour maps do represent mound-like/dish-like surfaces, in a significant sense; they are pervasive and important in economics. In fact they describe, respectively, what we call *quasi-concave* and *quasi-convex* functions:

3.7.9 Definition

$y = f(\underline{x})$ is quasi-concave if and only if, whenever

$$f(\underline{x}) \geqslant c \quad \text{and} \quad f(\underline{x}') \geqslant c$$

then also $f[k\underline{x} + (1 - k)\underline{x}'] \geqslant c$ for all k such that $0 < k < 1$.

3.7.10 Definition

$y = f(\underline{x})$ is quasi-convex if and only if, whenever

$$f(\underline{x}) \leqslant c \quad \text{and} \quad f(\underline{x}') \leqslant c$$

then also $f[k\underline{x} + (1-k)\underline{x}'] \leqslant c$ for all k such that $0 < k < 1$.

For the $n = 2$ case these criteria require that if two points on the surface, $\underline{x}$ and $\underline{x}'$, are each at least/at most c feet above sea level, then so is every point on the surface on a straight line between them.

For functions increasing away from the origin, Definition 3.7.9 is the minimum assumption needed to guarantee the sort of contour map shown in figure 3.5(a); similarly Definition 3.7.10 characterizes the sort shown in figure 3.5(b). These criteria imply that each contour line is itself *convex*/*concave* as a function $x_2 = x_2(x_1)$ of a single variable: see figure 3.6. The familiar term 'convex indifference map' applies to quasi-concave utility functions, an important class of utility functions in microeconomics.

Strict quasi-concavity/*strict quasi-convexity* would require a strict inequality, $f[k\underline{x} + (1-k)\underline{x}'] > c$ or $f[k\underline{x} + (1-k)\underline{x}'] < c$ respectively, in the relevant definition, and implies strictly convex/concave contours.

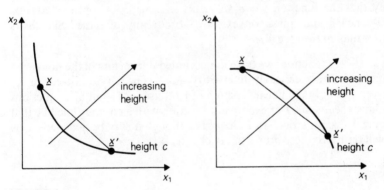

Figure 3.6

3.7.11 Exercise

(a) Show that the function $f(x_1, x_2) = x_1 x_2$ is strictly quasi-concave, for $x_1 > 0, x_2 > 0$.

(b) Show that if $y = f(\underline{x})$ is quasi-concave, then $y = -f(\underline{x})$ is quasi-convex.

There is no straightforward characterization of quasi-concavity/quasi-convexity in terms of partial derivatives: Katzner (1970, Appendix) details what *can* be said.

Finally, in this section, we examine the relationship between concavity/convexity and quasi-concavity/quasi-convexity:

3.7.12 Theorem

For a function of several variables.

$$\text{concave} \Rightarrow \text{quasi-concave} \not\Rightarrow \text{concave}$$
$$\text{convex} \Rightarrow \text{quasi-convex} \not\Rightarrow \text{convex}$$

Proof We shall prove the first part: statements about convexity and quasi-convexity will follow simply by reversing inequalities.

That quasi-concavity does not in general imply concavity is proved by the example $y = x_1 x_2$ of Exercises 3.7.4(a) and 3.7.11(a).

Suppose, then, that $y = f(\underline{x})$ is concave, and that $\underline{x}, \underline{x}'$ are two points such that $f(\underline{x}) \geqslant c$ and $f(\underline{x}') \geqslant c$. We must prove that $f[k\underline{x} + (1-k)\underline{x}'] \geqslant c$ in order to establish the theorem. Now from Definition 3.7.3, $f[k\underline{x} + (1-k)\underline{x}'] \geqslant kf(\underline{x}) + (1-k)f(\underline{x}')$; and in turn $kf(\underline{x}) + (1-k)f(\underline{x}') \geqslant kc + (1-k)c = c$ by assumption.   Q.E.D.

3.7.13 Exercise

Verify that the function $y = a_1 x_1 + a_2 x_2 + \ldots + a_n x_n$ is concave, convex, quasi-concave and quasi-convex. Is it *strictly* any of these? Sketch its contour map in the case $n = 2$.

This is a linear function; we have not excluded it from any of the non-strict definitions. *Strict* concavity/convexity/quasi-concavity/quasi-convexity rules out not only the linear function of Exercise 3.7.13 but also functions with linear segments. For example, a function with a contour line like that in figure 3.7 is not strictly quasi-concave, though it may be quasi-concave. We will return to these properties in chapter 4.

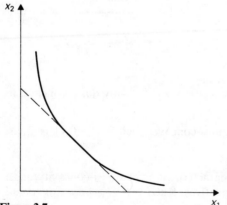

Figure 3.7

3.8 THE TOTAL DIFFERENTIAL

An obvious problem with the first- and second-order Taylor series approximations is that they are not exact: by having neglected a string of higher-order terms, there are always better approximations to be had, just around the corner (third order, fourth order, etc.).

We now present an elegant mathematical device that permits an *exact* use of the first-order Taylor series approximation for the increment to $f(\underline{a})$ that occurs when $\underline{a}$ changes slightly. We achieve this by using *infinitesimal numbers*: numbers that are smaller than finite non-zero numbers and yet not actually zero.

Mathematicians distinguish infinitesimal numbers from finite real numbers, and have rules for manipulating them. For example,

$$\text{(non-zero real)} \times \text{(infinitesimal)} = \text{(infinitesimal)},$$

and

$$\text{(zero)} \times \text{(infinitesimal)} = \text{(zero)}.$$

Division by zero is not permitted, but division by infinitesimals is possible: (infinitesimal) $\div$ (infinitesimal) can be finite. This is an area of mathematics called 'non-standard analysis'. See Robinson (1974) for a detailed exposition. At our level, we are content to treat infinitesimals somewhat casually; indeed we have already encountered them in chapter 1.

Recall that in equation (1.8), for a univariate function $y = f(x)$, we wrote $f'(x) = dy/dx = dy \div dx$ where dy, dx were infinitesimal. Given any small (finite) number Δx, let $\Delta y = [f(x + \Delta x) - f(x)]$. Then

$$f'(x) \doteq \Delta y / \Delta x, \quad \text{i.e.} \quad \Delta y \doteq f'(x) \Delta x. \tag{3.22}$$

The approximation becomes exact as $\Delta x \to 0$; but then all that remains in equation (3.22) is the trivial statement $0 = f'(x) \cdot 0$ or the meaningless one $f'(x) = 0/0$. By seeking exactness, and allowing Δx to reach zero, we have lost everything that was informative in approximation (3.22).

Instead we may let Δx become 'infinitesimal': call its value dx. Then (if $f'(x) \neq 0$) $f'(x) dx$ is also infinitesimal: call this dy. Then (3.22) becomes

$$dy = f'(x) dx. \tag{3.23}$$

Dividing, we recover equation (1.8):

$$dy \div dx = f'(x) = \frac{dy}{dx}. \tag{3.24}$$

Thus, we can interpret the familiar symbol dy/dx as a ratio of two infinitesimals.

3.8.1 Definition

The *total differential* of $y = f(x_1, x_2, \ldots, x_n)$ is

$$dy = \frac{\partial f}{\partial x_1} \cdot dx_1 + \frac{\partial f}{\partial x_2} \cdot dx_2 + \ldots + \frac{\partial f}{\partial x_n} \cdot dx_n \qquad (3.25)$$

where $dx_1, dx_2, \ldots, dx_n$ are infinitesimals.

You will recognize this both as an extension of the univariate equation (3.23) above, and as an 'exact' version of the first-order Taylor series expansion in equation (3.11). The inaccuracy in equation (3.11) has disappeared because we have taken the small changes in the variables 'almost all the way' to zero: but rather than ending up with $0 = \partial y/\partial x_1 . 0 + \partial y/\partial x_2 . 0 + \ldots$ we have retained the meaning in the expression.

Suppose that in fact only x_j is allowed to vary, and that dx_i is set *equal to zero* for $i \neq j$. Then equation (3.25) yields

$$\frac{\partial f}{\partial x_j} = dy \div dx_j, \qquad (3.26)$$

i.e. *partial derivatives can be viewed as ratios of infinitesimals* (with the other variables fixed).

(Second partial derivatives can also be interpreted as ratios, involving the differential of a differential, d^2y, and products of infinitesimals, $dx_i dx_j$, etc. (see Chiang, 1984, p. 309).)

3.8.2 Example

Let $y = 3x_1^2 + x_2^3 - 3x_1x_2$. Then the total differential is

$$dy = (6x_1 - 3x_2) dx_1 + (3x_2^2 - 3x_1) dx_2.$$

3.8.3 Exercise

Find the total differential of each of the functions in Exercises 3.3.2, *viz.*

(a) $y = 3x_1 + 2x_2 - x_3 + 6$.

(b) $y = x_1x_2x_3 - x_1x_2 + 2x_3 - x_3^2$.

(c) $y = 3x_1^2 + 2x_2^2 - 4x_2 + 1$.

Of what use is all of this to an economist? One particular use is in linearizing non-linear economic models; this was alluded to in chapter 2, section 2.1.

3.8.4 Application   IS–LM and aggregate demand

Suppose that the consumption, investment, money demand and tax functions in a closed economy with government are $C = C(Y_d, r)$, $I = I(Y, r)$, $L = L(Y, r)$ and $T = T(Y)$ where Y is total income, $Y_d = Y - T$ is disposable income and r is the interest rate. All variables are in real terms. Government spending is $\bar{G}$ and the money supply is $\bar{M}/P$ where P is the price level; $\bar{G}$ and $\bar{M}$ are autonomous. The equations in Y and r which define the IS and LM curves are

$$\text{IS} \qquad Y = C[Y - T(Y), r] + I(Y, r) + \bar{G} \qquad (3.27)$$

$$\text{LM} \quad L(Y, r) = \bar{M}/P. \qquad (3.28)$$

If the various functions are linear in Y and r, this pair of equations can easily be solved for equilibrium values. We could then examine the effect of changes in $\bar{G}$, $\bar{M}$, etc., upon the equilibrium level of income and upon the interest rate. If the functions are not linear we cannot do this readily, but we can linearize the equations by taking total differentials. It is then quite easy to quantify the effect on income and the interest rate of autonomous changes.

Suppose that $\bar{G}$, $\bar{M}$ and the price level P change infinitesimally (namely, by $d\bar{G}$, $d\bar{M}$ and dP). Denote $\partial C/\partial Y$ by C_Y, $\partial C/\partial r$ by C_r, etc., and take total differentials throughout equations (3.27) and (3.28):

$$[1 - C_Y(1 - T_Y) - I_Y]\, dY - (C_r + I_r)\, dr = d\bar{G} \qquad (3.29)$$

$$L_Y\, dY + L_r\, dr = d\bar{M}/P - \bar{M}\, dP/P^2. \qquad (3.30)$$

These can be solved for dY and dr, e.g. by using Cramer's rule. For larger systems of equations, for example those deriving from a three- or four-sector macroeconomic model, Cramer's rule may be the only practicable approach. In our particular case, elementary simultaneous equation methods suffice:

$$dY = [(d\bar{M}/P - \bar{M}\, dP/P^2)(C_r + I_r) + L_r\, d\bar{G}]/D \qquad (3.31)$$

$$dr = [(d\bar{M}/P - \bar{M}\, dP/P^2)[1 - C_Y(1 - T_Y) - I_Y] - L_Y\, d\bar{G}]/D \quad (3.32)$$

where $D = [1 - C_Y(1 - T_Y) - I_Y]L_r + (C_r + I_r)L_Y$. With usual assumptions about the signs of the various partial derivatives, D is negative.

From these equations we may discern the government spending multiplier $\partial Y/\partial \bar{G}$ (put $d\bar{M} = dP = 0$ in equation (3.31) and evaluate $dY \div d\bar{G}$); the money multiplier $\partial Y/\partial \bar{M}$ (put $d\bar{G} = dP = 0$ in equation (3.31) and evaluate $dY \div d\bar{M}$) as well as the effects of an increase in the price level, both upon Y and upon r.

The infinitesimals are easy to manipulate, and by setting their values appropriately, they yield a great deal of information.

See Burrows and Hitiris (1974) for an elegant exposition of macroeconomic theory in these terms.

3.8.5 Exercises

(a) Show that in the model developed above, with the usual assumptions about signs of partial derivatives, $\partial Y/\partial P$ is negative.

(b) Show that in the case of the liquidity trap (i.e. $L_r \to -\infty$) the aggregate demand curve becomes vertical (namely, prove that $\partial Y/\partial P \to 0$).

(c) Using the Patinkin (1965) consumption function $C = C(Y_d, r, A)$ where $A = M/P$ = real cash balances, re-work equations (3.29)–(3.32). Derive the expression for $\partial Y/\partial P$. Does the real balance effect remove the vertical section of the aggregate demand curve in the case of the liquidity trap?

Total differentials have many mathematical uses. One is in obtaining partial derivatives when a function is defined *implicitly* in terms of its variables. For example, suppose that y is defined as a function of two variables by

$$x_1^2 y^2 + y - x_2 = 6. \tag{3.33}$$

What are $\partial y/\partial x_1$ and $\partial y/\partial x_2$? It is hard to express y directly in terms of x_1 and x_2; but the total differential can help us obtain the partial derivatives.

Suppose that in general

$$F(y, x_1, x_2, \ldots, x_n) \equiv 0 \tag{3.34}$$

defines y implicitly as a function of $x_1, x_2, \ldots, x_n$. When the x_is vary in equation (3.34) so does y, in such a way that $F(y, x_1, x_2, \ldots, x_n)$ remains identically zero. In particular $dF = 0$ following infinitesimal changes in $y, x_1, x_2, \ldots, x_n$, since F does not vary. Then, applying equation (3.25) to F,

$$0 = \partial F/\partial y \cdot dy + \sum_i \partial F/\partial x_i \cdot dx_i. \tag{3.35}$$

For the partial derivative of y with respect to, say, x_j, we require the value of $dy \div dx_j$ when $dx_1 = \ldots = dx_{j-1} = dx_{j+1} = \ldots = dx_n = 0$.

3.8.6 Theorem (implicit function theorem)

If $F(y, x_1, x_2, \ldots, x_n) \equiv 0$, then

$$\partial y / \partial x_j = -(\partial F / \partial x_j)/(\partial F / \partial y). \tag{3.36}$$

3.8.7 Examples

(a) Consider the function $F(y, x_1, x_2) = x_1^2 y^2 + y - x_2 - 6$ suggested by equation (3.33). The partial derivative $\partial y / \partial x_1$ may be evaluated as

$$\frac{-(\partial F / \partial x_1)}{(\partial F / \partial y)} = \frac{-(2x_1 y^2)}{(2x_1^2 y + 1)}.$$

Similarly

$$\frac{\partial y}{\partial x_2} = \frac{1}{(2x_1^2 y + 1)}.$$

(b) Consider the function $y = x_1^{x_2}$ of Exercise 3.1.2(d). This is *not* an implicitly defined function: but let us take logarithms to make it so. We have:

$$F(y, x_1, x_2) = \ln(y) - x_2 . \ln(x_1) \equiv 0$$

whence the partial derivatives are

$$\frac{\partial y}{\partial x_1} = \frac{-(-x_2/x_1)}{(1/y)} = \frac{y x_2}{x_1} = x_2 . x_1^{x_2 - 1},$$

and

$$\frac{\partial y}{\partial x_2} = \frac{-[-\ln(x_1)]}{(1/y)} = y . \ln(x_1) = x_1^{x_2} . \ln(x_1).$$

3.8.8 Exercise

Find the partial derivatives when, (i) $\ln(y) - x_1 - x_2 - 6 = 0$, (ii) $y^3 x_1 + y^2 x_2 + y x_3 = 2$.

3.8.9 Application The slopes of IS–LM and the government spending and money multipliers

In the foregoing analysis, the IS and LM curves were defined implicitly by equations (3.27) and (3.28). Thus the slope of the IS curve, s_{IS} say, is given by

$$s_{IS} = \frac{-(\partial F/\partial Y)}{(\partial F/\partial r)}$$

where $F(Y,r) = Y - C[Y - T(Y), r] - I(Y,r) - \bar{G}$. That is,

$$s_{IS} = [1 - C_Y(1 - T_Y) - I_Y]/(C_r + I_r) \tag{3.37}$$

which is, of course, negative. Similarly the slope of the LM curve is

$$s_{LM} = \frac{-L_Y}{L_r} \tag{3.38}$$

using equation (3.28) and Theorem 3.8.6. This is positive. In particular

$$s_{LM} - s_{IS} = \frac{-D}{(C_r + I_r)L_r} \tag{3.39}$$

and we may write the government spending and money multipliers in terms of $s_{LM} - s_{IS}$, by substituting from equation (3.39) into equations (3.31) and (3.32):

$$\frac{\partial Y}{\partial \bar{G}} = \frac{-1}{(C_r + I_r)(s_{LM} - s_{IS})} \tag{3.40}$$

$$\frac{\partial Y}{\partial \bar{M}} = \frac{-1}{PL_r(s_{LM} - s_{IS})}. \tag{3.41}$$

In particular, *the flatter the IS curve (respectively, LM curve), the larger is the money (respectively, government spending) multiplier.*

These relationships between slopes and multipliers were first observed by Tobin (1947). But an assertion in a recent article on this subject, Meyer (1983, p. 228), to the effect that: 'the money multiplier is positively related to the slope of the LM curve only if the absolute value of the product of the slopes of the LM and IS curves exceeds unity' is wrong, as would have been clear to the author if he had used the highly elegant total differential approach to the problem.

3.9 THE CHAIN RULE

Another application of the total differential is to an analysis of the effects on $y = f(x_1, \ldots, x_n)$ of small changes in the variables $x_1, \ldots, x_n$ when $x_1, \ldots, x_n$ are not independent.

For example, suppose that $Y = Y(r)$ defines the IS curve explicitly. Then $Y(r)$ is the level of income that guarantees equilibrium in the expenditure sector of the economy given an interest rate of r. *Equilibrium consumption* is then $C_e = C\{Y(r) - T[Y(r)], r\}$ (neglecting the real balance effect). Although the consumption function $C = C(Y, r)$ is a function of two variables, equilibrium consumption C_e is not: it is a function of the interest rate r alone.

Consider in general a function

$$h(t) = f[x_1(t), x_2(t), \ldots, x_n(t)] \tag{3.42}$$

defined by a single variable t as the value of $y = f(x_1, x_2, \ldots, x_n)$ when for each independent variable x_i, the function $x_i(t)$ is substituted.

Suppose that t changes infinitesimally, to $t + dt$. Then $h(t)$ changes to $h(t) + dh$ where

$$dh = h'(t) \, dt. \tag{3.43}$$

Now if each $x_i(t)$ is differentiable, then $x_i(t)$ changes by

$$dx_i = x_i'(t) \, dt. \tag{3.44}$$

Thus all variables in $f(x_1, x_2, \ldots, x_n)$ change infinitesimally and the total effect is given by

$$dh = df = \sum_{i=1}^{n} \partial f / \partial x_i \cdot dx_i;$$

substituting from equations (3.43) and (3.44) and dividing by dt we have the following theorem.

3.9.1 Theorem   The chain rule

If $h(t) = f[x_1(t), x_2(t), \ldots, x_n(t)]$, then

$$h'(t) = \sum_{i=1}^{n} \partial f / \partial x_i \cdot dx_i / dt. \tag{3.45}$$

(Compare this chain rule with the one in Theorem 1.1.2.)

For example, the effect on equilibrium consumption of a change in the interest rate is

$$dC_e / dr = C_Y \cdot dY(r) / dr + C_r.$$

There is a direct interest rate effect upon consumption, and an indirect effect that arises via the income effect of a movement along the IS curve.

A useful application of the chain rule is to *homogeneous* functions of independent variables.

3.9.2 Definition

$y = f(x_1, x_2, \ldots, x_n)$ is *homogeneous of degree* r if and only if

$$f(kx_1, kx_2, \ldots, kx_n) = k^r f(x_1, x_2, \ldots, x_n) \tag{3.46}$$

for all real numbers k.

3.9.3 Examples

(a) The Cobb–Douglas production function $Q = K^a L^b$ is homogeneous of degree $a + b$. A production function which is homogeneous of degree 1 has constant returns to scale; homogeneity of degree greater/less than 1 implies increasing/decreasing returns to scale.

(b) Consider the tax function $T(X, \underline{b})$ mentioned earlier. Let b_1 be the (basic) allowance against income before tax, i.e. tax-free income, and $b_2, b_3, \ldots, b_n$ the thresholds for the sequence of increasing marginal tax rates which apply to income in excess of the basic allowance. If all incomes, allowances and thresholds doubled (more generally, increased by a factor k) then so would tax payments: $T(X, \underline{b})$ is homogeneous of degree 1 (assuming equiproportionate growth in individual incomes).

An important property of homogeneous functions is derived easily from the chain rule. It is known as *Euler's theorem*.

3.9.4 Theorem   (Euler's Theorem)

If $y = f(x_1, x_2, \ldots, x_n)$ is homogeneous of degree r, then

$$\sum_{i=1}^{n} x_i \cdot \partial f / \partial x_i = r f(x_1, x_2, \ldots, x_n) \tag{3.47}$$

for all $(x_1, x_2, \ldots, x_n)$.

Proof   Consider again equation (3.46), which is true of f by assumption:

$$f(kx_1, kx_2, \ldots, kx_n) = k^r f(x_1, x_2, \ldots, x_n). \tag{3.46}$$

Regard k as the variable. On the left-hand side the variables in f are all functions of k; the right-hand side is just k^r times a constant, as a function of k. Now differentiate equation (3.46) with respect to k:

$$\sum_i f_i(kx_1, kx_2, \ldots, kx_n) \cdot x_i = rk^{r-1} f(x_1, x_2, \ldots, x_n).$$

Finally, put $k = 1$. The result is immediate.
This result has many useful applications.

3.9.5 Examples

(a) If the production function $Q = F(K, L)$ has constant returns to scale then

$$Q = F_K . K + F_L . L$$

F_K and F_L are the marginal products of capital and labour. If each factor is paid its marginal product (i.e. MP_K = price of capital, and MP_L = wage) then total payments to factors just exhaust the value of output. What happens for increasing/decreasing returns to scale?

(b) For the tax function discussed in Example 3.9.3(b) we have from Euler's theorem

$$T = X . \partial T / \partial X + b_1 . \partial T / \partial b_1 + \sum_{j>1} b_j . \partial T / \partial b_j.$$

If we divide through by T then the terms on the right-hand side become elasticities of revenue with respect to income, the allowance and the marginal rate thresholds. All but the first of these are negative: increases in allowances/thresholds reduce revenue. Hence the income elasticity of revenue may be written

$$e_{\text{income}} = 1 + \bar{e}_{\text{allowances}} + \bar{e}_{\text{thresholds}} \tag{3.48}$$

each $\bar{e}$ denoting a positive quantity. In fact each $\bar{e}$ can be calculated easily and readily from published tax data; equation (3.48) is the basis for a recently proposed approach to the exact measurement of income tax revenue elasticity that avoids the statistical problems of existing estimation procedures (see Fries, Hutton and Lambert, 1982).

Part II

Static and Dynamic Optimization

4 Equality-constrained Optimization

In economics we frequently want to solve problems of the general form

$$\max_{x_1, x_2, \ldots, x_n} f(x_1, x_2, \ldots, x_n)$$

subject to $g(x_1, x_2, \ldots, x_n) = b$

or, indeed,

$$\min_{x_1, x_2, \ldots, x_n} f(x_1, x_2, \ldots, x_n)$$

subject to $g(x_1, x_2, \ldots, x_n) = b$.

The function $f(x_1, x_2, \ldots, x_n)$ is called the *objective function*, and $g(x_1, x_2, \ldots, x_n) = b$ is the *constraint*. This problem differs considerably from that of unconstrained or 'free' optimization considered in chapter 3.

4.1 THE TWO-VARIABLE CASE

Consider the $n = 2$ case. A free maximum of $f(x_1, x_2)$ is a mountain top on the surface in three dimensions that is the graph of $f(x_1, x_2)$; the constrained maximum is *the highest point on a path along the surface* (namely, the path defined by $g(x_1, x_2) = b$). Similarly for the free/constrained minimum.

The constraint $g(x_1, x_2) = b$ is simply the contour line at height b of the function $g(x_1, x_2)$. Suppose that $f(x_1, x_2)$ is an increasing function which is strictly quasi-concave and that $g(x_1, x_2)$ is strictly quasi-convex. Then the contour lines of $f(x_1, x_2)$, and the constraint $g(x_1, x_2) = b$, are as shown in figure 4.1.

This is a convenient way to represent the problem. Indeed the graph is a familiar one in economics; for example the constraint could be the production-possibilities frontier for an economy which produces two goods, and the convex contours societal indifference curves.

101

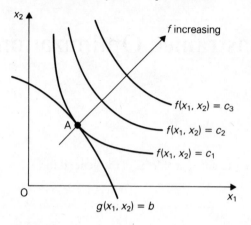

Figure 4.1

As shown in figure 4.1, the optimum occurs at A. We supposed that $f(x_1, x_2)$ was *strictly* quasi-concave and $g(x_1, x_2)$ *strictly* quasi-convex, to get figure 4.1; if we had not imposed strictness, we could have found a non-unique optimum: see figure 4.2(b).

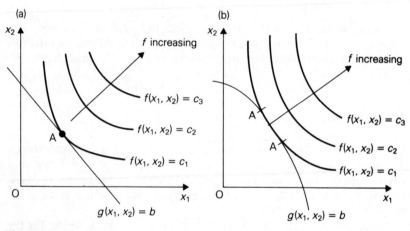

Figure 4.2

Constrained maxima/minima may not exist, or be unique. Assuming that there exists a unique constrained maximum (or constrained minimum) of $f(x_1, x_2)$, how do we find it mathematically? Plainly at the point A in figure 4.1 and similarly in figure 4.2(a), and at every point on the segment AA in figure 4.2(b), the slopes of the f-contours and of the constraint are the same. Also, of course, $g(x_1, x_2) = b$. Assuming non-zero partial derivatives with respect to x_1 at the optimum, the implicit function Theorem 3.8.6 yields a pair of conditions:

$$\frac{-(\partial f/\partial x_2)}{(\partial f/\partial x_1)} = \frac{-(\partial g/\partial x_2)}{(\partial g/\partial x_1)} \tag{4.1}$$

$$g(x_1, x_2) = b \tag{4.2}$$

which are necessary for the optimum.

(Note that we have excluded from consideration here certain possibilities called *corner solutions*. See figure 4.3, in which, as a result of confining both of the functions $f(x_1, x_2)$ and $g(x_1, x_2)$ to the positive quadrant $x_1 \geqslant 0$, $x_2 \geqslant 0$, the optimum is at a 'corner'. In this case the slopes of the contour of the objective function and of the constraint are *not* the same. We examine inequality constraints in detail in the next chapter.)

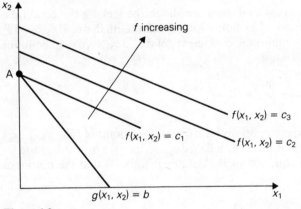

Figure 4.3

Conditions (4.1) and (4.2) are familiar in economics. Consider the case of utility maximization subject to a budget constraint. Put $f(x_1, x_2) = u(x_1, x_2)$ and $g(x_1, x_2) = p_1 x_1 + p_2 x_2$; b is income (see figure 4.2(a)). Equation (4.1) says that at the optimum the ratio of marginal utilities (the *marginal rate of substitution*, ignoring the minus sign) equals the price ratio. For the example of a two-good producer economy cited earlier, equation (4.1) says that at the optimum the marginal rate of technical transformation should equal society's marginal rate of substitution between the two goods.

4.2 THE GENERAL CASE

For the case of $n > 2$ variables we cannot argue graphically like this. But we can use the language of the total differential to approach the problem.

At the maximum (or minimum) of $f(x_1, x_2, \ldots, x_n)$ subject to $g(x_1, x_2, \ldots, x_n) = b$, infinitesimal movements in the variables $x_1, x_2, \ldots, x_n$ which satisfy the constraint must have no effect on the (stationary) value of the objective function.

Therefore a necessary condition for the optimum is that $df = 0$ whenever $dg = 0$. That is, we must have

$$\frac{\partial f}{\partial x_1} \cdot dx_1 + \frac{\partial f}{\partial x_2} \cdot dx_2 + \ldots + \frac{\partial f}{\partial x_n} \cdot dx_n \tag{4.3}$$

for all $dx_1, dx_2, \ldots, dx_n$ satisfying

$$\frac{\partial g}{\partial x_1} \cdot dx_1 + \frac{\partial g}{\partial x_2} \cdot dx_2 + \ldots + \frac{\partial g}{\partial x_n} \cdot dx_n. \tag{4.4}$$

If there were no constraint, then we should be seeking the conditions under which equation (4.3) holds for *all* infinitesimal $dx_1. dx_2, \ldots, dx_n$. Plainly this would require the coefficients of $dx_1, dx_2, \ldots, dx_n$ in equation (4.3) all to be zero. That is,

$$\frac{\partial f}{\partial x_1} = \frac{\partial f}{\partial x_2} = \ldots = \frac{\partial f}{\partial x_n} = 0;$$

the familiar first-order conditions for a free turning point of $f(x_1, x_2, \ldots, x_n)$.

Given the constraint (4.4) upon $dx_1, dx_2, \ldots, dx_n$, we may substitute for one of the dx_i into equation (4.3). Assuming $\partial g/\partial x_1 \neq 0$ at the optimum, substitute

$$dx_1 = \frac{-\left(\sum_{i>1} \partial g/\partial x_i . dx_i\right)}{(\partial g/\partial x_1)} \tag{4.5}$$

into equation (4.3); we then require

$$\sum_{i>1} \left[\partial f/\partial x_i - \frac{(\partial f/\partial x_1)(\partial g/\partial x_i)}{\partial g/\partial x_1} \right] dx_i = 0 \tag{4.6}$$

for *all* infinitesimals $dx_2, \ldots, dx_n$. The constraint $dg = 0$ has been taken care of, by substitution.

The solution is to set all coefficients to zero. So, now assuming $\partial g/\partial x_i \neq 0$ for all i at the optimum, we require

$$(\partial f/\partial x_i)/(\partial g/\partial x_i) = (\partial f/\partial x_1)/(\partial g/\partial x_1) \tag{4.7}$$

for $i = 2, \ldots, n$. This condition reduces to equation (4.1) for the case $n = 2$.

Of course, we also require the constraint itself to be satisfied (setting $dg = 0$ means that g is constant, but does not imply that $g(x_1, x_2, \ldots, x_n)$ equals b).

We now describe a simple technique for solving constrained optimization problems that generates these conditions – and rather more.

4.3 THE LAGRANGE MULTIPLIER APPROACH

In order to solve the problem

$$\max_{x_1, x_2, \ldots, x_n} f(x_1, x_2, \ldots, x_n)$$

$$\text{st } g(x_1, x_2, \ldots, x_n) = b$$

which we may write as

$$\max_{\underline{x}} f(\underline{x})$$

$$\text{st } g(\underline{x}) = b$$

or the analogous minimization problem, we define the *Lagrangean* by introducing a new variable λ, which we call the *Lagrange multiplier*. Let

$$L(\lambda, \underline{x}) = f(\underline{x}) - \lambda[g(\underline{x}) - b] \tag{4.8}$$

L is a function of $n + 1$ independent variables. Now we solve

$$\frac{\partial L}{\partial \lambda} = \frac{\partial L}{\partial x_1} = \frac{\partial L}{\partial x_2} = \ldots = \frac{\partial L}{\partial x_n} = 0, \tag{4.9}$$

i.e. we seek free turning points of the function L.

It is claimed that this will yield the solution we are looking for. If so, then we shall have turned the constrained optimization problem (in the n variables $x_1, x_2, \ldots, x_n$) into an unconstrained one (in the $n + 1$ variables λ, $x_1, x_2, \ldots, x_n$). This would represent a significant simplification in the mathematics.

First, note that $\partial L / \partial \lambda = -[g(\underline{x}) - b]$, so that the first condition in equation (4.9), $\partial L / \partial \lambda = 0$, yields $g(\underline{x}) = b$; it says that the constraint must be satisfied.

The remaining conditions in equation (4.9) are that $\partial L / \partial x_i = 0$ for $i = 1, 2, \ldots, n$. Now $\partial L / \partial x_i = \partial f / \partial x_i - \lambda \cdot \partial g / \partial x_i$. Hence (again assuming g

has non-zero partial derivatives) the remainder of equation (4.9) says that

$$\frac{\partial f/\partial x_i}{\partial g/\partial x_i} = \lambda \tag{4.10}$$

for each i. That is,

$$\frac{\partial f/\partial x_i}{\partial g/\partial x_i} = \lambda = \frac{\partial f/\partial x_1}{\partial g/\partial x_1} \tag{4.11}$$

for $i = 2,\ldots,n$.

This is precisely the content of the necessary condition (4.7). Hence a value of x, say $\hat{x}$, satisfying the first-order conditions for an unconstrained turning point of $L(\lambda, x)$ satisfies the necessary conditions for the constrained optimization problem under study: we have indeed found a simple approach to solving the problem.

4.3.1 Example

Let an individual's utility, defined over two goods whose prices in perfect markets are p_1 and p_2, be Cobb–Douglas, i.e. $u(x_1, x_2) = x_1^a x_2^b$. The individual has income m. Find his utility-maximizing demands for the two goods in terms of their prices.

First we define the Lagrangean:

$$L(\lambda, x_1, x_2) = x_1^a x_2^b - \lambda(p_1 x_1 + p_2 x_2 - m)$$

and obtain the necessary conditions

$$\frac{\partial L}{\partial \lambda} = \frac{\partial L}{\partial x_1} = \frac{\partial L}{\partial x_2} = 0.$$

Writing $u = x_1^a x_2^b$ for convenience the three conditions are

1. $p_1 x_1 + p_2 x_2 = m$

2. $\quad\dfrac{au}{x_1} = \lambda p_1$

3. $\quad\dfrac{bu}{x_2} = \lambda p_2.$

Cross-multiplying in 2 and 3 by x_1 and x_2 respectively, and adding, and using (1), we find:

4. $\quad (a+b)u = \lambda m.$

Substituting back from 4 into 2 and 3 yields the optimal values, say $\hat{x}_1$ and $\hat{x}_2$. They satisfy

5. $$\frac{p_1\hat{x}_1}{m} = \frac{a}{(a+b)}$$

6. $$\frac{p_2\hat{x}_2}{m} = \frac{b}{(a+b)}.$$

This shows that fixed shares $a/(a+b)$ and $b/(a+b)$ of the total budget are spent on each good, regardless of price. This property is peculiar to the Cobb–Douglas utility function.

The same technique, of course, applies to constrained minimization problems.

4.3.2 Exercises

(a) Maximize $a.\ln(x_1) + b.\ln(x_2)$ subject to $p_1x_1 + p_2x_2 = m$. Compare the solution to that obtained in Example 4.3.1 – and explain.

(b) Generalize the result in Example 4.3.1 to the utility function

$$u(x_1,\ldots,x_n) = x_1^{a_1} x_2^{a_2} \ldots x_n^{a_n}$$

defined over n goods.

(c) Minimize $y = x_1^2 + x_2^2$ subject to $x_1 + x_2 = 1$. Draw a graph and use geometric arguments to explain the values the Lagrange multiplier technique yields.

(d) Minimize $3x_1^2 + 2x_2^2 - x_3^2 + x_3$ subject to $x_1 + x_2 + x_3 = 1$. (Is there a maximum value? What is the value when $x_3 = 1$?)

(e) Find the stationary values of $y = 3x_1^2 + 2x_2^2 - 4x_2 + 1$ subject to $x_1^2 + x_2^2 = 16$ (there are four).

For any particular constrained optimization problem at hand, the value or values of $\underline{x}$ thrown up by the Lagrange multiplier approach could either maximize or, equally, minimize $f(\underline{x})$ subject to $g(\underline{x}) = b$. The same mathematics applies in both cases. In order to identify the nature of the solution we need to look at the second-order conditions for the turning point(s) of $L(\lambda, \underline{x})$.

Notice first of all that we are not necessarily looking for a maximum or a minimum of $L(\lambda, \underline{x})$. Let $\lambda = \hat{\lambda}$ and $\underline{x} = \hat{\underline{x}}$ be the values of λ and $\underline{x}$ at the turning point. Then certainly, for a maximum of $f(\underline{x})$ subject to $g(\underline{x}) = b$, we have

$$L(\hat{\lambda}, \underline{x}) \leqslant L(\hat{\lambda}, \hat{\underline{x}}) \text{ for all } \underline{x} \text{ such that } g(\underline{x}) = b \qquad (4.12)$$

(this just says that $f(\underline{x}) \leqslant f(\hat{\underline{x}})$ for all $\underline{x}$ satisfying the constraint); but also we have

$$L(\hat{\lambda}, \hat{\underline{x}}) = L(\lambda, \hat{\underline{x}}) = f(\hat{\underline{x}}) \text{ for all } \lambda. \tag{4.13}$$

So $(\hat{\lambda}, \hat{\underline{x}})$ is a rather special kind of turning point of $L(\lambda, \underline{x})$. It is not possible to give here full necessary and sufficient conditions for $(\hat{\lambda}, \hat{\underline{x}})$ to yield a maximum/minimum at $\hat{\underline{x}}$ of $f(\underline{x})$ subject to $g(\underline{x}) = b$, but we can give sufficient conditions in terms of the Hessian of $L(\lambda, \underline{x})$ at $(\hat{\lambda}, \hat{\underline{x}})$.

It is readily verified from the definition that the Hessian of $L(\lambda, \underline{x})$ is

$$H = \begin{bmatrix} 0 & -g_1 & -g_2 & & -g_n \\ \hline -g_1 & f_{11} - \lambda g_{11} & f_{12} - \lambda g_{12} & \cdots & f_{1n} - \lambda g_{1n} \\ -g_2 & f_{21} - \lambda g_{21} & f_{22} - \lambda g_{22} & \cdots & f_{2n} - \lambda g_{2n} \\ \vdots & \vdots & \vdots & \ddots & \vdots \\ -g_n & f_{n1} - \lambda g_{n1} & f_{n2} - \lambda g_{n2} & \cdots & f_{nn} - \lambda g_{nn} \end{bmatrix} \tag{4.14}$$

sometimes called, for obvious reasons, the *bordered Hessian* of $f(\underline{x}) - \lambda g(\underline{x})$. In some books the minus signs in the first row and column are omitted: this is immaterial in what follows (see Exercise 2.3.4(d), p. 48).

The sufficient (second-order) conditions on H at $(\hat{\lambda}, \hat{\underline{x}})$, for a maximum/minimum of $f(\underline{x})$ subject to $g(\underline{x}) = b$, resemble (at least superficially) those in conditions (3.21) for unconstrained turning points.

Again let H_i be the sub-determinant formed by the first i^2 elements in the top left-hand corner of H. Notice that $H_1 = 0$, and $H_2 = -(g_1)^2 \leqslant 0$. Then we have

$$\begin{array}{ll} \text{Suff. for max} & H_2 < 0, H_3 > 0, \dots \quad \text{signs alternating} \\ \text{Suff. for min} & H_2 < 0, H_3 < 0, \dots \quad \text{all signs negative.} \end{array} \tag{4.15}$$

See Chiang (1984) for a discussion of this result.

4.3.3 Exercises

(a) Check the second-order condition for a maximum in Example 4.3.1 or Exercise 4.3.2(a).

(b) Check the second-order conditions for Exercise 4.3.2(c) and Exercise 4.3.2(d).

(c) Examine the second-order conditions for the four extreme values obtained in Exercise 4.3.2(e).

4.4 THE MAXIMUM VALUE FUNCTION

The Lagrange multiplier technique just outlined yields not only the desired values $\hat{x}_1, \hat{x}_2, \ldots, \hat{x}_n$ of the variables in the original problem, but also an 'optimal' value $\hat{\lambda}$ for the Lagrange multiplier. This has a very particular significance; it makes the Lagrange multiplier approach extremely fruitful in economic applications.

Let the maximum (or, minimum) value of $f(\underline{x})$ subject to $g(\underline{x}) = b$, which is of course $f(\hat{\underline{x}})$, be denoted V. Then for all $\underline{x}$ such that $g(\underline{x}) = b$, we have

$$f(\underline{x}) \leqslant V. \tag{4.16}$$

4.4.1 Example

Find and identify the extreme value of $f(x, y) = x^2 y^2$ subject to $x^2 + y^2 = 1$. Deduce that for any $a, b > 0$,

$$(ab)^{\frac{1}{2}} \leqslant \frac{(a+b)}{2}.$$

The Lagrange multiplier conditions yield $\hat{x}^2 = \hat{y}^2 = \frac{1}{2}$. Thus for all (x, y) such that $x^2 + y^2 = 1$ we have $f(x, y) = x^2 y^2 \leqslant V = \frac{1}{4}$. Now put $x^2 = a/(a+b)$ and $y^2 = b/(a+b)$, which satisfies the constraint; the result is immediate.

4.4.2 Exercises

(a) Generalize the result in Example 4.4.1 to show that if $a_1, a_2, \ldots, a_n$ are any n positive numbers, then their geometric mean $(a_1 a_2 \ldots a_n)^{1/n}$ is less than, or equal to, their arithmetic mean $\Sigma_{i=1}^n a_i/n$ (max $x_1^2 x_2^2 \ldots x_n^2$ st $\Sigma_{i=1}^n x_i^2 = 1$).

(b) Show that the maximum of $\Sigma a_i x_i$ subject to $\Sigma x_i^p = 1$ ($p > 1$) is given by $V = (\Sigma a_i^q)^{1/q}$ where $q = p/(p-1)$. Deduce the Cauchy–Schwartz inequality:

$$\Sigma a_i b_i \leqslant [\sqrt{(\Sigma a_i^2)}] [\sqrt{(\Sigma b_i^2)}]$$

by considering the case $p = 2$ and comparing the value of $\Sigma a_i x_i$ when $x_i = b_i/\sqrt{(\Sigma b_i^2)}$ with the maximum value V. (Assume that $a_i > 0$ and $b_i > 0$ for $i = 1, 2, \ldots, n$).

Clearly the problem

$$\max_{\underline{x}} f(\underline{x})$$

$$\text{st } g(\underline{x}) = b,$$

and therefore its solution, depends critically upon the value of b. Similarly for the corresponding minimization problem. Any change in b specifies a different problem and a different solution emerges. We may therefore write the solution as

$$\hat{\underline{x}} = \hat{\underline{x}}(b) \quad \text{and} \quad V = f(\hat{\underline{x}}) = V(b). \tag{4.17}$$

$V(b)$ is called the *maximum* (or *minimum*) *value function*.

The Lagrange multiplier $\hat{\lambda}$ tells us how the maximum (or minimum) value V changes in response to a change in the value of b (e.g. how maximum utility responds to an increase in the individual's money income).

4.4.3 Theorem

$\hat{\lambda} = V'(b)$.

Proof   Differentiate $V(b) = f[\hat{\underline{x}}(b)]$ with respect to b, using the chain rule in equation (3.45). We find that

$$V'(b) = \sum_i \left(\frac{\partial f}{\partial x_i} \cdot \frac{\mathrm{d}\hat{x}_i}{\mathrm{d}b} \right). \tag{4.18}$$

Now $\partial f/\partial x_i = \hat{\lambda} \cdot \partial g/\partial x_i$ when $\underline{x} = \hat{\underline{x}}$: see equation (4.10). Thus

$$V'(b) = \hat{\lambda} \cdot \sum_i \left(\frac{\partial g}{\partial x_i} \cdot \frac{\mathrm{d}\hat{x}_i}{\mathrm{d}b} \right) = \hat{\lambda} \cdot \frac{\mathrm{d}}{\mathrm{d}b} \{ g[\hat{\underline{x}}(b)] \}. \tag{4.19}$$

But $g[\hat{\underline{x}}(b)] = b$ and so the result follows.   Q.E.D.

4.4.4 Example

For the Cobb–Douglas utility maximization problem in Example 4.3.1 we have $\hat{\lambda} = (a+b)V/m$ (e.g. from 2 and 5). Also

$$V = \hat{x}_1^a \hat{x}_2^b = (a/p_1)^a (b/p_2)^b [m/(a+b)]^{a+b}.$$

Thus we can verify directly that $\hat{\lambda} = \mathrm{d}V/\mathrm{d}m$. V is called the *indirect utility function.* Marginal utility of income is increasing/decreasing with income according as $a+b$ exceeds/is less than 1.

4.4.5 Exercise

Consider the firm's cost minimization problem

$$\min_{K,L} rK+wL$$

st $F(K,L) = Q$

where r and w are the prices of capital K and labour L respectively in perfect markets (and $F(K,L)$ is the production function). Show that at the optimum the ratio MP_K/MP_L of marginal products equals r/w and interpret.

By examining second-order conditions show that if $F_{KL} = 0$ then a sufficient condition for the optimum to be cost-minimizing is that $(F_K)^2 F_{LL} + (F_L)^2 F_{KK} < 0$.

Denote by $V(Q)$ the minimum cost $r\hat{K} + w\hat{L}$. Then V is the conventional total cost function. Use Theorem 4.4.3 to show that marginal cost equals r/MP_K or w/MP_L, and interpret.

4.4.6 Exercise

Find the stationary value of $y = cx_1 + x_2$ subject to the constraint $x_1 + \ln(x_2) = b$, where $b, c > 0$. Identify it as a maximum or minimum from second-order conditions. Letting V be the stationary value, verify that $\partial V/\partial b = \hat{\lambda}$. What is $\partial V/\partial c$?

4.5 MORE THAN ONE CONSTRAINT

We can deal with optimization problems with two or more constraints simply by using two or more Lagrange multipliers. Thus for the problem

$$\max_{\underline{x}} f(\underline{x})$$

st $g(\underline{x}) = b$ $h(\underline{x}) = c$

we define the Lagrangean

$$L(\lambda, \mu, \underline{x}) = f(\underline{x}) - \lambda[g(\underline{x}) - b] - \mu[h(\underline{x}) - c]$$

and solve the necessary conditions $\partial L/\partial \lambda = \partial L/\partial \mu = \partial L/\partial x_i = 0$.

4.5.1 Example

Find the maximum and minimum of $x - y + 2z$ subject to the constraints $x^2 + y^2 + z^2 = 1$ and $x + y + z = 0$.
First define the Lagrangean

$$L(\lambda, \mu, x, y, z) = x - y + 2z - \lambda(x^2 + y^2 + z^2 - 1) - \mu(x + y + z)$$

and obtain the necessary conditions $\partial L/\partial \lambda = \partial L/\partial \mu = \partial L/\partial x = \partial L/\partial y = \partial L/\partial z = 0$. These are

1. $x^2 + y^2 + z^2 = 1$

2. $\quad x + y + z = 0$

3. $\quad 1 - 2\lambda x - \mu = 0$

4. $-2 - 2\lambda y - \mu = 0$

5. $\quad 1 - 2\lambda z - \mu = 0.$

Adding 3, 4 and 5 and using 2, we find $\hat{\mu} = 0$. Now use 3, 4 and 5 to determine $\hat{x}$, $\hat{y}$ and $\hat{z}$ in terms of $\hat{\lambda}$. This implies $\hat{x} = \hat{z} = -\hat{y}/2$. From 1, $(\hat{x}, \hat{y}, \hat{z}) = (1/\sqrt{6}, -2/\sqrt{6}, 1/\sqrt{6})$ or $(-1/\sqrt{6}, 2/\sqrt{6}, -1/\sqrt{6})$. The stationary values of the function at these points are, respectively, $+\sqrt{6}$ and $-\sqrt{6}$. We shall take it that the first is the maximum, and the second the minimum value of $x - 2y + z$ subject to the two constraints, without examining second-order conditions.

We must, however, be rather careful about this use of the Lagrange multiplier approach for more than one constraint. For example in the $n = 2$ case, two constraints in two variables will in general determine a unique point: so that if both constraints are satisfied at once, then there is nothing left to maximize over! A good example of this situation is when *ration coupons* are introduced into the utility maximization problem of Example 4.3.1.

4.5.2 Example

(a) Let $u(x_1, x_2) = x_1 x_2$ and suppose that the prices of goods 1 and 2 are £5, £4 respectively. The individual has income £50.
Then we know from Example 4.3.1 that he spends £25 on each good; we also can calculate his indirect utility. Thus we find:

$$\hat{x}_1 = 5 \qquad \hat{x}_2 = 6.25 \qquad V = 31.250. \tag{4.20}$$

(b) A system of ration coupons is introduced. In addition to the money price the individual must now surrender three ration coupons for each unit of good 1, and six ration coupons for each unit of good 2. He is given forty ration coupons.

He has insufficient ration coupons to sustain his previous levels of consumption. In fact if he uses all of his income and all of his ration coupons then the two constraints

$$5x_1 + 4x_2 = 50$$
$$3x_1 + 6x_2 = 40$$

both hold at once and determine the quantities of each good purchased. We may also compute the utility level in this case:

$$\bar{x}_1 = \tfrac{70}{9} \qquad \bar{x}_2 = \tfrac{25}{9} \qquad u = 21.605. \tag{4.21}$$

What happens if the individual uses all of his ration tickets optimally, ignoring the income constraint? He will spend twenty ration tickets on each good (the result in Example 4.3.1 still holds; put $p_1 = 3$ and $p_2 = 6$). We can also calculate utility:

$$\tilde{x}_1 = \tfrac{20}{3} \qquad \tilde{x}_2 = \tfrac{10}{3} \qquad V = 22.222. \tag{4.22}$$

Furthermore, the individual still has some income left (£3.33 in fact). He raises his utility by keeping some of his income back (compare equations (4.21) and (4.22)). But utility is still lessened by the introduction of the rationing system (compare equation (4.20)).

The lesson to draw from this example is clear. In the presence of the extra constraint, an *inequality-constrained* specification for the optimization problem becomes more appropriate:

$$\max_{x_1, x_2} x_1 x_2$$
$$\text{st } 5x_1 + 4x_2 \leqslant 50 \qquad 3x_1 + 6x_2 \leqslant 40.$$

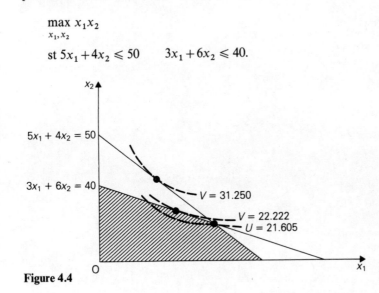

Figure 4.4

In figure 4.4 the region in which (x_1, x_2) satisfies both inequality constraints is shaded. Also shown are the three 'solutions' (4.20), (4.21) and (4.22). It is clear which of these solves the inequality-constrained problem.

In the next chapter, we deal more fully with the general problem of inequality-constrained optimization. The mathematics becomes slightly more complex, but a similar Lagrangean-based approach can be adopted. Equality-constrained optimization problems will be encountered again in chapter 6.

4.5.3 Exercises

(a) Use Exercises 4.3.2(e) and 4.3.3(c) to obtain the minimum of $y = 3x_1^2 + 2x_2^2 - 4x_2 + 1$ subject to the constraint $x_1^2 + x_2^2 = 16$. What is the minimum subject to the constraint $x_1^2 + x_2^2 \leqslant 16$? (*Hint*: what is the free minimum? Recall Exercise 3.3.2(c), p. 17.)

(b) Maximize utility $u(x_1, x_2) = x_2 + \ln(x_1)$ subject to the budget constraint $p_1 x_1 + p_2 x_2 = m$. Find the optimal quantities $\hat{x}_1, \hat{x}_2$ and the marginal utility of income.

If $m < p_2$, what is a more appropriate specification for this problem?

5 Inequality-constrained Optimization

5.1 COMPLEMENTARY SLACKNESS

In the last chapter we saw an example in which the problem of utility maximization subject to two linear budget constraints was incorrectly specified using equality constraints. By treating the constraints as inequalities, utility achieved was higher than if both of them were binding.

Another example where inequality constraints are appropriate, this time for a single linear budget constraint, is provided by a utility function with closed contours, i.e. having a bliss point beyond which there is satiation (see figure 5.1).

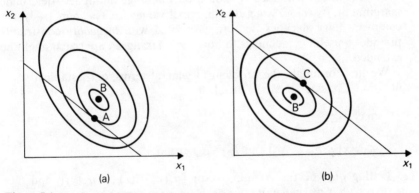

Figure 5.1

If the individual has insufficient income to reach the bliss point B, then A is optimal; if he has more than enough income to reach the bliss point then clearly he should stop there and not go beyond to C which is the optimal point on the budget line. His problem can therefore be specified as

$$\max_{x_1, x_2} u(x_1, x_2)$$

$$\text{st } p_1 x_1 + p_2 x_2 \leqslant m.$$

115

What is the marginal utility of income in this problem? In figure 5.1(a), when the budget constraint binds, it is clearly positive. In figure 5.1(b), where the budget constraint is 'slack', it is zero. Thus we have

$$MU_{inc} \geqslant 0 \quad p_1 x_1 + p_2 x_2 \leqslant m \quad \text{and} \quad MU_{inc}(p_1 x_1 + p_2 x_2 - m) = 0 \quad (5.1)$$

in either case.

Similarly for the two-constraint problem in chapter 4. In that case all ration coupons were used ($MU_{rat} \geqslant 0$) but some income was left over ($MU_{inc} = 0$). An essential feature of this optimum is thus given by

$$MU_{inc} \geqslant 0 \quad p_1 x_1 + p_2 x_2 \leqslant m \quad \text{and} \quad MU_{inc}(p_1 x_1 + p_2 x_2 - m) = 0 \quad (5.2)$$

$$MU_{rat} \geqslant 0 \quad r_1 x_1 + r_2 x_2 \leqslant n \quad \text{and} \quad MU_{rat}(r_1 x_1 + r_2 x_2 - n) = 0 \quad (5.3)$$

(using an obvious notation). This would have been equally true had the numbers in the problem been such that all income was used, and not all ration coupons – or if both constraints had been binding.

The relationships between inequalities that characterizes conditions (5.1)–(5.3) is called *complementary slackness*. If one inequality is slack (non-binding) then the other must bind (but you may *not* argue conversely that if one inequality is binding, then the other is slack: both could bind).

For *equality*-constrained optimization Lagrange multipliers determine marginal utility (more generally, marginal value: see Theorem 4.4.3); the complementary slackness feature associated with *inequality* constraints provides a useful guideline as to how the Lagrangean approach might be extended.

We first formulate the problem in general terms, and establish some notation. Consider, then, the problem

$$\max_{\underline{x}} f(\underline{x})$$

$$\text{st } g_1(\underline{x}) \leqslant b_1 \quad g_2(\underline{x}) \leqslant b_2 \ldots g_m(\underline{x}) \leqslant b_m. \quad (5.4)$$

Letting $\underline{g}(\underline{x})$ be the column vector $[g_1(\underline{x}), g_2(\underline{x}), \ldots, g_m(\underline{x})]^t$ and $\underline{b} = (b_1, b_2, \ldots, b_m)^t$ we may write this problem more compactly as

$$\max_{\underline{x}} f(\underline{x})$$

$$\text{st } \underline{g}(\underline{x}) \leqslant \underline{b}. \quad (5.5)$$

(Recall the definition of vector inequalities in Example 2.7.2.) Let X be the subset of vectors $\underline{x}$ that satisfy the constraints $\underline{g}(\underline{x}) \leqslant \underline{b}$. Then problem (5.5) could equally be written

$$\max_{\underline{x} \in X} f(\underline{x}). \quad (5.6)$$

Note that this formulation does not exclude inequality constraints of the opposite kind $g(\underline{x}) \geqslant b$: we may replace such a constraint by the equivalent one $-g(\underline{x}) \leqslant -b$. We may also admit equality constraints in this framework, since $g(\underline{x}) = b$ is equivalent to the pair

$$g(\underline{x}) \leqslant b$$

$$-g(\underline{x}) \leqslant -b$$

of inequality constraints.

5.2 THE LAGRANGEAN APPROACH

What we are about to do is define the Lagrangean and explore a technique suggested by the complementary slackness property: namely, instead of finding a free turning point of the Lagrangean, as we did by solving

$$\frac{\partial L}{\partial \lambda} = \frac{\partial L}{\partial x_i} = 0$$

for the case of an equality constraint, we shall maximize L over $\underline{x}$ only, seeking complementary slackness relationships for the Lagrange multipliers.

The Lagrangean is simply

$$L(\lambda_1, \lambda_2, \ldots, \lambda_m, \underline{x}) = f(\underline{x}) - \lambda_1[g_1(\underline{x}) - b_1]$$
$$- \lambda_2[g_2(\underline{x}) - b_2] \ldots - \lambda_m[g_m(\underline{x}) - b_m]$$

or

$$L(\underline{\lambda}, \underline{x}) = f(\underline{x}) - \underline{\lambda}^t[\underline{g}(\underline{x}) - \underline{b}] \tag{5.7}$$

in vector notation.

5.2.1 Definition   The Lagrangean conditions

A vector $\underline{\hat{x}} \in X$ and a multiplier $\underline{\hat{\lambda}} \geqslant \underline{0}$ (i.e. $\hat{\lambda}_j \geqslant 0$ for all j) satisfy the *Lagrangean conditions* if

1. $L(\underline{\hat{\lambda}}, \underline{\hat{x}}) \geqslant L(\underline{\hat{\lambda}}, \underline{x})$ for all $\underline{x}$, and

2. $\underline{\hat{\lambda}}^t[\underline{g}(\underline{\hat{x}}) - \underline{b}] = 0$.

Part 1 says that $\underline{\hat{x}}$ maximizes $L(\underline{\hat{\lambda}}, \underline{x})$ freely over all $\underline{x}$ (not just over $\underline{x} \in X$). This we can find using the differential calculus. As before, it makes solving the problem significantly easier. Part 2, together with the requirements $\hat{\underline{x}} \in X$ and $\hat{\underline{\lambda}} \geqslant \underline{0}$, is the complementary slackness condition. If we write it out in full, this becomes plain. Since $\hat{\underline{x}} \in X$ and $\hat{\underline{\lambda}} \geqslant \underline{0}$ we have

$$g_j(\hat{\underline{x}}) \leqslant b_j$$
$$\hat{\lambda}_j \geqslant 0$$

whilst $\hat{\underline{\lambda}}'[g(\hat{\underline{x}}) - \underline{b}] = 0$ says that

$$\sum_j \hat{\lambda}_j[g_j(\hat{\underline{x}}) - b_j] = 0.$$

In the summation, each term is the product of a non-negative factor and a non-positive factor. Thus the whole expression is non-positive, and the only way it can be zero is if each term is zero. Hence we have complementary slackness

$$\hat{\lambda}_j \geqslant 0 \qquad g_j(\hat{\underline{x}}) \leqslant b_j \quad \text{and} \quad \hat{\lambda}_j[g_j(\hat{\underline{x}}) - b_j] = 0 \tag{5.8}$$

for $j = 1, 2, \ldots, m$, i.e. for each constraint. If a constraint is slack, then $\hat{\lambda}_j = 0$ and if $\hat{\lambda}_j > 0$ then the constraint binds (compare conditions (5.1)–(5.3)).

This is, of course, merely the definition of a condition. It carries with it no guarantee that we can find such an $\hat{\underline{x}}$ and $\hat{\underline{\lambda}}$; nor, indeed, that if we do find them, they will solve the maximization problem at hand. Still less does it entitle us to regard the multipliers as marginal valuations, as we would like to.

We deal with each of these aspects in turn, in what follows. We devote the rest of the present chapter to establishing the validity of the technique, and using it; in chapter 6 we turn to the interpretation of the multipliers.

5.2.2 Theorem

If $\hat{\underline{x}}$ and $\hat{\underline{\lambda}}$ exist satisfying the Lagrangean conditions then

$$f(\hat{\underline{x}}) = \max_{\underline{x} \in X} f(\underline{x}).$$

Proof   Because of 2, $f(\hat{\underline{x}}) = L(\hat{\underline{\lambda}}, \hat{\underline{x}})$. From 1, $L(\hat{\underline{\lambda}}, \hat{\underline{x}}) \geqslant L(\hat{\underline{\lambda}}, \underline{x})$ for all $\underline{x}$. Now $L(\hat{\underline{\lambda}}, \underline{x}) = f(\underline{x}) - \hat{\underline{\lambda}}'[g(\underline{x}) - \underline{b}]$. For $\underline{x} \in X$, therefore, $L(\hat{\underline{\lambda}}, \underline{x}) \geqslant f(\underline{x})$ since, as pointed out above, $\hat{\underline{\lambda}}'[g(\underline{x}) - \underline{b}]$ is non-positive when $\underline{x} \in X$. Putting this chain of inequalities together, we have $f(\hat{\underline{x}}) \geqslant f(\underline{x})$ for all $\underline{x} \in X$.
                                                                        Q.E.D.

Therefore *if we can solve them* the Lagrangean conditions do indeed lead to the optimum we seek. But suppose that we do not succeed in solving the Lagrangean conditions: what then? There are three possibilities.

1. The failure to solve the Lagrangean conditions is due to our own mathematical inadequacy: a solution exists.
2. There is no solution to the Lagrangean conditions, even though the optimization problem has a solution.
3. There is no solution to the Lagrangean conditions, and the optimization problem cannot be solved either.

An approach to problem-solving that does not resolve the uncertainty between 1, 2 and 3 is not very helpful when difficulties arise: we need further results to make the Lagrangean approach more useful.

Results of the following general form would be ideal:

> If ****************, and if $\max_{x \in X} f(x)$ exists, and equals $f(\hat{x})$, say, then the Lagrangean conditions will be satisfied by $x = \hat{x}$ and by some $\lambda \geqslant 0$.

Then, to solve the optimization problem, we need only check ****************, and apply the Lagrangean conditions: we will know that *if a solution exists, the Lagrangean approach will find it.*

The criterion ****************, whatever it may be, represents our guarantee that following the Lagrangean approach will not be needlessly fruitless. It is a *sufficient condition* to ensure that the Lagrangean approach will lead to the optimum; in conjunction with Theorem 5.2.2, it ensures that the Lagrangean conditions themselves are *necessary and sufficient* for the optimum.

In the Appendix, we describe an elegant and powerful new approach to constrained optimization, that of Clarke (1979), which validates the use of a Lagrangean under very weak conditions on the functions $f(x)$ and $g(x)$.

But a more easily understood result, which is very useful in economics and is in precisely the form we require, is as follows.

5.2.3 Theorem

If (a) $f(x)$ is concave, (b) each $g_j(x)$ is convex, and (c) there exists an x such that $g(x) < b$; and if $\max_{x \in X} f(x)$ exists, and equals $f(\hat{x})$, say, then the Lagrangean conditions are satisfied by $x = \hat{x}$ and by some $\lambda \geqslant 0$.

The last condition, (c), is called the *constraint qualification*. It is essentially a non-degeneracy condition, and will usually be true of the sort of economic problems we wish to consider (but see Exercise 5.4.4(a), p. 131; and Example 6.1.2, p. 142).

There are other forms of constraint qualification for constrained optimization. One is given in the Appendix which is sufficient to make the generalized gradient vector approach of Clarke (1979) yield Lagrangean conditions.

Problems which satisfy (a)–(c) in Theorem 5.2.3 fall under the generic heading of *concave programming problems*.

The proof of Theorem 5.2.3 is rather long. It involves some *m*-dimensional geometry (*m* is the number of constraints) and may go beyond the resources of some readers. But the ideas in the proof are perfectly accessible, even to the least technically sophisticated reader.

Proof of Theorem 5.2.3   The proof proceeds in stages.

1. Define a set A to comprise all values that the constants $\underline{b}$ in the constraints $g(\underline{x}) \leqslant \underline{b}$ could meaningfully take. In mathematical terms,

$$A = \{\underline{a} \in \mathbf{R}^m : \exists \underline{x} : g(\underline{x}) \leqslant \underline{a}\}.$$

2. For each $\underline{a} \in A$ define $V(\underline{a})$ as the maximum value for the problem

$$\max f(\underline{x})$$

$$\text{st } g(\underline{x}) \leqslant \underline{a}. \tag{5.9}$$

It is clear that V is non-decreasing in each a_j, since the set X of vectors $\underline{x}$ satisfying the constraints enlarges when any a_j increases.

3. Prove that $V(\underline{a})$ is concave. This is quite easy. We want to show that

$$V[k\underline{c} + (1-k)\underline{d}] \geqslant kV(\underline{c}) + (1-k)V(\underline{d})$$

for all $\underline{c}, \underline{d}$ in A and for $0 < k < 1$ (see Definition 3.7.1). Now if $\underline{x} = \underline{u}, \underline{v}$ is optimal for problem (5.9) when $\underline{a} = \underline{c}, \underline{d}$ and if $\underline{z}$ is optimal when $\underline{a} = k\underline{c} + (1-k)\underline{d}$, then we have

$$V[k\underline{c} + (1-k)\underline{d}] = f(\underline{z}).$$

Since each $g_j(\underline{x})$ is convex,

$$g_j[k\underline{u} + (1-k)\underline{v}] \leqslant kg_j(\underline{u}) + (1-k)g_j(\underline{v}) \leqslant kc_j + (1-k)d_j$$

by the definition of $\underline{u}$ and $\underline{v}$. Thus $\underline{x} = k\underline{u} + (1-k)\underline{v}$ satisfies the constraints when $\underline{a} = k\underline{c} + (1-k)\underline{d}$, and so

$$V[k\underline{c} + (1-k)\underline{d}] = f(\underline{z}) \geqslant f[k\underline{u} + (1-k)\underline{v}] \geqslant kf(\underline{u}) + (1-k)f(\underline{v})$$

$$= kV(\underline{c}) + (1-k)V(\underline{d})$$

by the concavity of f.

4. Establish some properties of the set A: in fact that A is 'convex' and has 'non-empty interior'. Being convex means that if $\underline{c}$ and $\underline{d}$ belong to A, then so does $k\underline{c} + (1-k)\underline{d}$. This is easy to visualize when $m = 2$: the point $k\underline{c} + (1-k)\underline{d}$ traces out the chord between $\underline{c}$ and $\underline{d}$, as k runs from 1 to 0 (see figure 5.2).

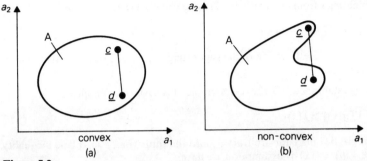

Figure 5.2

Having a non-empty interior means that there are non-boundary points in A. Proving convexity of A is routine and rather similar to III above; the constraint qualification ensures a non-empty interior. When $m = 1$ these properties of A mean that A is essentially an interval.

5. Using 1–4 we prove that there exists a $\underline{\lambda} \geqslant \underline{0}$ such that $V(\underline{a}) - V(\underline{b}) \leqslant \underline{\lambda}'(\underline{a} - \underline{b})$. This is where the m-dimensional geometry comes in: the proposition is known as the *supporting hyperplane theorem*.

For $m = 1$ it is easily appreciated. In figure 5.3 the maximum value function $V(a)$ is graphed (recall $V(a)$ is concave and non-decreasing from 2 and 3). The set A is the interval from a_1 to a_2; b is contained within it. The dotted line is a tangent at b ('supporting hyperplane'); it has positive slope λ, with equation $y = \lambda a + e$, say. Then

$$V(b) = \lambda b + e. \tag{5.10}$$

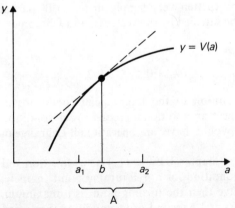

Figure 5.3

If a general point (a, y) lies above/below the dotted tangent line then y is greater/less than $\lambda a + e$. In particular, since $[a, V(a)]$ is below the tangent for each $a \in A$, we have

$$V(a) \leqslant \lambda a + e. \tag{5.11}$$

Eliminating e from inequality (5.11) using equation (5.10) we have

$$V(a) - V(b) \leqslant \lambda(a - b)$$

which is the $m = 1$ version of the supporting hyperplane theorem. We omit the general proof.

6. Having established 1–5, the rest is simple. It is trivial that for all $\underline{x}$

$$V[\underline{g}(\underline{x})] \geqslant f(\underline{x}). \tag{5.12}$$

Then put $\underline{a} = \underline{g}(\underline{x})$, for arbitrary $\underline{x}$, into the supporting hyperplane inequality. Since $V(\underline{b}) = f(\hat{\underline{x}})$ by assumption, we have

$$f(\hat{\underline{x}}) \geqslant f(\underline{x}) - \hat{\underline{\lambda}}^t[\underline{g}(\underline{x}) - \underline{b}]. \tag{5.13}$$

The right-hand side of inequality (5.13) is $L(\hat{\underline{\lambda}}, \underline{x})$, and for $\underline{x} \in X$ it is greater than or equal to $f(\underline{x})$, with equality if and only if $\hat{\underline{\lambda}}^t[\underline{g}(\underline{x}) - \underline{b}] = 0$. Now put $\underline{x} = \hat{\underline{x}} \in X$: the conclusion is that $\hat{\underline{\lambda}}^t[\underline{g}(\hat{\underline{x}}) - \underline{b}] = 0$. Since we also have, directly from inequality (5.13), that $f(\hat{\underline{x}}) = L(\hat{\underline{\lambda}}, \hat{\underline{x}}) \geqslant L(\hat{\underline{\lambda}}, \underline{x})$ for all $\underline{x}$, we have established that $\hat{\underline{\lambda}}$ and $\hat{\underline{x}}$ satisfy the Lagrangean conditions.   Q.E.D.

Theorem 5.2.3 could be called the *concave programming theorem*. It validates the Lagrangean conditions as *necessary* for the inequality-constrained optimization problem in the particular case that (a), (b) and the constraint qualification (c) are satisfied (*sufficiency* is Theorem 5.2.2).

It is not very obvious how to apply these conditions in practice, however. But when all of the functions are differentiable, the first-order conditions for part 1 of the Lagrangean conditions in Definition 5.2.1 can be applied; part 2 can also be written very simply in terms of partial derivatives. The conditions to be satisfied by the vectors $\hat{\underline{\lambda}}$ and $\hat{\underline{x}}$ become:

$$\begin{aligned} \partial L/\partial x_i &= 0 \qquad i = 1, 2, \ldots, n \\ \lambda_j &\geqslant 0 \qquad \partial L/\partial \lambda_j \geqslant 0 \text{ and } \lambda_j . \partial L/\partial \lambda_j = 0 \qquad j = 1, 2, \ldots, m. \end{aligned} \tag{5.14}$$

These are *necessary* for the solution to the Lagrangean conditions in Definition 5.2.1. We would expect an additional second-order condition to give sufficiency. Then we would have an operational Lagrangean approach.

Let us recall here a result from chapter 3. If $y = f(\underline{x})$ is any function and $\underline{x} = \underline{a}$ satisfies the first-order condition for a *free* turning point (namely, $\nabla f(\underline{a}) = \underline{0}$) and if $f(\underline{x})$ is concave then the turning point is a maximum. Concavity ensures that the appropriate second-order condition is satisfied (see the discussion around Definition 3.7.5, p. 84).

Happily a similar result applies for constrained maximization. If conditions (a), (b) and the constraint qualification (c) in the concave programming Theorem 5.2.3 are satisfied, then the partial derivative conditions (5.14) are *necessary and sufficient* for a (unique) optimum.

In fact we can go further. Arrow and Enthoven (1961) have shown that condition (a) can be weakened to *quasi-concavity*. Thus we may replace (a) and (b) in Theorem 5.2.3 by

(a*) f is differentiable and quasi-concave,
(b*) each g_j is differentiable and convex,

with (c) as before. Indeed (b*) can also be weakened, to

(b**) each g_j differentiable and quasi-convex,

if we add to the constraint qualification (c) a technical restriction on partial derivatives. Problems that are covered by these criteria are known as *quasi-concave programming* problems. Conditions (5.14) (which in some books are known as the *Arrow–Enthoven conditions*) are necessary and sufficient for their solution.

This result is very useful to us as economists: it tells us conditions we may impose on objective and constraint functions, in theoretical work (e.g. in consumer theory), that will ensure the Lagrangean approach is valid. We shall see in the next chapter that the Lagrangean approach yields powerful insights – especially in consumer theory (where the quasi-concave programming assumptions are quite acceptable).

It is as well to remember, however, that even if the criteria for concave/quasi-concave programming do not hold, for a particular problem, the Lagrangean conditions are worth pursuing. By Theorem 5.2.2, if they have a solution, it will be the right one; and (see the Appendix) it will be among the solutions to conditions (5.14).

5.2.4 Example

Maximize $x_1 + x_2$ subject to the constraints $4x_1 - x_2 - x_1^2 \leqslant 0$, $2x_1 + 3x_2 \leqslant 8$ and $x_1 \leqslant 3$.

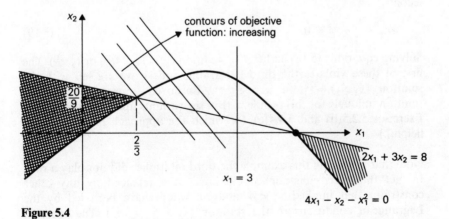

Figure 5.4

Note first that this problem has a *concave* constraint: see Exercise 3.7.4(c): hence the Arrow–Enthoven conditions do not necessarily lead to a unique solution.

The feasible region for the problem is graphed (cross-hatched) with contours of the objective function, in figure 5.4. It is clear that the problem has a solution, in fact at $(\hat{x}_1, \hat{x}_2) = (\frac{2}{3}, \frac{20}{9})$; let us explore conditions (5.14).

First we define the Lagrangean

$$L(\lambda_1, \lambda_2, \lambda_3, x_1, x_2) = x_1 + x_2 - \lambda_1(4x_1 - x_2 - x_1^2)$$
$$- \lambda_2(2x_1 + 3x_2 - 8) - \lambda_3(x_1 - 3)$$

and then we write down equations (5.14):

$$\partial L/\partial x_1 = 1 - 4\lambda_1 + 2\lambda_1 x_1 - 2\lambda_2 - \lambda_3 = 0 \tag{5.15}$$

$$\partial L/\partial x_2 = 1 + \lambda_1 - 3\lambda_2 = 0 \tag{5.16}$$

and

$$\lambda_j \geq 0 \quad \partial L/\partial \lambda_j \geq 0 \quad \text{and} \quad \lambda_j . \partial L/\partial \lambda_j = 0 \qquad j = 1, 2, 3. \tag{5.17}$$

Note immediately from equation (5.16) that $\lambda_2 \neq 0$, otherwise $\lambda_1 = -1$ which violates conditions (5.17). Hence, again from conditions (5.17), $\partial L/\partial \lambda_2 = 0$, i.e. the second constraint is binding:

$$2x_1 + 3x_2 = 8. \tag{5.18}$$

Now suppose that $\lambda_1 = 0$. Then from equations (5.15) and (5.16) $\lambda_2 = \lambda_3 = \frac{1}{3}$; and from conditions (5.17) $\partial L/\partial \lambda_3 = 0$, i.e. $x_1 = 3$. Then from equation (5.18) $x_2 = \frac{2}{3}$. But then the first constraint is violated. So λ_1 cannot be zero.

Therefore $\partial L/\partial \lambda_1 = 0$, i.e. the first constraint binds (in addition to the second):

$$4x_1 - x_2 - x_1^2 = 0. \tag{5.19}$$

Solving equations (5.18) and (5.19), we find $(x_1, x_2) = (4, 0)$ or $(\frac{2}{3}, \frac{20}{9})$. The first of these violates the third constraint, and so we are left with the solution $(\hat{x}_1, \hat{x}_2) = (\frac{2}{3}, \frac{20}{9})$: the Arrow–Enthoven approach yields the solution uniquely for this problem. (But see variants upon this problem in Exercises 5.2.5(b) and 5.4.4(c), for which the approach is *not* quite so helpful.)

Note that in solving this example the third multiplier did not play a role. In fact the third constraint could have been replaced by any other constraint that implied $x_1 < 4$, and we would have been led by the Lagrangean conditions to the solution $(\hat{x}_1, \hat{x}_2) = (\frac{2}{3}, \frac{20}{9})$. The effect of such a third constraint is simply to confine the feasible region for the problem to the cross-hatched area in figure 5.4, excluding the single-shaded region that also satisfies the first two constraints. In the absence of *any* third constraint, the problem clearly has no maximum, and we could not expect the Lagrangean conditions to lead us to one.

5.2.5 Exercises

(a) Verify that in Example 5.2.4 the conditions (5.14) are satisfied by $(\hat{\lambda}_1, \hat{\lambda}_2, \hat{\lambda}_3) = (3\lambda - 1, \lambda, -10\lambda + \frac{11}{3})$ for any $\lambda \in (\frac{10}{30}, \frac{11}{30})$.

(b) Show that in the absence of any third constraint in Example 5.2.4, there is a unique solution to conditions (5.14), given by $(\hat{x}_1, \hat{x}_2, \hat{\lambda}_1, \hat{\lambda}_2) = (\frac{2}{3}, \frac{20}{9}, \frac{1}{10}, \frac{11}{30})$; but no finite solution to the optimization problem.

We said earlier that the Lagrangean approach allowed equality constraints within the constraint set $g(\underline{x}) \leqslant \underline{b}$. It is reassuring to note that, for such an equality constraint, say $h(\underline{x}) = c$, conditions (5.14) reduce to the familiar ones we used in chapter 4.

To see this, suppose that the constraints $g(\underline{x}) \leqslant \underline{b}$ contain the pair $g_k(\underline{x}) = h(\underline{x}) \leqslant b_k = c$ and $g_{k+1}(\underline{x}) = -h(\underline{x}) \leqslant b_{k+1} = -c$. (Note that if both $h(\underline{x})$ and $-h(\underline{x})$ are to satisfy the conditions for concave/quasi-concave programming, then $h(\underline{x})$ must be concave and convex, i.e. linear: see Exercise 3.7.4(b).) Conditions (5.14) contain the pair $\partial L/\partial \lambda_k \geqslant 0$ and $\partial L/\partial \lambda_{k+1} \geqslant 0$; but since $\partial L/\partial \lambda_k = -\partial L/\partial \lambda_{k+1}$, both must be zero. Thus we have $\partial L/\partial \lambda = 0$ for the equality constraint, as in chapter 4. The following example is one which mixes equality and inequality constraints.

5.2.6 Example

Maximize utility $u(x_1, x_2) = x_2 + \ln(x_1)$ subject to the budget constraint $p_1 x_1 + p_2 x_2 = m$ and subject to $x_2 \geqslant 0$, when $m < p_2$ (see Exercise 4.5.3(b)).

First note that $u(x_1, x_2)$ is concave by Exercise 3.7.7(b). The constraint is linear. Hence the Arrow–Enthoven conditions (5.14) yield the solution uniquely. The Lagrangean is:

$$L = x_2 + \ln(x_1) - \lambda_1(p_1 x_1 + p_2 x_2 - m) + \lambda_2 x_2$$

(writing the non-negativity constraint on x_2 as $-x_2 \leqslant 0$). The equations to be satisfied are $\partial L/\partial x_1 = \partial L/\partial x_2 = \partial L/\partial \lambda_1 = 0$, and $\lambda_2 \geqslant 0$, $\partial L/\partial \lambda_2 \geqslant 0$ and $\lambda_2 . \partial L/\partial \lambda_2 = 0$. These say that:

$$\frac{1}{x_1} - \lambda_1 p_1 = 0 \tag{5.20}$$

$$1 - \lambda_1 p_2 + \lambda_2 = 0 \tag{5.21}$$

$$\lambda_2 \geqslant 0 \qquad x_2 \geqslant 0 \quad \text{and} \quad \lambda_2 x_2 = 0 \tag{5.22}$$

and that the budget constraint is satisfied.

Suppose $x_2 > 0$. Then, from conditions (5.22), $\lambda_2 = 0$. From equation (5.21), $\lambda_1 = 1/p_2$. Thus, from equation (5.20), $x_1 = p_2/p_1$. From the budget constraint $x_2 = (m - p_2)/p_2$. But since $m < p_2$ this is a contradiction.

Hence $\hat{x}_2 = 0$. From the budget constraint, $\hat{x}_1 = m/p_1$. Thus $\hat{\lambda}_1 = 1/m$.

In Exercise 4.5.3(b) the restriction $x_2 \geqslant 0$ was not imposed, and the optimal quantities were $x_1 = p_2/p_1$ and $x_2 = (m - p_2)/p_2 < 0$. The Lagrange multiplier in that case was $\lambda = 1/p_2$ and it could be interpreted as the marginal utility of income (Theorem 4.4.3). With the non-negativity constraint imposed upon x_2, the budget constraint multiplier *rises*, to $\hat{\lambda}_1 = 1/m$. We may still interpret it as the marginal utility of income (this is shown in the next chapter): the imposition of the additional constraint forces the individual to a lower level of utility, but the increment to utility derivable from extra income goes up.

5.3 NON-NEGATIVITY CONSTRAINTS ON VARIABLES

There is a further general simplification we can make in the Lagrangean conditions 5.2.1 when, as in Example 5.2.5, some of the inequality constraints are of the form $x_k \geqslant 0$.

This type of constraint is often necessary in economic applications, with variables such as capital, labour, consumption goods, etc. Even when absent from the mathematical specification of a problem, non-negativity constraints may be implicit or understood, only being included after negative optimal values are encountered (as in Exercises 4.5.3(b) and 4.2.5).

Suppose that the constraints $\underline{g}(\underline{x}) \leqslant \underline{b}$ divide into two types: some of the form $g_k(\underline{x}) = -x_k \leqslant b_k = 0$, i.e. representing $x_k \geqslant 0$, and other inequalities $g_j(\underline{x}) \leqslant b_j$ not of this kind.

One approach would be to ignore the $x_k \geqslant 0$ constraints altogether, and solve the problem without them, hoping for a solution $x_i = x_i^*$ which is in accord (i.e. for which $x_k^* \geqslant 0$ for each such k). Whereas the full Lagrangean including all constraints is

$$L = f(\underline{x}) - \sum_j \lambda_j [g_j(\underline{x}) - b_j] + \sum_k \mu_k x_k \tag{5.23}$$

(distinguishing the multipliers for the two kinds of constraints as λs and μs), the Lagrangean that excludes the non-negative variable constraints would be

$$L^* = f(\underline{x}) - \sum_j \lambda_j [g_j(\underline{x}) - b_j]. \tag{5.24}$$

Solving this according to the conditions (5.14) requires

$$\frac{\partial L^*}{\partial x_1} = \frac{\partial L^*}{\partial x_2} = \ldots = \frac{\partial L^*}{\partial x_n} = 0$$

$$\lambda_j \geqslant 0 \qquad \frac{\partial L^*}{\partial \lambda_j} \geqslant 0 \quad \text{and} \quad \lambda_j\left(\frac{\partial L^*}{\partial \lambda_j}\right) = 0$$

for all j. Let $x_i = x_i^*$ be the solution that emerges.

If $x_k^* \geqslant 0$, well and good: we have 'got away' with ignoring the non-negativity constraint on x_k (and reduced the amount of computation in the process), and the solution to the full problem is simply $\hat{x}_i = x_i^*$, $i = 1, 2, \ldots, n$. This happy situation is shown in figure 5.5(a).

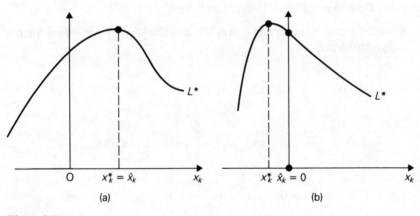

Figure 5.5

If one or more of the x_k^* is negative, then the situation is as depicted in figure 5.5(b). In order to maximize L^* over $x_k \geqslant 0$ we should clearly have set $\hat{x}_k = 0$. At $\hat{x}_k = 0$, in figure 5.5(b), we have $\partial L^*/\partial x_k < 0$. If $x_k^* \geqslant 0$ as in figure 5.5(a), then we have $\partial L^*/\partial x_k = 0$. Therefore the correct optimum for the problem is described by

$$x_k \geqslant 0 \qquad \frac{\partial L^*}{\partial x_k} \leqslant 0 \quad \text{and} \quad x_k\left(\frac{\partial L^*}{\partial x_k}\right) = 0 \qquad (5.25)$$

in either case. This is simply a complementary slackness condition. We have arrived at a set of conditions known as the *Kuhn–Tucker conditions*. Let us summarize the process we have followed.

5.4 THE KUHN–TUCKER CONDITIONS

For the problem

$$\max_{x_i, i = 1,\ldots,n} f(\underline{x})$$

st $x_k \geqslant 0$ for certain $k \in \{1, 2, \ldots, n\}$ and $g_j(\underline{x}) \leqslant b_j$

(additional constraints $j = 1, 2, \ldots, m$)

the (modified) Lagrangean is

$$L^* = f(\underline{x}) - \underline{\lambda}^t[\underline{g}(\underline{x}) - \underline{b}]. \tag{5.26}$$

5.4.1 Definition   Kuhn–Tucker conditions

A vector $\underline{x}$ and a multiplier $\underline{\lambda}$ satisfy the *Kuhn–Tucker conditions* for the above problem if

$$\frac{\partial L^*}{\partial x_i} = 0 \qquad i \neq k \in \{1, 2, \ldots, n\}$$

$$x_k \geqslant 0 \qquad \frac{\partial L^*}{\partial x_k} \leqslant 0 \quad \text{and} \quad x_k\left(\frac{\partial L^*}{\partial x_k}\right) = 0 \qquad \text{for all } k$$

$$\lambda_j \geqslant 0 \qquad \frac{\partial L^*}{\partial \lambda_j} \geqslant 0 \quad \text{and} \quad \lambda_j\left(\frac{\partial L^*}{\partial \lambda_j}\right) = 0 \qquad j = 1, 2, \ldots, m.$$

The problem has a unique solution, uniquely satisfying the Kuhn–Tucker (henceforth: K–T) conditions, if the quasi-concave programming conditions hold.

Although we have reduced the number of multipliers, and thereby the complexity of the mathematics, it can nevertheless be a complex matter to address this stack of equations.

The more *inequalities* we have to handle in solving the K–T conditions, the more case-by-case analysis we may have to carry out in search of the solution. It is usually best to argue each case from the assumption of a *strict inequality*, e.g. from $x_k > 0$ or $\lambda_j > 0$. If true, this yields an additional *equality* (namely $\partial L^*/\partial x_k = 0$ or $\partial L^*/\partial \lambda_j = 0$) that must be satisfied, making the mathematics that much easier; if false, we also get an equality to work with (i.e. $x_k = 0$ or $\lambda_j = 0$). In the next example, we rework the ration coupons Example 4.5.2 using the K–T conditions.

5.4.2 Example

Solve the problem

$$\max_{x_1, x_2} x_1 x_2$$

$$\text{st } 5x_1 + 4x_2 \leqslant 50 \qquad 3x_1 + 6x_2 \leqslant 40 \quad \text{and} \quad x_1 \geqslant 0 \qquad x_2 \geqslant 0.$$

First, note that the quasi-concave programming criteria are met by this problem (see Exercise 3.7.11(a)). The modified Lagrangean is

$$L^* = x_1 x_2 - \lambda_1 (5x_1 + 4x_2 - 50) - \lambda_2 (3x_1 + 6x_2 - 40)$$

ignoring the $x_k \geqslant 0$ constraints (in this case, on all variables). Now we write down the K–T conditions:

$$x_1 \geqslant 0 \qquad \frac{\partial L^*}{\partial x_1} \leqslant 0 \quad \text{and} \quad x_1 \left(\frac{\partial L^*}{\partial x_1} \right) = 0$$

$$x_2 \geqslant 0 \qquad \frac{\partial L^*}{\partial x_2} \leqslant 0 \quad \text{and} \quad x_2 \left(\frac{\partial L^*}{\partial x_2} \right) = 0$$

$$\lambda_1 \geqslant 0 \qquad \frac{\partial L^*}{\partial \lambda_1} \geqslant 0 \quad \text{and} \quad \lambda_1 \left(\frac{\partial L^*}{\partial \lambda_1} \right) = 0$$

$$\lambda_2 \geqslant 0 \qquad \frac{\partial L^*}{\partial \lambda_2} \geqslant 0 \quad \text{and} \quad \lambda_2 \left(\frac{\partial L^*}{\partial \lambda_2} \right) = 0.$$

Let us try $x_1 > 0$, $x_2 > 0$ and see whether this provides a solution (in which case we need go no further) or a contradiction. (In fact it is obvious that both variables must be positive as the objective function would be zero if not, and this is certainly not the maximum value it can take.)

Then $\partial L^* / \partial x_1 = \partial L^* / \partial x_2 = 0$. These tell us that

1. $x_2 - 5\lambda_1 - 3\lambda_2 = 0$
2. $x_1 - 4\lambda_1 - 6\lambda_2 = 0$

which is useful information. In particular λ_1 and λ_2 cannot both be zero. This leaves three possibilities for the multipliers:

A $\lambda_1 > 0 \qquad \lambda_2 > 0$

B $\lambda_1 > 0 \qquad \lambda_2 = 0$

C $\lambda_1 = 0 \qquad \lambda_2 > 0$

which we investigate in turn. As soon as we reach a solution, rather than a contradiction, we can stop.

A From the K–T conditions we have $\partial L^*/\partial \lambda_1 = \partial L^*/\partial \lambda_2 = 0$, i.e. both constraints bind. This means $(x_1, x_2) = (\frac{70}{9}, \frac{25}{9})$ and 1, 2 can be solved for the multipliers. In particular $\lambda_1 = -\frac{20}{54}$, a contradiction.
B From 1 and 2 $4x_2 = 5x_1$, and from the K–T conditions the first constraint binds. Then $(x_1, x_2) = (5, \frac{25}{4})$. But this violates the second constraint (which is $\partial L^*/\partial \lambda_2 \geqslant 0$).
C We leave it as an exercise for the reader to verify that in this case all of the K–T conditions hold at $(\hat{x}_1, \hat{x}_2) = (\frac{20}{3}, \frac{10}{3})$: we thus locate the solution.

Recalling the context of this example, case C is where ration coupons are exhausted ($\lambda_2 > 0$) and some income is left over ($\lambda_1 = 0$). With the benefit of hindsight, we could have gone straight to case C without first eliminating A and B. Indeed we might have listed the cases in the reverse order. But the roundabout approach is useful in that it serves to illustrate the sort of case-by-case analysis that the K–T conditions often demand.

5.4.3 Example

A firm has total revenue $TR = 10Q - Q^2 + A/2$ where Q is its output and A is its advertising expenditure. Its total costs are $TC = Q^2/2 + 5Q + 1 + A$. The managers of the firm have to maximize total revenue subject to the minimum profit constraint $\pi \geqslant \pi_0$; Q and A are required to be non-negative. What levels of Q and A will the managers choose if, (i) $\pi_0 = \frac{1}{2}$, (ii) $\pi_0 = 3$?

The problem is

$$\max_{Q, A} 10Q - Q^2 + A/2$$

$$\text{st } 3Q^2/2 - 5Q + A/2 + 1 + \pi_0 \leqslant 0 \qquad Q \geqslant 0 \qquad A \geqslant 0.$$

The objective function is concave, and the constraint convex, in Q and A by Exercise 3.7.4(c), p. 84, and Example 3.7.3(b), p. 83, respectively. So the K–T conditions have a unique solution, which we now find.

The Lagrangean is

$$L^* = 10Q - Q^2 + A/2 - \lambda(3Q^2/2 - 5Q + A/2 + 1 + \pi_0)$$

and the K–T conditions are

$$Q \geqslant 0 \qquad \frac{\partial L^*}{\partial Q} \leqslant 0 \quad \text{and} \quad Q\left(\frac{\partial L^*}{\partial Q}\right) = 0$$

$$A \geqslant 0 \qquad \frac{\partial L^*}{\partial A} \leqslant 0 \quad \text{and} \quad A\left(\frac{\partial L^*}{\partial A}\right) = 0$$

$$\lambda \geqslant 0 \qquad \frac{\partial L^*}{\partial \lambda} \geqslant 0 \quad \text{and} \quad \lambda\left(\frac{\partial L^*}{\partial \lambda}\right) = 0.$$

We try first the possibility $Q > 0$. This should yield the solution: zero output is unlikely. Then $\partial L^*/\partial Q = 0$, i.e.

1. $10 - 2Q - 3\lambda Q + 5\lambda = 0$.

We also have $\partial L^*/\partial A \leqslant 0$:

2. $\frac{1}{2} - \lambda/2 \leqslant 0$.

Hence $\lambda \geqslant 1$ and so $\partial L^*/\partial \lambda = 0$: the constraint binds. If 2 is an equality, then $\lambda = 1$ and from 1 $Q = 3$. This implies $A = 1 - 2\pi_0$, which is perfectly consistent with all K–T conditions if $\pi_0 \leqslant \frac{1}{2}$, as in case (i), but is a contradiction in case (ii) when $\pi_0 = 3$.

We have, therefore, solved case (i) of the problem. Assuming still that $Q > 0$, we must have $A = 0$ in case (ii) (otherwise 2 is an equality). Since the constraint binds, we find

3. $Q = \dfrac{5 \pm \sqrt{(19 - 6\pi_0)}}{3}$.

We have $\pi_0 = 3$. Then $Q = 2$ or $\frac{4}{3}$. In the latter case, $\lambda = -\frac{22}{3}$ from 1, which contradicts 2. Hence the overall solution to the problem is: (i) $\hat{Q} = 3$, $\hat{A} = 0$; (ii) $\hat{Q} = 2$, $\hat{A} = 0$.

5.4.4 Exercises

(a) In the problem above, can the square root in 3 go negative? What is the absolute maximum level of profit the firm can earn? What happens if the managers are constrained to make *at least* this much profit? What value of the Lagrange multiplier does equation 1 suggest in that case?

(b) Check the quasi-concave programming conditions for the problem: maximize $x_1 + x_2$ subject to $x_1^2 + x_2 \leqslant 1$, $x_1 - 2x_2 \leqslant -1$ and $x_1 \geqslant 0$, $x_2 \geqslant 0$, and solve it.

(c) Consider the problem of Example 5.2.4, replacing the third constraint by non-negativity constraints on the variables:

$$\max_{x_1, x_2} x_1 + x_2$$

$$\text{st } 4x_1 - x_2 - x_1^2 \leqslant 0 \qquad 2x_1 + 3x_2 \leqslant 8 \quad \text{and} \quad x_1 \geqslant 0, x_2 \geqslant 0.$$

Show that the K–T conditions are satisfied by $(x_1, x_2, \lambda_1, \lambda_2) = (\frac{2}{3}, \frac{20}{9}, \frac{1}{10}, \frac{11}{30})$ and by $(x_1, x_2, \lambda_1, \lambda_2) = (4, 0, \lambda, [1 + 4\lambda]/2)$ for any $\lambda \geq 0$. What is the solution to the problem (draw the feasible region on a graph like figure 5.4)?

(d) The following question appeared in a Finals paper in Mathematical Economics at a British university some years ago:

> The demand q for a firm's product depends upon the area, with radius r, within which it is prepared to deliver, i.e.
>
> $$q = ar^2 \qquad a > 0.$$
>
> The firm employs the services of a delivery company which charges at the rate of br per unit of output delivered. The firm has a capacity constraint $q \leq q_0$ and its only direct cost is delivery. The firm wishes to choose its delivery radius r^* so as to maximize its profits, given that it sells its output (inclusive of delivery) at a constant price p. Show that it will not use its entire capacity if $br^* = 2p/3$.

Is the question correctly formulated?

(e) Show that for a constrained maximization problem with non-negative variables constraints, the Arrow–Enthoven conditions (5.14) on the full Lagrangean L defined in equation (5.23) are equivalent to the K–T conditions on the modified Lagrangean L^* given in equation (5.24). (Note that $\partial L/\partial x_k = \partial L^*/\partial x_k + \mu_k$ for each variable x_k that is constrained to be non-negative.)

Finally, in this section, we note that everything we have said about constrained maximization problems, and Arrow–Enthoven/Kuhn–Tucker conditions, has a natural analogue for constrained *minimization* problems. To see this, note that

$$\min_x f(\underline{x})$$
$$\text{st } \underline{g}(\underline{x}) \geq \underline{b} \quad \text{and} \quad x_k \geq 0 \tag{5.27}$$

and

$$\max_x -f(\underline{x})$$
$$\text{st } -\underline{g}(\underline{x}) \leq -\underline{b} \quad \text{and} \quad x_k \geq 0 \tag{5.28}$$

are the same problem. The natural Lagrangean for the minimization problem (5.27), $L^* = f(\underline{x}) - \underline{\lambda}^t[\underline{g}(\underline{x}) - \underline{b}]$, is simply the negative of the Lagrangean appropriate for the maximization problem (5.28), to which the K–T conditions in Definition 5.4.1 apply. Thus the inequalities in Definitions 5.4.1 merely get reversed for the minimization problem.

5.4.5 Definition   Kuhn–Tucker conditions for constrained minimization

For the problem

$$\min_{\underline{x}} f(\underline{x})$$

$$\text{st } \underline{g}(\underline{x}) \geqslant \underline{b} \quad \text{and} \quad x_k \geqslant 0$$

the (modified) Lagrangean is $L^* = f(\underline{x}) - \underline{\lambda}'[\underline{g}(\underline{x}) - \underline{b}]$, and the K–T conditions are as follows:

$$\frac{\partial L^*}{\partial x_i} = 0 \qquad i \neq k \in \{1, 2, \ldots, n\}$$

$$x_k \geqslant 0 \qquad \frac{\partial L^*}{\partial x_k} \geqslant 0 \quad \text{and} \quad x_k \left(\frac{\partial L^*}{\partial x_k} \right) = 0 \qquad \text{for all } k$$

$$\lambda_j \geqslant 0 \qquad \frac{\partial L^*}{\partial \lambda_j} \leqslant 0 \quad \text{and} \quad \lambda_j \left(\frac{\partial L^*}{\partial \lambda_j} \right) = 0 \qquad j = 1, 2, \ldots, m.$$

These conditions will be necessary and sufficient for the problem if $-f$ and $-g$ satisfy the concave or quasi-concave programming conditions: for example, if

(a*) f is differentiable and quasi-con*vex*
(b**)   each g_j is differentiable and quasi-con*cave*

(plus an appropriate constraint qualification).

5.4.6 Exercise

Minimize the function $(x_1 - 1)^2 + (x_2 - 1)^2$ subject to the constraints $x_1^2 \leqslant x_2 \leqslant 2$ and $x_1 \geqslant 0$. Check first that the K–T conditions will be necessary and sufficient, and sketch the feasible region and contours of the objective function.

5.5 LINEAR PROGRAMMING

Constrained optimization problems, for which the objective function $f(\underline{x})$ and each constraint $g_j(\underline{x})$ are linear, are called *linear programming* problems. The K–T conditions are evidently necessary and sufficient for the solution of linear programming problems, and they contain interesting insights, to be explored here. There are also other approaches in this special case.

Suppose then that

$$f(\underline{x}) = c_1 x_1 + c_2 x_2 + \ldots + c_n x_n = \underline{c}^t \underline{x}$$

and that for each $j = 1, 2, \ldots, m$ we have

$$g_j(\underline{x}) = a_{j1} x_1 + a_{j2} x_2 + \ldots + a_{jn} x_n.$$

The problem we shall explore here is the one with non-negativity constraints on *all* variables:

$$\max_{\underline{x}} \underline{c}^t \underline{x}$$

$$\text{st } A\underline{x} \leqslant \underline{b} \quad \text{and} \quad \underline{x} \geqslant \underline{0}.$$

(5.29)

We first note that such a problem is particularly easy to handle graphically in the case of $n = 2$ variables. Recall the example already seen in chapter 2.

5.5.1 Example

A.company manufactures two products X_1 and X_2. Each X_1 requires 6 hours on the company's machines and each X_2 requires 5 hours, and there is a maximum of 6000 machine hours available every month. There are two basic raw materials, A and B, used in manufacture. To make each X_1, 3 lb of A and 1 lb of B are used, and to make each X_2, 1 lb of A and 2 lb of B are used. In this particular month, the company has available 2400 lb of A and 2000 lb of B. If the profit on each X_1 is £3 and the profit on each X_2 is £2, find how many of each product the company should manufacture this month to maximize profit.

The problem may be specified as

$$\max_{x_1, x_2} 3x_1 + 2x_2$$

$$\text{st } 6x_1 + 5x_2 \leqslant 6000 \qquad 3x_1 + x_2 \leqslant 2400 \qquad x_1 + 2x_2 \leqslant 2000$$

$$\text{and} \quad x_1, x_2 \geqslant 0$$

and the feasible region is as shown in figure 5.6.

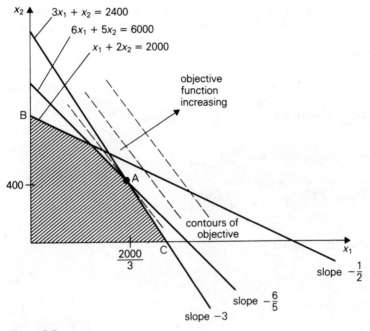

Figure 5.6

Note particularly the *slopes* of the three linear constraints that bound the feasible region: they are $-\frac{1}{2}$, $-\frac{6}{5}$ and -3. Now the contours of the objective function, given by $3x_1 + 2x_2 = $ constant, have slope $-\frac{3}{2}$. They are therefore *steeper than the first two, and shallower than the last* of these boundary constraints. Hence the maximum of the objective function occurs at A: the contours are shown as dotted lines. The solution is $(\hat{x}_1, \hat{x}_2) = (\frac{2000}{3}, 400)$.

Had the slope of the contours of the objective function been *shallower than all three* boundary constraints, the optimum would have been at B; if *steeper than all three*, at C; etc. Linear programming for $n = 2$ variables is thus particularly easy to handle, by comparing the slopes of the objective contours and boundary constraints with the aid of a graph.

5.5.2 Exercise

Write down the Lagrangean for the above problem. Find the Lagrange multipliers for the three constraints. Anticipating the results in the next chapter, interpret these as the marginal effect on profit of an additional machine hour; unit of A; and unit of B respectively. If the firm could acquire one extra machine hour *or* an extra 2 lb of raw material A, at a cost of 50 pence, which alternative (if either) should it choose?

For $n > 2$ variables we may resort to the K–T conditions to find the solution. Let us examine these more closely for the general linear programming problem (5.29).

The Lagrangean is

$$L^* = \underline{c}'\underline{x} - \underline{\lambda}'(A\underline{x} - \underline{b}) \tag{5.30}$$

and the conditions to solve are

$$x_i \geqslant 0 \qquad \frac{\partial L^*}{\partial x_i} \leqslant 0 \quad \text{and} \quad x_i\left(\frac{\partial L^*}{\partial x_i}\right) = 0 \qquad \text{for all } i$$

$$\lambda_j \geqslant 0 \qquad \frac{\partial L^*}{\partial \lambda_j} \geqslant 0 \quad \text{and} \quad \lambda_j\left(\frac{\partial L^*}{\partial \lambda_j}\right) = 0 \qquad j = 1, 2, \ldots, m.$$

These yield matrix equations:

$$\underline{c} - A'\underline{\lambda} \leqslant \underline{0} \tag{5.31}$$

$$\underline{x}'(\underline{c} - A'\underline{\lambda}) = 0 \tag{5.32}$$

$$\underline{b} - A\underline{x} \geqslant \underline{0} \tag{5.33}$$

$$\underline{\lambda}'(\underline{b} - A\underline{x}) = 0. \tag{5.34}$$

Suppose the solution is at $\underline{\lambda} = \hat{\underline{\lambda}}$ and $\underline{x} = \hat{\underline{x}}$. Let the maximum value be

$$V = \underline{c}'\hat{\underline{x}}. \tag{5.35}$$

Then we can prove very simply a rather interesting proposition:

5.5.3 Theorem

$$V = \min_{\underline{y}} \underline{b}'\underline{y}$$

$$\text{st } A'\underline{y} \geqslant \underline{c} \quad \text{and} \quad \underline{y} \geqslant \underline{0}$$

and this minimum occurs at $\underline{y} = \hat{\underline{\lambda}}$.

Proof Suppose that $A'\underline{y} \geqslant \underline{c}$, i.e. $\underline{y}$ is feasible for the minimization problem. Then consider the following:

$$\underline{b}'\underline{y} = \underline{y}'\underline{b} \geqslant \underline{y}'A\hat{\underline{x}} = \hat{\underline{x}}'A'\underline{y} \geqslant \hat{\underline{x}}'\underline{c} = \underline{c}'\hat{\underline{x}} = V \tag{5.36}$$

using equations (5.33) and (5.35) (and Exercise 2.2.2(e)). Hence V is a *lower bound* for $\underline{b}^t\underline{y}$; it remains to prove that V is achieved, at $\underline{y} = \hat{\underline{\lambda}}$. This follows directly from equations (5.34) and (5.32):

$$\underline{b}^t\hat{\underline{\lambda}} = \hat{\underline{\lambda}}^t\underline{b} = \hat{\underline{\lambda}}^t A\hat{\underline{x}} = \hat{\underline{x}}^t A^t\hat{\underline{\lambda}} = \hat{\underline{x}}^t\underline{c} = \underline{c}^t\hat{\underline{x}} = V. \qquad \text{Q.E.D.}$$

Hence every maximization problem goes hand in hand with a minimization problem having the same solution. We call the two problems respectively the *primal* and the *dual*.

5.5.4 Definition

If the PRIMAL is

$$\max_{x} \underline{c}^t\underline{x}$$

$$\text{st } A\underline{x} \leqslant \underline{b} \quad \text{and} \quad \underline{x} \geqslant \underline{0}$$

then the DUAL is

$$\min_{\underline{y}} \underline{b}^t\underline{y}$$

$$\text{st } A^t\underline{y} \geqslant \underline{c} \quad \text{and} \quad \underline{y} \geqslant \underline{0}.$$

There is a one-to-one correspondence between the variables of one problem and the constraints of the other: the primal has n variables and m constraints, the dual m variables and n constraints.

Not only do the Lagrange multipliers for the primal solve the dual, yielding the same optimum value V for both problems, but also the complementary slackness conditions for the multipliers and variables of the primal determine further interrelationships between the solutions to the two problems.

5.5.5 Theorem

At the joint optimum for the two problems, we have:

(a) if a variable in one problem is NON-ZERO, the corresponding constraint in the other problem BINDS, and
(b) if a constraint in one problem is SLACK, the corresponding variable in the other problem is ZERO.

These properties relating the primal and dual are extremely useful. For instance, we can turn a problem with many variables and few constraints into one with few variables and many constraints – and the latter may be much easier to solve. Having solved it, we can infer the solution to the original problem from the interrelationships above.

5.5.6 Example

Solve the following linear programming problem:

$$\max 3x_1 + 4x_2 + 3x_3$$

$$\text{st } x_1 + x_2 + 3x_3 \leqslant 12 \qquad 2x_1 + 4x_2 + x_3 \leqslant 42 \quad \text{and} \quad x_1, x_2, x_3 \geqslant 0.$$

This problem has three variables and two constraints. If we go to the dual, we will have only two variables (and three constraints) and we may use the graphical approach.

For this problem,

$$\underline{c} = \begin{bmatrix} 3 \\ 4 \\ 3 \end{bmatrix} \qquad A = \begin{bmatrix} 1 & 1 & 3 \\ 2 & 4 & 1 \end{bmatrix} \quad \text{and} \quad \underline{b} = \begin{bmatrix} 12 \\ 42 \end{bmatrix}$$

and the dual is

$$\min 12y_1 + 42y_2$$

$$\text{st } y_1 + 2y_2 \geqslant 3 \qquad y_1 + 4y_2 \geqslant 4 \qquad 3y_1 + y_2 \geqslant 3 \qquad y_1, y_2 \geqslant 0.$$

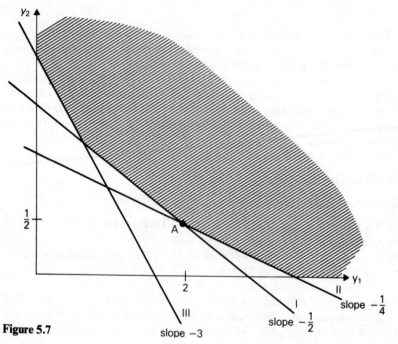

Figure 5.7

Check this for yourself. Denoting the constraints I, II and III, figure 5.7 depicts the feasible region (shaded).

The slope of the contours of the objective function is $-\frac{2}{7}$, steeper than boundary constraint II but shallower than I and III: the optimum is at A.

Hence $\hat{y}_1 = 2$, $\hat{y}_2 = \frac{1}{2}$ and the minimum value is $\underline{b}'\hat{y} = 45$. Both variables are NON-ZERO; constraints I, II bind and constraint III is SLACK.

Returning to the primal, Theorems 5.5.3 and 5.5.5 imply that: (i) the maximum value of the primal is 45, (ii) both constraints BIND, and (iii) the third variable $\hat{x}_3$ is ZERO.

It is now trivial that the solution is $(\hat{x}_1, \hat{x}_2, \hat{x}_3) = (3, 9, 0)$.

5.5.7 Exercises

(a) Minimize $34y_1 + 18y_2 + 48y_3 + 10y_4$ subject to the constraints

$$3y_1 + y_2 + y_3 + y_4 \geqslant 1 \qquad 2y_1 + 2y_2 + 6y_3 \geqslant 1 \quad \text{and} \quad y_1, y_2, y_3, y_4 \geqslant 0$$

by solving graphically the constrained maximization problem of which this is the dual. *Verify that the K–T approach yields the same answer, and that the multipliers equal the dual variables at the optimum.*

(b) Minimize $x + 2y + z$ subject to the constraints

$$x + 3y + z \geqslant 2 \qquad x - y \geqslant 4 \quad \text{and} \quad x, y, z \geqslant 0.$$

If a particular problem at hand cannot be reduced to one with just *two* variables, other approaches may be adopted. One such is the *simplex method* (see Chiang, 1984, p. 671 *et seq*). In macro-economic modelling very high dimensional linear programs can arise. As one might expect, there are computer algorithms for solving such problems. Numerical computational techniques have also been developed for *non-linear programming*, and indeed for *dynamic programming* problems, which we shall encounter in chapter 7 (see, for example, Hadley, 1962, 1964).

6 The Maximum Value Function

In the last chapter we said that, when using the Lagrangean approach to solve the problem

$$\max_{x} f(\underline{x})$$

$$\text{st } \underline{g}(\underline{x}) \leqslant \underline{b} \tag{6.1}$$

each Lagrange multiplier $\hat{\lambda}_j$ could be interpreted as the marginal effect on maximum value of a small relaxation in the relevant constraint (i.e. increase in b_j).

We shall now establish this assertion, and also several other useful properties of maximum value functions. The effect upon maximum value of changes in parameters in the objective function is important for comparative static analysis in economics, and this will be explored. Also, we shall consider the effect upon maximum value of differing degrees of constraint.

In the final part of the chapter, we shall note an important, and very fruitful, application of the results obtained. There is a natural duality in the microeconomic theory of consumer choice between the utility-maximizing problem:

$$\max_{x} u(\underline{x})$$

$$\text{st } \underline{p}^t \underline{x} \leqslant m \tag{6.2}$$

(where $\underline{p}^t \underline{x} = p_1 x_1 + p_2 x_2 + \ldots + p_n x_n = $ total expenditure on the n available commodities), and the expenditure-minimizing problem:

$$\min_{x} \underline{p}^t \underline{x}$$

$$\text{st } u(\underline{x}) \geqslant \bar{u} \tag{6.3}$$

(which can, of course, be written in the format of problem (6.1) as:

$$\max_{x} - \underline{p}^t \underline{x}$$

$$\text{st } -u(\underline{x}) \leqslant -\bar{u} \tag{6.4}$$

140

as noted generally for constrained minimization in problems (5.27) and (5.28), p. 132. Exploiting this duality, we shall apply the Lagrangean approach to the expenditure problem; and find that many insights and results in consumer theory, whose derivation can otherwise be quite difficult, 'drop out' as immediate consequences of the theoretical results on maximum value.

At this point we will leave the topic that has concerned us for the last three chapters, that of *static optimization*, in which the objective function and constraints have been timeless. In the final chapter we shall explore the Lagrangean and other approaches to *dynamic optimization*, where objective function and constraints are variable and interdependent through time.

6.1 THE MAXIMUM VALUE FUNCTION AND THE LAGRANGEAN

Returning now to the constrained maximization problem (6.1), it will be helpful for what follows if we distinguish the particular problem at hand,

$$\max_{\underline{x}} f(\underline{x}) \tag{6.1}$$

$$\text{st } \underline{g}(\underline{x}) \leqslant \underline{b}$$

for which $\underline{b}$ is a given vector of *numbers* (for example, in Example 5.4.2, $\underline{b} = \begin{bmatrix} 50 \\ 40 \end{bmatrix}$), from the general problem

$$\max_{\underline{x}} f(\underline{x}) \tag{6.5}$$

$$\text{st } \underline{g}(\underline{x}) \leqslant \underline{a}$$

where $\underline{a}$ is free to range over the set A of all values that $\underline{b}$ could possibly take.

The maximum value *function* is then $V(\underline{a})$, whilst the maximum value for the problem at hand is $V(\underline{b})$. Two properties of the function V which are easily established are given in the next theorem.

6.1.1 Theorem

(i) $V(\underline{a})$ is non-decreasing in each a_j; and
(ii) if f is concave and each g_j is convex, then $V(\underline{a})$ is concave.

Proof See the proof of Theorem 5.2.3, parts 2 and 3, p. 120.

If within the set of constraints $\underline{g}(\underline{x}) \leqslant \underline{b}$ for problem (6.1) there are some non-negativity constraints on variables, then the particular g_js associated with these constraints are linear. Such constraints evidently satisfy the condition in part (ii) of Theorem 6.1.1; the convexity requirement for the constraints g_j in this theorem is therefore significant only for constraints other than non-negativity constraints on variables.

6.1.2 Example

Consider again the profit-constrained revenue maximization problem in Example 5.4.3, p. 130. This may be stated as

$$\max_{Q, A} R(Q, A)$$

$$\text{st} -\pi(Q, A) \leqslant -\pi_0$$

with non-negativity constraints on both variables, where $R(Q, A) = 10Q - Q^2 + A/2$, and $\pi(Q, A) = -3Q^2/2 + 5Q - A/2 - 1$ are revenue and profit respectively. Recall that $R(Q, A)$ is concave and $-\pi(Q, A)$ is convex. We also found in Exercise 5.4.4(a), p. 131, that the constraint qualification is satisfied for this problem provided $\pi_0 < \frac{19}{6}$. The solution to the problem was as follows: if $\pi_0 \leqslant \frac{1}{2}$, then

$$\hat{A} = 1 - 2\pi_0 \qquad \hat{Q} = 3 \Rightarrow V(b) = V(-\pi_0) = R(3, 1 - 2\pi_0) = -\pi_0 + \frac{43}{2}$$

whilst if $\frac{1}{2} < \pi_0 \leqslant \frac{19}{6}$ then

$$\hat{A} = 0$$

$$\hat{Q} = [5 + \sqrt{(19 - 6\pi_0)}]/3 \Rightarrow V(-\pi_0) = R([5 + \sqrt{(19 - 6\pi_0)}]/3, 0).$$

Thus $V(-\pi_0)$ is *non-decreasing and concave* in $-\pi_0$ (see figure 6.1).

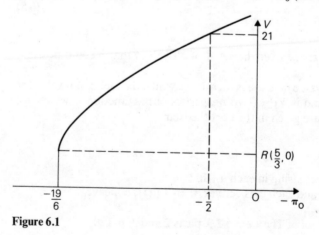

Figure 6.1

In solving this problem, in Example 5.4.3, we used the modified Lagrangean $L^* = R(Q, A) - \lambda[-\pi(Q, A) + \pi_0]$ which neglects the $Q \geqslant 0$ and $A \geqslant 0$ constraints. Had we not done so, then there would have been three multipliers and the maximum value function would have been a vector function of the form $V(\underline{a}) = V(a_1, a_2, a_3)$, the maximum value for the problem at hand being $V(-\pi_0, 0, 0)$, obtained by setting $a_1 = -\pi_0$ and $a_2 = a_3 = 0$ in the more general problem with constraints

$$-\pi(Q, A) \leqslant a_1 \qquad -Q \leqslant a_2 \qquad -A \leqslant a_3.$$

The theorem we have been anticipating, connecting maximum value and Lagrange multipliers, is as follows.

6.1.3 Theorem

If $\hat{\underline{\lambda}}$ are the Lagrange multipliers for problem (6.1) and if $V(\underline{a})$ is differentiable at $\underline{a} = \underline{b}$, then

$$\hat{\lambda}_j = V_j(\underline{b})$$
$$= \frac{\partial V}{\partial a_j}\bigg|_{\underline{a} = \underline{b}}$$

for each $j = 1, 2, \ldots, m$.

We shall see that V need not be differentiable. But assuming that it is, the theorem says that each Lagrange multiplier $\hat{\lambda}_j$ measures the marginal change in value with respect to b_j.

(This includes the multipliers for non-negative-variable constraints $g_k(\underline{x}) = -x_k \leqslant b_k = 0$, if the *full* Lagrangean L is used, rather than the modified one L^*. An increase in such a b_k, from zero to, say, Δb, means a relaxation in the constraint to $x_k \geqslant -\Delta b$, and a possible increase in value, i.e. non-negative multiplier.)

A proof of the result follows easily from the version of the *supporting hyperplane theorem* (SHT for short) quoted in the proof of Theorem 5.2.3, for which the concave programming assumptions, that f is concave and each g_j convex, were required. But we do not need to assume this in order to prove Theorem 6.1.3: only that the Lagrangean approach is valid for the problem. Accordingly we give below two proofs, one following from the concave programming assumptions, the other slightly longer but requiring only differentiability of f and each g_j.

Proof using SHT   Let $\underline{a} = \underline{b} + \underline{h}$, where $\underline{h} = (0, 0, \ldots, 0, h_j, 0, \ldots, 0)$, i.e. with non-zero entry only in the jth place. Then by the SHT in part 5 of the proof of Theorem 5.2.3, we have

$$V(\underline{b} + \underline{h}) - V(\underline{b}) \leqslant \hat{\underline{\lambda}}^t(\underline{a} - \underline{b}) = \hat{\lambda}_j h_j \tag{6.6}$$

for all such $\underline{h}$, i.e. for all h_j. When $h_j > 0$ this yields

$$\frac{V(\underline{b}+\underline{h})-V(\underline{b})}{h_j} \leqslant \hat{\lambda}_j \tag{6.7}$$

and when $h_j < 0$ it yields

$$\frac{V(\underline{b}+\underline{h})-V(\underline{b})}{h_j} \geqslant \hat{\lambda}_j. \tag{6.8}$$

Letting $h_j \searrow 0$ and $h_j \nearrow 0$ in inequalities (6.7) and (6.8) respectively, and recalling the definitions of left and right partial derivatives in chapter 3 (p. 73), we have, at the point $\underline{a} = \underline{b}$,

$$\left(\frac{\partial V}{\partial a_j}\right)^{+} \leqslant \hat{\lambda}_j \leqslant \left(\frac{\partial V}{\partial a_j}\right)^{-} \tag{6.9}$$

provided only that these derivatives exist at $\underline{a} = \underline{b}$. If V is differentiable at $\underline{a} = \underline{b}$, then the left and right derivatives are equal, and the theorem is proved.

Alternative proof Let us first distinguish the Lagrangean for problem (6.1) from the Lagrangean for the general problem (6.5). Let the general Lagrangean be

$$L(\underline{\lambda}, \underline{x} \mid \underline{a}) = f(\underline{x}) - \underline{\lambda}'[\underline{g}(\underline{x}) - \underline{a}] \tag{6.10}$$

and let $\underline{\lambda} = \hat{\underline{\lambda}}(\underline{a})$, $\underline{x} = \hat{\underline{x}}(\underline{a})$ solve the Lagrangean conditions (5.14) for this general problem. Then

$$V(\underline{a}) = f[\hat{\underline{x}}(\underline{a})] \tag{6.11}$$

and the Lagrangean and maximum value for our particular problem (6.1) are $L(\underline{\lambda}, \underline{x}) = L(\underline{\lambda}, \underline{x} \mid \underline{b})$ and $V(\underline{b}) = f[\hat{\underline{x}}(\underline{b})]$ respectively.

Now consider the function $W(\underline{a})$ defined by

$$W(\underline{a}) = L[\hat{\underline{x}}(\underline{a}), \hat{\underline{\lambda}}(\underline{b}) \mid \underline{a}] = f[\hat{\underline{x}}(\underline{a})] - \hat{\underline{\lambda}}(\underline{b})'\{\underline{g}[\hat{\underline{x}}(\underline{a})] - \underline{a}\} \tag{6.12}$$

for each $\underline{a}$. Since $\hat{\underline{x}}(\underline{a})$ satisfies the constraints for problem (6.5) we have $\underline{g}[\hat{\underline{x}}(\underline{a})] \leqslant \underline{a}$. Also from the Lagrangean conditions for problem (6.1) we have $\hat{\underline{\lambda}}(\underline{b}) \geqslant 0$. These two inequalities together imply that

$$W(\underline{a}) \geqslant f[\hat{\underline{x}}(\underline{a})] = V(\underline{a}) \tag{6.13}$$

for each $\underline{a}$. In particular, when $\underline{a} = \underline{b}$ we have

$$
\begin{aligned}
W(\underline{b}) &= f[\hat{\underline{x}}(\underline{b})] - \hat{\underline{\lambda}}(\underline{b})'\{g[\hat{\underline{x}}(\underline{b})] - \underline{b}\} \\
&= f[\hat{\underline{x}}(\underline{b})] = V(\underline{b})
\end{aligned}
\tag{6.14}
$$

from the complementary slackness between $\hat{\underline{\lambda}}(\underline{b})$ and $g[\hat{\underline{x}}(\underline{b})] - \underline{b}$.

Now let $\underline{a} = (b_1, b_2, \ldots, b_{j-1}, a_j, b_{j+1}, \ldots, b_m)$. Assuming differentiability of $V(\underline{a})$ at $\underline{a} = \underline{b}$, i.e. at $a_j = b_j$, then because of equations (6.13) and (6.14) we must have the situation shown in figure 6.2: not only does $W(\underline{a})$ equal $V(\underline{a})$ at $a_j = b_j$, but the two functions W and V have the same slopes in the a_j-direction, i.e.

$$
\left. \frac{\partial W}{\partial a_j} \right|_{a=b} = \left. \frac{\partial V}{\partial a_j} \right|_{a=b}.
\tag{6.15}
$$

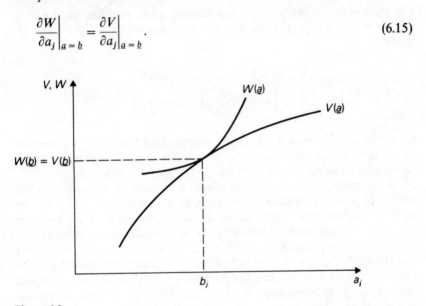

Figure 6.2

This condition generates the result we require. Differentiating equation (6.12), we have

$$
\begin{aligned}
\frac{\partial W}{\partial a_j} &= \sum_i \left(\frac{\partial f}{\partial x_i} \right) \left(\frac{\partial \hat{x}_i(\underline{a})}{\partial a_j} \right) - \sum_k \hat{\lambda}_k(\underline{b}) \left\{ \sum_i \left[\frac{\partial g_k}{\partial x_i} \right] \left[\frac{\partial \hat{x}_i(\underline{a})}{\partial a_j} \right] \right\} + \hat{\lambda}_j(\underline{b}) \\
&= \sum_i \left[\frac{\partial f}{\partial x_i} - \sum_k \hat{\lambda}_k(\underline{b}) \left(\frac{\partial g_k}{\partial x_i} \right) \right] \left[\frac{\partial \hat{x}_i(\underline{a})}{\partial a_j} \right] + \hat{\lambda}_j(\underline{b}) \\
&= \sum_i \left\{ \frac{\partial L[\hat{\underline{\lambda}}(\underline{b}), \underline{x} \mid \underline{a}]}{\partial x_i} \right\} \left(\frac{\partial \hat{x}_i(\underline{a})}{\partial a_j} \right) + \hat{\lambda}_j(\underline{b}).
\end{aligned}
$$

When we evaluate this at $\underline{a} = \underline{b}$ the first term drops out: this is because the Lagrangean conditions (5.14) for the problem (6.1) include the condition that $\partial L/\partial x_i = 0$ at $\underline{\lambda} = \hat{\underline{\lambda}}(\underline{b})$ and $\underline{x} = \hat{\underline{x}}(\underline{b})$, i.e. that $\partial L[\hat{\underline{\lambda}}(\underline{b}), \underline{x} | \underline{b}]/\partial x_i = 0$.
It follows that

$$\left.\frac{\partial V}{\partial a_j}\right|_{\underline{a}=\underline{b}} = \left.\frac{\partial W}{\partial a_j}\right|_{\underline{a}=\underline{b}} = \hat{\lambda}_j \tag{6.16}$$

as the theorem claims.

6.1.4 Example

For the profit-constrained revenue maximization problem in Example 6.1.2 note that $V(-\pi_0)$ is differentiable except possibly at $\pi_0 = \frac{1}{2}$ and $\frac{19}{6}$.
In fact

$$\frac{dV}{d(-\pi_0)} = -\frac{dV}{d\pi_0} = \begin{cases} +1 & \pi_0 < \frac{1}{2} \\ -\frac{\partial R}{\partial Q}\left(\frac{d\hat{Q}}{d\pi_0}\right) & \frac{1}{2} < \pi_0 < \frac{19}{6}. \end{cases}$$

Using the definitions of R and $\hat{Q}$ it is easy to check that as $\pi_0 \to \frac{1}{2}$, the two values become the same, i.e. V is differentiable at $\pi_0 = \frac{1}{2}$. We may readily verify from Example 5.4.3, p. 130, that $dV/d\pi_0 = \hat{\lambda}$ for all values of $\pi_0 < \frac{19}{6}$. Thus the multiplier expresses the effect on revenue of a *decrease* in the minimum profit demanded of the firm's managers (increase in $-\pi_0$). At $\pi_0 = \frac{19}{6}$ profit is constrained to be *at least* the maximum the problem will bear. In that case output is at the profit-maximizing level, $\hat{Q} = \frac{5}{3}$, and since from equation 1 in Example 5.4.3 we have in general that $\lambda = (10 - 2Q)/(3Q - 5)$, $\hat{\lambda} \to \infty$ in this case. The interpretation is that if the minimum profit demanded of the managers were to be further increased, beyond the profit-maximizing level, then the effect $dV/d(-\pi_0)$ on revenue would become infinite, i.e. the problem (or the managers) would collapse, having no solution.

We saw in the first proof of Theorem 6.1.3 that even if $V(\underline{a})$ is not differentiable at $\underline{a} = \underline{b}$, then provided the left and right derivatives exist, the Lagrange multiplier lies between them:

$$\left(\frac{\partial V}{\partial a_j}\right)^+ \leqslant \hat{\lambda}_j \leqslant \left(\frac{\partial V}{\partial a_j}\right)^-. \tag{6.9}$$

We can illustrate this situation very easily, by reference to a utility-maximization problem with two linear budget constraints, as in the rationing example of Example 4.5.2, p. 112. Let the constraints be

$$p_1 x_1 + p_2 x_2 \leqslant m_0 \qquad\qquad (6.17)$$

$$r_1 x_1 + r_2 x_2 \leqslant n_0 \qquad\qquad (6.18)$$

and suppose that (unlike Example 4.5.2) the number of ration coupons n_0 in constraint (6.18) is just enough for the individual to purchase the quantities which would maximize utility subject to the income constraint (6.17) alone. Thus the optimum for both constraints is the one that would have occurred in the absence of the ration, but just exhausts the ration too: see figure 6.3.

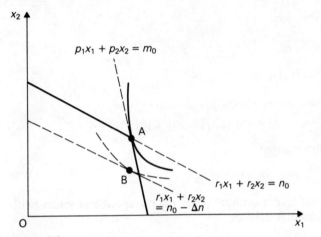

Figure 6.3

It is clear that if we *increased* the ration n_0, the optimum would stay where it is, at A. If we *decreased* n_0, the ration constraint would bind and the optimum would move (e.g. to B): a lower level of utility would be achieved. But the utility level clearly responds smoothly to increases/decreases in income m_0. Therefore the maximum value function $V(m, n)$ is not differentiable in the n-direction at (m_0, n_0): see figure 6.4.

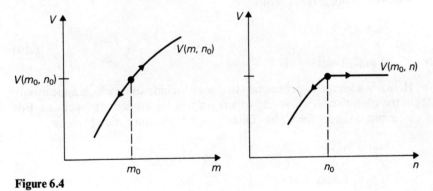

Figure 6.4

6.1.5 Exercise

Recall the problem in Example 5.2.6, p. 125, namely

$$\max_{\underline{x}} x_2 + \ln(x_1)$$

$$\text{st } p_1 x_1 + p_2 x_2 = m \qquad -x_2 \leqslant 0$$

for which $m < p_2$. Show that the maximum value function for the *more general problem*:

$$\max_{\underline{x}} x_2 + \ln(x_1)$$

$$\text{st } p_1 x_1 + p_2 x_2 = m \qquad -x_2 \leqslant a$$

(again with $m < p_2$) is given by

$$V(m, a) = \begin{cases} (m - p_2)/p_2 + \ln(p_2/p_1) & a \geqslant (p_2 - m)/p_2 \\ -a + \ln[(m + ap_2)/p_1] & a < (p_2 - m)/p_2. \end{cases}$$

Show by differentiating that

$$V_1(m, 0) = \hat{\lambda}_1 \quad \text{and} \quad V_2(m, 0) = \hat{\lambda}_2$$

where $\hat{\lambda}_1, \hat{\lambda}_2$ are the Lagrange multipliers for the specific problem (with $a = 0$) solved in Example 5.2.6.

6.2 MAXIMUM VALUE AND COMPARATIVE STATICS

We now turn to the broader issue of the effect on maximum value of changes in parameters in the objective function of the problem. As a matter of fact, we can also encompass the effect of changes in parameters in the constraint functions $g_j(\underline{x})$, if we re-specify the problem in the following more general form:

$$\max_{\underline{x}} f(\underline{x}, \underline{c})$$

$$\text{st } \underline{g}(\underline{x}, \underline{c}) \leqslant \underline{0}. \tag{6.19}$$

Here $\underline{c}$ is a vector of parameters that may include some which appear only in the objective function and others only in the constraint functions. For example, consider the Cobb–Douglas utility maximization problem

$$\max_{\underline{x}} x_1^a x_2^b$$

$$\text{st } p_1 x_1 + p_2 x_2 \leqslant m.$$

If we are interested in the effect on the solution to this problem of changes in prices, or in the utility (taste) parameters a and b, then we could write $\underline{c} = (a, b, p_1, p_2, m)$ and put $f(\underline{x}, \underline{c}) = x_1^a x_2^b$, $g(\underline{x}, \underline{c}) = p_1 x_1 + p_2 x_2 - m$. Some components of $\underline{c}$ do not figure in the objective function, and others do not affect the constraints. Another problem that benefits considerably from being expressed in this more general form is the expenditure minimization problem (6.3)/(6.4):

$$\max_{\underline{x}} \ -\underline{p}^t \underline{x}$$

$$\text{st } -u(\underline{x}) \leqslant -\bar{u}.$$

Here we can write $\underline{c} = (\underline{p}, \bar{u})$, $f(\underline{x}, \underline{c}) = -\underline{p}^t \underline{x}$ and $g(\underline{x}, \underline{c}) = \bar{u} - u(\underline{x})$, and this permits study of the effect on the solution of changes in prices and minimum utility level.

The Lagrangean for the general problem (6.19) is

$$L(\underline{\lambda}, \underline{x}) = f(\underline{x}, \underline{c}) - \underline{\lambda}^t g(\underline{x}, \underline{c}). \tag{6.20}$$

If at the solution to the Lagrangean conditions we have $\underline{x} = \hat{\underline{x}}(\underline{c})$, then the maximum value function is

$$V(\underline{c}) = f[\hat{\underline{x}}(\underline{c}), \underline{c}]. \tag{6.21}$$

There are two ways a change in a parameter c_j of the *objective function* can effect maximum value. Applying the chain rule (Theorem 3.9.1, p. 95) to equation (6.21) we have:

$$\frac{\partial V}{\partial c_j} = \sum_i \left(\frac{\partial f}{\partial x_i} \right) \left(\frac{\partial \hat{x}_i(\underline{c})}{\partial c_j} \right) + \frac{\partial f}{\partial c_j}, \tag{6.22}$$

i.e. a change in c_j affects the objective function *directly* (the effect is $\partial f / \partial c_j$, evaluated at $[\hat{\underline{x}}(\underline{c}), \underline{c}]$), and indirectly through the effect upon the solution $\hat{\underline{x}}(\underline{c})$ (the other term in equation (6.22)).

We can no longer expect $V(\underline{c})$ to be increasing in each c_j. Concavity of $V(\underline{c})$ may be established, though under rather strong conditions:

6.2.1 Theorem

If $f(\underline{x}, \underline{c})$ is concave, and each $g_j(\underline{x}, \underline{c})$ is convex, *jointly in x and c*, then $V(\underline{c})$ is concave.

If $\underline{c}$ consists of, say, r parameters, then these conditions require concavity/convexity of the objective/constraint functions *as functions of* $n + r$ *variables*. For example, f must satisfy

$$f[k\underline{x} + (1-k)\underline{x}', k\underline{c} + (1-k)\underline{c}'] \geqslant kf(\underline{x}, \underline{c}) + (1-k)f(\underline{x}', \underline{c}')$$

for all $\underline{x}, \underline{x}', \underline{c}, \underline{c}'$ and for $0 < k < 1$.

This certainly is not true of the expenditure function $p^t\underline{x} = \Sigma_{i=1}^{n} p_i x_i$ as a function of the $2n$ variables $x_1, \ldots, x_n, p_1, \ldots, p_n$ (see Exercise 3.7.4(a)), nor is it true of the Cobb–Douglas utility $x_1^a x_2^b$ as a function of the four variables x_1, x_2, a, b.

6.2.2 Exercise

Prove Theorem 6.2.1, following exactly the line of argument used in the proof of Theorem 5.2.3, part 3.

Further progress with the general specification

$$\max_{\underline{x}} f(\underline{x}, \underline{c})$$

$$\text{st } \underline{g}(\underline{x}, \underline{c}) \leq \underline{0} \tag{6.19}$$

is difficult. But if we are prepared to regard only *some* of the parameters in $\underline{c}$ as (potential) variables, and others as part of the functions, then an assortment of substantive further results obtain. Another weakening of problem (6.19) that generates further results is to go back to *equality* constraints again. Consider, then, the following three special cases of problem (6.19):

Case I   Parameters in objective function only:

$$\max_{\underline{x}} f(\underline{x}, \underline{c})$$
$$\text{st } \underline{g}(\underline{x}) \leq \underline{0}. \tag{6.23}$$

Case II   Parameters in constraint functions only:

$$\max_{\underline{x}} f(\underline{x})$$

$$\text{st } \underline{g}(\underline{x}, \underline{c}) \leq 0. \tag{6.24}$$

Case III   Parameters in both objective and constraint functions, but *equality* constraints only:

$$\max_{\underline{x}} f(\underline{x}, \underline{c})$$

$$\text{st } \underline{g}(\underline{x}, \underline{c}) = 0. \tag{6.25}$$

We do not mean by Case I that the constraint functions should be *parameter-free*, only that in specifying the problem as in problem (6.23) we are prepared to forgo any interest in the effect of changes in constraint parameters on the solution to the problem. Similarly for Case II. These specifications I, II and III are particularly apt, as we shall see, for certain economic problems. By sacrificing total generality, we can obtain some very simple and important results, which we now describe.

Case I   Parameters in objective function only

For this special case, i.e.

$$\max_{\underline{x}} f(\underline{x}, \underline{c})$$

$$\text{st } g(\underline{x}) \leqslant \underline{0}$$

(6.23)

we can establish a perhaps surprising result, *convexity* of the maximum value function, under very mild conditions:

6.2.3 Theorem

If $f(\underline{x}, \underline{c})$ is convex in $\underline{c}$ alone, for each $\underline{x}$, then $V(\underline{c})$ is convex.

The result holds no matter what properties f and $\underline{g}$ may possess as functions of $\underline{x}$.

Proof of Theorem 6.2.3   We are required to prove that

$$V[k\underline{c}^1 + (1-k)\underline{c}^2] \leqslant kV(\underline{c}^1) + (1-k)V(\underline{c}^2)$$

for all $\underline{c}^1, \underline{c}^2$ and for $0 < k < 1$.
   Suppose that $\underline{x} = \underline{x}^1, \underline{x}^2$ are optimal when $\underline{c} = \underline{c}^1, \underline{c}^2$ and that $\underline{x}^0$ is optimal when $\underline{c} = k\underline{c}^1 + (1-k)\underline{c}^2 = \underline{c}^0$, say. Then $g(\underline{x}^0) \leqslant \underline{0}, g(\underline{x}^1) \leqslant \underline{0}$ and $g(\underline{x}^2) \leqslant \underline{0}$. Furthermore,

$$V(\underline{c}^0) = f[\underline{x}^0, k\underline{c}^1 + (1-k)\underline{c}^2] \leqslant kf(\underline{x}^0, \underline{c}^1) + (1-k)f(\underline{x}^0, \underline{c}^2)$$

by the convexity of f in $\underline{c}$. But since $\underline{x}^0$ was feasible when $\underline{c} = \underline{c}^1$ or $\underline{c}^2$, we have $f(\underline{x}^0, \underline{c}^i) \leqslant V(\underline{c}^i), i = 1, 2$, i.e.

$$V[k\underline{c}^1 + (1-k)\underline{c}^2] \leqslant kV(\underline{c}^1) + (1-k)V(\underline{c}^2)$$

as required.   Q.E.D.

This result is extremely useful for the expenditure minimization problem (6.3)/(6.4), i.e. for the maximization problem

$$\max_{\underline{x}} -\underline{p}^t \underline{x}$$

$$\text{st } -u(\underline{x}) \leqslant -\bar{u}.$$

If prices are the only parameters of interest, i.e. $\underline{c} = \underline{p}$ and $g(\underline{x}) = \bar{u} - u(\underline{x})$, the objective function is *linear* in prices alone and therefore convex (Exercise 3.7.13, p. 88). Thus by Theorem 6.2.3 the maximum value function $V(\underline{p}) = -\underline{p}^t \underline{\hat{x}}(\underline{p})$ is convex. Writing $E(\underline{p})$ for minimized expenditure, i.e. $E(\underline{p}) = \underline{p}^t \underline{\hat{x}}(\underline{p}) = -V(\underline{p})$, we have the useful result that *the expenditure function* $E(\underline{p})$ *is concave in prices* (recall Exercise 3.7.4(b), p. 84).

6.2.4 Exercise

For the general Case I problem (6.23), show that if $\underline{x} = \underline{x}^1, \underline{x}^2$ are optimal when $\underline{c} = \underline{c}^1, \underline{c}^2$, then $V(\underline{c}^1) \geqslant f(\underline{x}^2, \underline{c}^1)$ and $V(\underline{c}^2) \geqslant f(\underline{x}^1, \underline{c}^2)$.

Case II Parameters in constraints only

The further result available in this special case,

$$\max_{\underline{x}} f(\underline{x})$$

$$\text{st } g(\underline{x}, \underline{c}) \leqslant \underline{0}$$

(6.24)

is very simple. We leave its proof to the reader.

6.2.5 Exercise

Prove the following: Let $\underline{x} = \underline{x}^1, \underline{x}^2$ be optimal when $\underline{c} = \underline{c}^1, \underline{c}^2$; if $V(\underline{c}^1) \neq V(\underline{c}^2)$ and $g(\underline{x}^1, \underline{c}^2) \leqslant \underline{0}$, then we must have $g(\underline{x}^2, \underline{c}^1) > \underline{0}$.

(Argue by contradiction: assume that $g(\underline{x}^2, \underline{c}^1) \leqslant \underline{0}$, i.e. that $\underline{x}^2$ is feasible when $\underline{c} = \underline{c}^1 \ldots$.)

This result is interesting in so far as it applies to the utility maximization problem

$$\max_{\underline{x}} u(\underline{x})$$

$$\text{st } \underline{p}^t \underline{x} \leqslant m.$$

Here $\underline{c} = (\underline{p}, m)$ and $V = V(\underline{p}, m)$ is the indirect utility function. Suppose that the individual chooses bundle of goods $\underline{x}^1$ when the budget constraint is $\Sigma_i p_i x_i \leqslant m$, and the bundle $\underline{x}^2$ when the budget constraint is, say, $\Sigma_i q_i x_i \leqslant n$. The result says that *if* $\underline{x}^1$ *is available when* $\underline{x}^2$ *is chosen, then* $\underline{x}^2$ *cannot have been available when* $\underline{x}^1$ *was chosen*. Replacing the word 'chosen' by the phrase 'revealed preferred', this is a central tenet of *revealed preference theory* (in fact, it is the Weak Axiom of Revealed Preference) (see Henderson and Quandt, 1980, p. 45 *et seq.*).

Case III Parameters in both objective and constraint functions, but equality constraints only

Here we are faced with the problem

$$\max_{\underline{x}} f(\underline{x}, \underline{c})$$

$$\text{st } \underline{g}(\underline{x}, \underline{c}) = \underline{0}. \tag{6.25}$$

Recall the result that gave the effect on maximum value of a change in one of the parameters c_j of the general problem:

$$\frac{\partial V}{\partial c_j} = \sum_i \left(\frac{\partial f}{\partial x_i} \right) \left(\frac{\partial \hat{x}_i(\underline{c})}{\partial c_j} \right) + \frac{\partial f}{\partial c_j}. \tag{6.22}$$

The derivatives are evaluated at the point $[\hat{\underline{x}}(\underline{c}), \underline{c}]$. We may fruitfully pursue this equation further in the particular case of equality constraints. The Lagrangean for the problem is

$$L(\underline{\lambda}, \underline{x}) = f(\underline{x}, \underline{c}) - \underline{\lambda}' \underline{g}(\underline{x}, \underline{c}) \tag{6.26}$$

and one of the Lagrangean conditions holding at the optimum $\underline{\lambda} = \hat{\underline{\lambda}}$, $\underline{x} = \hat{\underline{x}}(\underline{c})$ is:

$$\frac{\partial L}{\partial x_i} = \frac{\partial f}{\partial x_i} - \sum_k \hat{\lambda}_k \left(\frac{\partial g_k}{\partial x_i} \right) = 0 \tag{6.27}$$

for $1 \leqslant i \leqslant n$. Substituting into equation (6.22) for $\partial f / \partial x_i$, we have

$$\frac{\partial V}{\partial c_j} = \sum_k \hat{\lambda}_k \sum_i \left(\frac{\partial g_k}{\partial x_i} \right) \left(\frac{\partial \hat{x}_i(\underline{c})}{\partial c_j} \right) + \frac{\partial f}{\partial c_j}$$

$$= \sum_k \hat{\lambda}_k \left(\frac{\partial \{ g_k[\hat{\underline{x}}(\underline{c}), \underline{c}] \}}{\partial c_j} - \frac{\partial g_k}{\partial c_j} \right) + \frac{\partial f}{\partial c_j}$$

using the chain rule (Theorem 3.9.1, p. 95). Since $g_k[\hat{\underline{x}}(\underline{c}), \underline{c}]$ is identically zero for all $\underline{c}$, this reduces to

$$\frac{\partial V}{\partial c_j} = \frac{\partial f}{\partial c_j} - \sum_k \hat{\lambda}_k \cdot \frac{\partial g_k}{\partial c_j} = \frac{\partial L}{\partial c_j} \bigg|_{\hat{\underline{\lambda}}, \hat{\underline{x}}(\underline{c})}. \tag{6.28}$$

The effect on maximum value of a change in the parameter c_j is determined by the *direct* effects on objective and constraint functions. In fact, it equals the *direct effect on the Lagrangean* L (evaluated at the optimum).

In the particular case that c_j is a parameter in the objective function, not present in the constraint functions, we have $\partial g_k/\partial c_j = 0$ for all k. Then

$$\frac{\partial V}{\partial c_j} = \frac{\partial f}{\partial c_j}. \tag{6.29}$$

The effect on maximum value of a change in a parameter of the objective function is given simply by the direct effect on the objective function, evaluated at the optimum.

A very useful application of this is to the expenditure minimization problem (6.3)/(6.4) *with equality constraint,* namely to

$$\max_{\underline{x}} \ -\underline{p}^t\underline{x}$$

$$\text{st } u(\underline{x}) = \bar{u}.$$

Equation (6.29) says that if $E(\underline{p}) = \underline{p}^t\underline{\hat{x}}(\underline{p})$ is the minimum expenditure needed to attain *exactly* utility $\bar{u}$, then

$$\frac{\partial E}{\partial p_k} = \hat{x}_k(\underline{p}), \tag{6.30}$$

i.e. *the derivative of the expenditure function in the* p_k *direction is the utility-compensated demand for good* k. We shall return to this property in section 6.4.

6.2.6 Exercises

(a) For the Cobb–Douglas utility maximization problem

$$\max_{\underline{x}} \ x_1^a x_2^b$$

$$\text{st } p_1 x_1 + p_2 x_2 = m$$

we found in Exercise 4.3.1 (p. 106) and Exercise 4.4.4 (p. 110) that the demand for x_1 was given by $p\hat{x}_1/m = a/(a+b)$, and maximum value by

$$V = \hat{x}_1^a \hat{x}_2^b = \left(\frac{a}{p_1}\right)^a \left(\frac{b}{p_2}\right)^b \left[\frac{m}{(a+b)}\right]^{a+b}.$$

Verify by direct computation that

$$\frac{\partial V}{\partial a} = \frac{\partial}{\partial a}[\hat{x}_1^a \hat{x}_2^b] = \frac{\partial}{\partial a}[x_1^a x_2^b]\,|_{\hat{\underline{x}}} = \hat{x}_1^a \hat{x}_2^b \cdot \ln(\hat{x}_1) = V \cdot \ln(\hat{x}_1)$$

(see Exercise 3.8.7(b), p. 93). (*Hint*: evaluate the derivative with respect to a of $\ln(V)$, and then set this equal to $(1/V) \cdot \partial V/\partial a$.)

(b) For the problem of Exercise 4.4.6, p. 111, namely

$$\min_{x} cx_1 + x_2$$

$$\text{st } x_1 + \ln(x_2) = b$$

verify that $\partial V/\partial c = \hat{x}_1$.

(c) For the problem

$$\max_{x} u(\underline{x})$$

$$\text{st } \underline{p}^t \underline{x} = m$$

show that the total differential of the maximum value V is:

$$dV = \hat{\lambda} \left[dm - \sum_i \hat{x}_i(\underline{p}) dp_i \right]$$

where $\hat{\lambda}$ is the Lagrange multiplier and $\hat{\underline{x}}(\underline{p})$ is the optimal value of $\underline{x}$.

6.3 MAXIMUM VALUE AND DEGREES OF CONSTRAINT

We return to the general problem:

$$\max_{x} f(\underline{x},\underline{c}) \tag{6.19}$$

$$\text{st } g(\underline{x},\underline{c}) \leqslant \underline{0}.$$

Our purpose now is to examine how the maximum value function is affected by the addition (or removal) of constraints.

The basic idea we shall explore is very simple: if constraints are added that happen to be satisfied at the existing optimum $\underline{x} = \hat{\underline{x}}(\underline{c}^0)$, for a certain parameter configuration $\underline{c} = \underline{c}^0$, this will not affect the maximum value $V(\underline{c}^0)$ attainable for that parameter configuration; but the new constraints *will* affect the maximum value *function* $V(\underline{c})$, in general reducing maximum value for problems whose original optimum $\underline{x} = \hat{\underline{x}}(\underline{c})$ may not satisfy the added constraints when $\underline{c} \neq \underline{c}^0$.

We can illustrate the central idea most easily for the case of a single parameter c, using a graph. Let $\tilde{V}(c)$ be the new maximum value function, in the presence of additional constraints which are satisfied at the

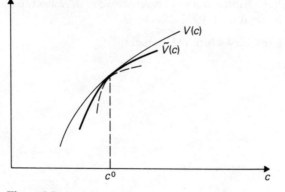

Figure 6.5

optimum for the problem when $c = c^0$ (see figure 6.5). Assuming smoothness (differentiability) of $V(c)$ and $\tilde{V}(c)$, $\tilde{V}(c)$ will be tangent to $V(c)$ at $c = c^0$ and below $V(c)$ elsewhere. In many situations $V(c)$ is concave (e.g. this is true for problem (6.1) if the concave programming assumptions hold); then $\tilde{V}(c)$ will be *more concave* than $V(c)$, having greater curvature at $\underline{c} = \underline{c}^0$ (see figure 6.5).

The more constraints we add, each one of them being satisfied at the original optimum $\underline{x} = \hat{\underline{x}}(c^0)$, the more concave $\tilde{V}(c)$ will become, whilst always remaining tangent to $V(c)$ at $c = c^0$ (see the dotted line in figure 6.5). Bearing in mind the discussion about concavity and second derivatives in chapters 1 and 3, our simple graphical example suggest that as constraints get added, the following mathematical relations should hold between successive maximum value functions:

$$V(c^0) = \tilde{V}^1(c^0) = \tilde{V}^2(c^0) = \ldots \tag{6.31}$$

$$\left(\frac{\mathrm{d}V}{\mathrm{d}c}\right)_{c\,=\,c^0} = \left(\frac{\mathrm{d}\tilde{V}^1}{\mathrm{d}c}\right)_{c\,=\,c^0} = \left(\frac{\mathrm{d}\tilde{V}^2}{\mathrm{d}c}\right)_{c\,=\,c^0} = \ldots \tag{6.32}$$

$$\left(\frac{\mathrm{d}^2V}{\mathrm{d}c^2}\right)_{c\,=\,c^0} \geqslant \left(\frac{\mathrm{d}^2\tilde{V}^1}{\mathrm{d}c^2}\right)_{c\,=\,c^0} \geqslant \left(\frac{\mathrm{d}^2\tilde{V}^2}{\mathrm{d}c^2}\right)_{c\,=\,c^0} \geqslant \ldots \tag{6.33}$$

the superscripts denoting the number of added constraints, each satisfied at the original optimum $\underline{x} = \hat{\underline{x}}(c^0)$. Equation (6.31) says that maximum value is unaffected at $c = c^0$; equation (6.32) expresses the tangency of maximum value functions and (6.33) the concavity condition.

Of course, we have not proved these mathematical properties. The problem is too general, and the nature of the added constraints too vague, to hope that an easy proof could be given. But we shall encounter (and prove) a special case of equations (6.31)–(6.33) soon. A general result in precisely the form of equations (6.31)–(6.33) has been proved rigorously, for a maximization problem with equality constraints, under certain carefully defined conditions, by Silberberg (1971). His result is known as a *generalized envelope theorem*; a problem satisfying equations (6.31)–(6.33) could be said to obey the *generalized envelope property*.

For minimization problems, the inequalities (6.33) must be reversed, and the minimum value functions $\tilde{V}$ lie above, and tangent to, V: recall problems (5.27) and (5.28). We shall see later how to apply the generalized envelope theorem in consumer theory.

A particularly simple and interesting case of the generalized envelope theorem, and one we shall examine here in some detail, obtains if we modify the original optimization problem

$$\max_{x} \text{ (or min) } f(\underline{x}, \underline{c})$$

$$\text{st } \underline{g}(\underline{x}, \underline{c}) \leqslant \underline{0}$$

by keeping some of the x_i fixed.

We have in mind the short-run/long-run distinction between the variable inputs capital and labour in a firm's production process. Recalling the cost minimization problem, Exercise 4.4.5 (p. 111),

$$\min_{K, L} rK + wL$$

$$\text{st } F(K, L) = Q$$

suppose that (in the short run) capital is fixed at K_0 and costs are minimized over labour L only. If K_0 is the long-run optimal value of capital when output is Q_0, then the minimized cost of producing output with K fixed at K_0 is higher than if K can be varied *except when Q_0 is produced*. Then the short-run optimum for labour coincides with the long-run optimum (see figure 6.6).

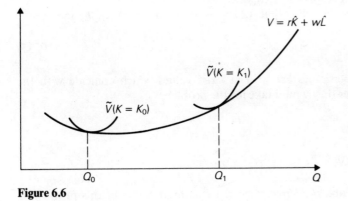

Figure 6.6

As Q_0 varies through all positive values, the long-run minimum cost is achievable in the short run only if fixed capital takes on the correct long-run value, and the familiar short-run/long-run envelope results.

The general problem here, that of optimization over a restricted subset of variables, with others held fixed, i.e. with varying degrees of *choice*, provides a particular instance of the generalized envelope property. We now examine this problem more closely.

For notational convenience and ease of exposition, we confine ourselves to problems in the format (6.5) (this in fact describes the least-cost production problem just discussed):

$$\max f(\underline{x})$$

$$\text{st } \underline{g}(\underline{x}) \leqslant \underline{a},$$

i.e. neglecting parameters in objective and constraint functions. But nothing we do below will depend significantly on this restriction.

Suppose, then, that $\underline{x} = (x_1, x_2, \ldots, x_n)$ is partitioned into two subsets of variables: some, say y_k, which are to remain fixed and others, z_k, which are to be allowed to vary. Then, writing $\underline{x} = (\underline{y}, \underline{z})$, the problem becomes:

$$\max_{z} f(\underline{y}, \underline{z})$$

$$\text{st } \underline{g}(\underline{y}, \underline{z}) \leqslant \underline{a}. \tag{6.34}$$

Thus the fixed values of the y-variables become parameters in both the objective and constraint functions of the problem.

Supposing that this problem can be solved, let $\underline{z} = \underline{\tilde{z}}(\underline{a}, \underline{y})$ be the solution, and $\tilde{V}(\underline{a}, \underline{y}) = f[\underline{y}, \underline{\tilde{z}}(\underline{a}, \underline{y})]$ the maximum value function.

Further, let $\underline{\hat{x}}(\underline{a}) = [\underline{\hat{y}}(\underline{a}), \underline{\hat{z}}(\underline{a})]$ be the solution when *all variables are free*. This is the case we have become familiar with, and the maximum value function is $V(\underline{a}) = f[\underline{\hat{x}}(\underline{a})]$.

It is immediately clear that: (i) if $\underline{y} = \underline{\hat{y}}(\underline{b})$ then $\underline{\tilde{z}}(\underline{b}, \underline{y}) = \underline{\hat{z}}(\underline{b})$ and

$$\tilde{V}[\underline{b}, \underline{\hat{y}}(\underline{b})] = V(\underline{b}) \tag{6.35}$$

(i.e. if the y-variables are held at *fixed* values which coincide with the optimal values they would take for the problem

$$\max_{x} f(\underline{x})$$

$$\text{st } \underline{g}(\underline{x}) \leqslant \underline{b}$$

when all variables are *free*, then the maximum value of this problem is achievable); and (ii) in general, for all $\underline{y}$, and all $\underline{a}$,

$$\tilde{V}(\underline{a},\underline{y}) \leqslant V(\underline{a}) \tag{6.36}$$

(we cannot do better with some variables fixed than if all are free).

In particular, put $\underline{y} = \hat{\underline{y}}(\underline{b})$ in inequality (6.36). Then from equation (6.35) and inequality (6.36) we have:

$$\tilde{V}[\underline{a},\hat{\underline{y}}(\underline{b})] \leqslant V(\underline{a}) \qquad \text{with equality when } \underline{a} = \underline{b}. \tag{6.37}$$

This is a familiar sort of statement: see the second proof of Theorem 6.1.3. We shall use it to prove that the generalized envelope properties (6.31)–(6.33) apply to the two maximum value functions $V(\underline{a})$ and $\tilde{V}[\underline{a},\hat{\underline{y}}(\underline{b})]$. Note first that equation (6.35) is the equivalent of equation (6.31). Now let

$$\underline{a} = (b_1, b_2, \ldots, b_{j-1}, a_j, b_{j+1}, \ldots, b_m). \tag{6.38}$$

Assuming differentiability of the two functions of $\underline{a}$, $\tilde{V}[\underline{a},\hat{\underline{y}}(\underline{b})]$ and $V(\underline{a})$, we have the situation shown in figure 6.7. In particular, from (6.37):

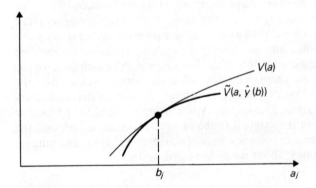

Figure 6.7

$$\left(\frac{\partial \tilde{V}}{\partial a_j}\right)_{\underline{a}=\underline{b}} = \left(\frac{\partial V}{\partial a_j}\right)_{\underline{a}=\underline{b}}. \tag{6.39}$$

This is a special case of generalized envelope property (6.32).

Now put $a_j = b_j + db$ in equation (6.38), and expand each side of the inequality

$$\tilde{V}[\underline{a},\hat{\underline{y}}(\underline{b})] \leqslant V(\underline{a}) \tag{6.37}$$

using Taylor's theorem, about $\underline{a} = \underline{b}$. The vectors $\underline{a}$ and $\underline{b}$ only differ in the a_j-direction, and so

$$\tilde{V}[\underline{a}, \hat{\underline{y}}(\underline{b})] \doteqdot \tilde{V}[\underline{b}, \hat{\underline{y}}(\underline{b})] + \left(\frac{\partial \tilde{V}}{\partial a_j}\right)_{\underline{a}=\underline{b}} \cdot db + \left(\frac{\partial^2 \tilde{V}}{\partial a_j^2}\right)_{\underline{a}=\underline{b}} \cdot \frac{(db)^2}{2} \quad (6.40)$$

to a second-order approximation, whilst

$$V(\underline{a}) \doteqdot V(\underline{b}) + \left(\frac{\partial V}{\partial a_j}\right)_{\underline{a}=\underline{b}} \cdot db + \left(\frac{\partial^2 V}{\partial a_j^2}\right)_{\underline{a}=\underline{b}} \cdot \frac{(db)^2}{2} \quad (6.41)$$

(see equation (3.6)). From equations (6.35) and (6.39), the first two terms on the right-hand side of each of these Taylor series approximations are the same. Since the neglected third- and higher-order terms could not dominate the remaining second-order terms in approximations (6.40) and (6.41), the inequality (6.37) reduces to

$$\left(\frac{\partial^2 \tilde{V}}{\partial a_j^2}\right)_{\underline{a}=\underline{b}} \leqslant \left(\frac{\partial^2 V}{\partial a_j^2}\right)_{\underline{a}=\underline{b}}. \quad (6.42)$$

This is the generalized envelope property (6.33) claimed earlier.

This exploration has highlighted the basic idea behind the generalized envelope theorem: if we add to any particular problem under study some extra constraints which are satisfied at the existing optimum (in the case just considered, extra constraints of the form $x_k = \hat{x}_k(\underline{b})$ which hold for the $\underline{a} = \underline{b}$ problem) then these will not affect maximum value. But the maximum value *function*, expressing the solution in terms of the parameters of the problem, *is* affected, maximum value being reduced for parameter values 'near' those of the original problem. Under certain conditions, the maximum value function becomes more concave, lying below, and tangent to, that which obtains without the added constraints.

6.3.1 Exercise

Consider a production process with three inputs, K_1, K_2 and L, whose prices in competitive markets are r_1, r_2 and $w = 1$ per unit. The production function is $Q = (K_1 K_2 L)^{\frac{1}{6}}$. Let $V(Q)$ be the minimum cost of producing Q. Show that $V(Q) = 3(r_1 r_2)^{\frac{1}{3}} Q^2$ and find the optimal value of K_2 as a function of Q. Call this $\hat{K}_2(Q)$.

Now let K_2 be fixed, $K_2 = \bar{K}_2$, and let $\tilde{V}(Q, \bar{K}_2)$ be the minimum cost of producing Q when only K_1 and L are variable. Show that $\tilde{V}(Q, \bar{K}_2) = r_2 \bar{K}_2 + 2(r_1/\bar{K}_2)^{\frac{1}{2}} Q^3$.

Finally, fix $\bar{K}_2$ at the optimal value for this input when $Q = Q_0$: $\bar{K}_2 = \hat{K}_2(Q_0)$. Letting $V = V(Q)$ and $\tilde{V} = \tilde{V}[Q, \hat{K}_2(Q_0)]$, show that (i)

$\tilde{V} > V$ for all $Q \neq Q_0$, and $\tilde{V} = V$ when $Q = Q_0$; (ii) $\partial \tilde{V}/\partial Q = V'(Q)$ at $Q = Q_0$; and (iii) $\partial^2 \tilde{V}/\partial Q^2 > V''(Q)$ at $Q = Q_0$. Draw a graph showing V and $\tilde{V}$ as functions of Q.

6.4 MAXIMUM VALUE FUNCTIONS IN CONSUMER THEORY

We conclude by applying some of the results on maximum value obtained in this chapter to consumer theory. We mentioned earlier the duality between the utility-maximizing problem:

$$\max_{\underline{x}} u(\underline{x})$$

$$\text{st } \underline{p}^t \underline{x} \leqslant m \tag{6.2}$$

and the expenditure-minimizing problem:

$$\min_{\underline{x}} \underline{p}^t \underline{x}$$

$$\text{st } u(\underline{x}) \geqslant \bar{u} \tag{6.3}$$

equivalently:

$$\max_{\underline{x}} -\underline{p}^t \underline{x}$$

$$\text{st } -u(\underline{x}) \leqslant -\bar{u}. \tag{6.4}$$

These two ways of looking at the consumer's problem are equivalent, and will yield the same answer if the utility function has no unusual properties, e.g. if it is increasing and quasi-concave: see figure 6.8. In particular we lose nothing by respecifying the problems with *equality* constraints; in fact we gain because we can then apply some of the results of section 6.2, Case III, to the maximum value functions.

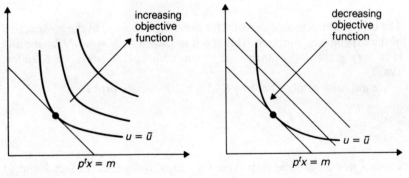

Figure 6.8

Let the optimal quantities for the utility-maximizing problem (6.2) be $\hat{\underline{x}}(\underline{p}, m)$ and the maximum value function be

$$V(\underline{p}, m) = u[\hat{\underline{x}}(\underline{p}, m)]. \tag{6.43}$$

The $\hat{x}_k(\underline{p}, m)$, $k = 1, 2, \ldots, n$, are the *uncompensated* or *Marshallian* demands functions, and $V(\underline{p}, m)$ is the *indirect utility function*.

Further, writing u for $\bar{u}$ for convenience in problems (6.3) and (6.4), let the optimal quantities for the expenditure-minimizing problem be $\underline{x} = \underline{x}^*(\underline{p}, u)$, and the minimum value function

$$E(\underline{p}, u) = \underline{p}^t \underline{x}^*(\underline{p}, u) \tag{6.44}$$

(so that $-E(\underline{p}, u)$ is the maximum value function for problem (6.4)). The $x_k^*(\underline{p}, u)$ are the *utility-compensated* or *Hicksian* demand functions, and $E(\underline{p}, u)$ is the *expenditure function*.

The duality between these two approaches to the consumer's problem can be expressed mathematically by the two equations:

$$V[\underline{p}, E(\underline{p}, u)] = u \tag{6.45}$$

and

$$E[\underline{p}, V(\underline{p}, m)] = m \tag{6.46}$$

which must hold for all m and all u. Thus, as functions of m and u respectively, V and E are *inverse mappings*: application of one, and then the other (with p fixed), leads back to the starting point.

We now summarize some other properties of $V(\underline{p}, m)$ and $E(\underline{p}, u)$ which follow from the earlier analysis. First, we showed in equation (6.30) that

1. $x_k^*(\underline{p}, u) = \dfrac{\partial E}{\partial p_k}.$

The utility-compensated demand for good k is the slope in the p_k-direction of the expenditure function. This result is known as *Shephard's lemma* and is of very great importance (not just in consumer theory: see Madden, 1985).

We may also apply Theorem 4.4.3 (p. 110) to both problems;

2. $\dfrac{\partial V}{\partial m} = \hat{\lambda}$ and $\dfrac{\partial E}{\partial u} = \lambda^*$

where $\hat{\lambda}$ and λ^* are the respective Lagrange multipliers. In fact $\hat{\lambda}$ and λ^* are inverses: $\hat{\lambda} = 1/\lambda^*$. See ahead to Exercise 6.4.1(c).

We can evaluate $\partial V/\partial p_k$ using equation (6.28): it equals the direct effect $\partial L/\partial p_k$ upon the Lagrangean $L(\lambda, \underline{x}) = u(\underline{x}) - \lambda(\underline{p}'\underline{x} - m)$ evaluated at the optimum $(\hat{\lambda}, \hat{\underline{x}})$:

3. $\dfrac{\partial V}{\partial p_k} = -\hat{\lambda} \cdot \hat{x}_k(\underline{p}, m).$

Combining 2 and 3 we obtain the result that is analogous to 1, expressing uncompensated demands in terms of partial derivatives of indirect utility:

4. $\hat{x}_k(\underline{p}, m) = -\dfrac{\partial V/\partial p_k}{\partial V/\partial m}.$

This is *Roy's identity*.

6.4.1 Exercises

(a) Verify that $V(\underline{p}, m)$ is homogeneous of degree zero in $\underline{p}$ and m, and that $E(\underline{p}, u)$ is homogeneous of degree 1 in $\underline{p}$ alone. Now apply Euler's Theorem 3.9.4 (p. 96) to V and E. What do you conclude?

(b) Differentiate equation (6.45) with respect to p_k, using the chain rule (Theorem 3.9.1, p. 95). By using 1–4 above, show that $\hat{x}_k(\underline{p}, m) = x_k^*(\underline{p}, u)$ whenever $V(\underline{p}, m) = u$. This confirms that the dual approaches to the consumer's problem yield the same solution; does it say that the Marshallian and Hicksian demand functions are the same?

(c) Differentiate equation (6.46) partially with respect to m, and conclude that $\hat{\lambda} = 1/\lambda^*$.

If we go much further into consumer theory using uncompensated (Marshallian) demand functions, the mathematics starts to get complicated (see for example, Henderson and Quandt, 1980, chapter 2). But we may proceed, at very little mathematical expense, in terms of utility-compensated demand functions.

Recall that $E(\underline{p}, u)$ is concave in prices (this was shown after Theorem 6.2.3). Since concavity in $\underline{p}$ implies, in particular, concavity in the p_k-direction (see remarks on p. 84), we have

$$\frac{\partial^2 E}{\partial p_k^2} \leqslant 0. \tag{6.47}$$

Using 1, we obtain

5. $\dfrac{\partial x_k^*(\underline{p}, u)}{\partial p_k} \leqslant 0.$

That is, the *own-substitution effect* is *non-positive* for each good.

Furthermore, we may apply Young's theorem (equation (3.2), p. 74). This tells us that, provided E and its derivatives are continuously differentiable, $\partial^2 E/\partial p_i \partial p_k = \partial^2 E/\partial p_k \partial p_i$ for $i, k = 1, 2, \ldots, n$. Again using 1, this yields

6. $\dfrac{\partial x_k^*(p, u)}{\partial p_i} = \dfrac{\partial x_i^*(p, u)}{\partial p_k}$

which implies *symmetry of cross-substitution effects*.

For a detailed account of consumer theory see Deaton and Muellbauer (1980, chapter 2); this lays out very clearly the relationships between the dual approaches and results obtainable.

We turn finally to an application of the generalized envelope theorem. This is particularly appropriate for examining the effect upon an individual's behaviour of the imposition of rationing constraints. Suppose that in the absence of rationing constraints, the individual's demands are $z_k = x_k^*(p, u) = \hat{x}_k(p, m)$, where $V(p, m) = u$ (see Exercise 6.4.1(b)). Now let rationing constraints be added, one by one, which permit the individual to continue to purchase z_k, $k = 1, 2, \ldots, n$, but which constrain his responses to any parameter changes, e.g. price changes (recall figure 6.3). What is the effect upon the individual's demand *functions* (compensated and uncompensated)?

It is intuitively appealing *a priori* to suppose that demand should become more price-inelastic, the larger the number of constraints placed upon the individual's ability to respond.

Samuelson (1972) has explored and verified propositions in several economic contexts, including this proposition in consumer theory, which formally relate number of constraints to responsiveness. The central idea is closely analogous to an established principle of thermodynamics, called the *le Chatelier principle*. As a result, this nomenclature has come to be applied to economic problems; the rationing result is but one example of it.

The result can be derived very easily from the generalized envelope theorem. Silberberg (1971) shows that problem (6.4),

$$\max_{x} \; -p^t x$$
$$\text{st} \; -u(x) \leqslant -\bar{u} \tag{6.4}$$

satisfies the conditions of his generalized envelope theorem. Putting $V(p, u) = -E(p, u)$ in conditions (6.31)–(6.33), and noting that

$$\partial^2 V/\partial p_k^2 = -\partial x_k^*(p, u)/\partial p_k \geqslant 0 \tag{6.48}$$

we can say from condition (6.33) that

$$-\frac{\partial x_k^*}{\partial p_k} = -\left(\frac{\partial x_k^*}{\partial p_k}\right)^0 \geqslant -\left(\frac{\partial x_k^*}{\partial p_k}\right)^1 \geqslant -\left(\frac{\partial x_k^*}{\partial p_k}\right)^2 \geqslant \ldots \qquad (6.49)$$

the superscripts denoting the number of rationing constraints (of whatever kind, so long as they are satisfied at the original optimum). Now multiply through inequality (6.49) by p_k/x_k^*. The terms become price elasticities of demand (see Example 1.5.4, p. 18). Thus we have

$$e = e^0 \geqslant e^1 \geqslant e^2 \geqslant \ldots, \qquad (6.50)$$

i.e. the more rationing restrictions placed upon the individual's ability to respond to price changes, the more (own-price) inelastic the (utility-compensated) demands for all goods become.

See Deaton and Muellbauer (1980, section 4.3), for another account of this. There is also a related result for cross-elasticities of demand (see Silberberg, 1971). To derive such results for uncompensated demands requires a number of strong mathematical assumptions (again see Silberberg, 1971, and associated references, for a discussion).

The consumer theory results and insights we have gained here are quite powerful, but they have come cheaply with the aid of the maximum value tool-kit. This can be a highly elegant approach to economic problem-solving, subsuming entirely the underlying optimizing behaviour.

7 Dynamic Optimization

The constrained optimization problems we considered in the last three chapters were representative of *static* or *timeless* economic problems. In economic analysis we need also to address *dynamic* problems. Given an *inter-temporal* scenario, i.e. one with variables and an objective function that are not timeless, how do we choose optimally the time-paths of the variables, which may react to each other through time? And under what conditions is a steady state achievable? These sort of questions are the concern of the final chapter in this book.

The simplest multi-period optimization problems do not extend the static analysis at all. Consider for example problems in the general form

$$\max_{x_t : 1 \leqslant t \leqslant T} \sum_{t=1}^{T} f(t, x_t)$$

$$\text{st } g(t, x_t) \leqslant b_t \qquad t = 1, 2, \ldots, T. \tag{7.1}$$

We have allowed t as a variable in $f(\ )$ and $g(\ )$, as well as x_t, for greater generality. For example, the objective function could represent a present value summation by taking

$$f(t, x_t) = \frac{1}{(1+r)^t} \cdot h(x_t)$$

where r is an appropriate discount rate (recall Example 1.8.2, p. 27).

Problems in this format are *separable across time*: the optimal choice of x_t at time t is unaffected by the constraints at times $s \neq t$ and is quite independent of what goes on in these other time periods. Clearly the solution derives from the solutions to the T static problems in the unrelated time periods. Namely, the solution to problem (7.1) is a *function* $x_t = \hat{x}(t)$, such that for each t_0, $\hat{x}(t_0)$ solves the time-t_0 static problem:

$$\max_{x} f(t_0, x)$$

$$\text{st } g(t_0, x) \leqslant b_t. \tag{7.2}$$

Recalling our discussion in Chapter 1 of the use of alternative con-

166

tinuous and discrete time specifications for economic problems, we may also include in this category of separable (essentially static) multi-period problems those of the equivalent form:

$$\max_{x(t):0 \leqslant t \leqslant T} \int_0^T f[t, x(t)]\,\mathrm{d}t$$

$$\text{st } g[t, x(t)] \leqslant b(t) \qquad 0 \leqslant t \leqslant T. \tag{7.3}$$

Of course dynamic economic problems are rarely separable over time, and they present themselves in many different formats. Even within the format of problems (7.1) or (7.3), the time t constraint could depend upon what has gone before, e.g.

$$g(t, \ ) = g(t, x_t, x_{t-1}) \quad \text{or} \quad g[t, x(t), x'(t)]$$

as could the time t summand (or integrand) $f(t, \ )$ in the objective function. More general formulations might involve additional variables, constraints which are differential equations, end-point restrictions (e.g. upon $x(0)$ and/or $x(T)$) and an infinite or even variable time horizon T.

We are going to examine three approaches to solving dynamic optimization problems in this chapter. The first, *optimal control theory*, is an extension of the Lagrangean technique already discussed at such length in this book, and it will be our main focus. The others, which we discuss briefly in section 7.9, are the historically prior *calculus of variations* approach, and *dynamic programming*. Continuous time is assumed throughout, but at the very end we indicate how dynamic programming applies to discrete time problems (indeed it provides essentially the only solution technique for such problems).

7.1 SOME EXAMPLES OF DYNAMIC OPTIMIZATION PROBLEMS

In order to evolve a general format for the sort of problems in dynamic economic analysis that can be addressed using optimal control theory, we shall present here three particular economic problems in detail. These will be denoted Problem A, Problem B and Problem C. When we have discerned a general formulation for dynamic optimization problems that covers these three particular ones, and explored the Lagrangean approach to its solution, we shall return to Problems A, B and C and solve them carefully to illustrate the practical use of the technique evolved.

The problems to be considered are:

A An individual maximizing his discounted utility stream from consumption.

B A firm maximizing its net profit stream.
C A society maximizing welfare in the presence of pollution from production.

We will find that all three problems can be specified in a common format.
There is a *choice variable* (in each case a flow variable), to be determined
optimally at every moment of time, and yielding the solution to the
problem. The constraints to be satisfied will be expressible in terms of the
initial and final values of *another variable*, and a differential equation for
its time-path. This other variable (in our examples, a stock variable) is
guided along from $t = 0$ to $t = T$ by the time-path of the choice variable.
    These features will become clear when we outline the three specific
problems A, B and C mathematically.
    In the general formulation which is suggested by our observations, the
choice variable will be called the *control*, and the other variable the *state*
variable; they need not be characterized as flow and stock variables
respectively, but this will often be the case. The problem is to find the
optimal control, which maximizes the objective function subject to con-
sistency with the differential equation and terminal conditions for the state
variable. Hence the generic label *optimal control theory* for this approach
to dynamic optimization.

Problem A   An individual with no earned income derives income from
the interest paid at rate i on his savings $S = S(t)$. This is to be allocated
between consumption $C(t)$ and new saving $I(t) = S'(t) \geqq 0$ (i.e. dissaving
is allowed). Initially the individual has savings of S_0, and he chooses his
consumption rate to maximize his discounted utility stream over a finite
horizon:

$$\max_{C(t)} \int_0^T e^{-rt} U[C(t)] \, dt \tag{7.4}$$

(recall our discussion in Exercise 1.8.2, p. 28, on the use of e^{-rt} as a continuous time-discounting factor). There is no restriction upon the savings
remaining at time $t = T$. The choice of time-path for $C(t)$ in maximization (7.4) is constrained by the relationship:

$$C(t) = iS(t) - S'(t)$$

which may be written as:

$$S'(t) = iS(t) - C(t) \tag{7.5}$$

and by the end-point conditions:

$$S(0) = S_0 \qquad S(T) \text{ free.} \tag{7.6}$$

In this problem the flow variable $C(t)$ is the *control* (or choice) *variable* for the objective function (7.4), and the constraints of the problem are given by the differential equation (7.5), and end-point condition (7.6), upon the stock variable $S(t)$, which is the *state variable* for the problem. Note that the problem is not separable through time, even though the objective function (7.4) is.

Problem B A firm has capital stock $K = K(t)$ and a profit rate of $P(K)$. Capital depreciates at a constant proportionate rate b, and the cost of gross investment $I = K' + bK$ is $C = C(I)$. The problem is to maximize the present value of the net profit stream over a fixed planning period, by choice of an investment plan:

$$\max_{I(t)} \int_0^T e^{-rt}[P(K) - C(I)] \, dt. \tag{7.7}$$

Initial capital stock is K_0 and the terminal value $K(T)$ may not be negative.

Investment $I(t)$ is clearly the *control variable* for the problem, and the constraints upon its choice can be expressed by the differential equation

$$K' = I - bK \tag{7.8}$$

on the *state variable*, capital stock, together with the end-point conditions

$$K(0) = K_0 \qquad K(T) \geqslant 0. \tag{7.9}$$

Note that in this case the objective function is not separable over time (substitute for I from equation (7.8) into expression (7.7)).

This problem was anticipated in Examples 1.5.2 and 1.8.2. The particular specification (7.7)–(7.9) appears in a variety of contexts in economics, many of which are explored in Kamien and Schwartz (1981). For example, specification (7.7)–(7.9) may be applied to problems in human capital theory and health economics; by letting K = stock of human capital/stock of health, $P(K)$ = earnings rate achievable and I = training acquired/use of medical care, the problem becomes one of determining an individual's demand over time for education/medical services.

Problem C We base this example upon a recent article, 'How fast should we graze the global commons?', by Nordhaus (1982). This concerns the effect on society of pollution of the air by carbon dioxide (CO_2) from the combustion of fossil fuels (coal, oil). In a simple inter-temporal model, consumption (which determines social welfare) is achieved by production (through which the pollution is incurred): the pollution affects the ability of the labour force to work and thereby the production/consumption stream. What should be the strategy, taking into account these damaging effects of the build-up of CO_2?

The production process involves fossil fuel and manpower. Fossil fuels emit CO_2, and the greater the concentration $M(t)$ of CO_2 in the air the less efficiently the labour force works. Let $E(t)$ be the current rate of emission of CO_2, and let the production function be

$$C(t) = f[E(t)] - h[M(t)]. \tag{7.10}$$

Thus $f[E(t)]$ measures (or proxies) the contribution of coal and oil, and $h[M(t)]$ the deleterious effect of atmospheric CO_2 on the (fixed) labour force. We may suppose further, and reasonably, that $f(.)$ is increasing and concave while $h(.)$ is increasing and convex. The choice problem for society is

$$\max_{C(t)} \int_0^T e^{-rt} U[C(t)] \, dt \tag{7.11}$$

subject to (7.10) and the differential equation

$$M'(t) = aE(t) - bM(t) \tag{7.12}$$

and end-point conditions

$$M(0) = M_0 \qquad M(T) \leqslant M_T \tag{7.13}$$

which govern the time-path for the build-up of atmospheric CO_2. In this simple model the rate of build-up thus depends positively and linearly upon industrial emissions, and there is a constant proportionate rate b of dissipation (into the outer atmosphere).

In the end-point conditions (7.13), M_0 could equal zero (or the pre-industrial level) if the problem is being used to examine the past; or it could be set to the current level if the idea is to determine a policy for the future. M_T is the fatal concentration level. T need not be finite (representing a fixed planning period): it could be set to infinity (as Nordhaus does). Indeed, in a more sophisticated problem, T could be variable: the first moment of time at which the fatal level is reached then terminates the problem. (How long have we got?)

The problem is not quite yet in the format of Problems A and B. The *control variable*, in a practical sense, should be the rate of use of fossil fuel: we may take it to be $E(t)$, the rate of emission of CO_2. By substituting from equation (7.10) into maximization (7.11) the problem becomes

$$\max_{E(t)} \int_0^T e^{-rt} U[f(E) - h(M)] \, dt$$

$$\text{st } M' = aE - bM \qquad M(0) = M_0 \qquad M(T) \leqslant M_T \qquad 0 \leqslant t \leqslant T. \tag{7.14}$$

The constraints are, once again, in the form of a differential equation and end-point conditions upon the *state variable* $M(t)$, which is the 'stock' of CO_2 in the air.

7.2 THE OPTIMAL CONTROL THEORY FORMAT

In each of the three problems A, B and C we used continuous time. We shall continue to do so here; many discrete time problems are more appropriately dealt with using the dynamic programming technique, which we shall encounter later.

The format in which problems A, B and C were specified suggests a general one. Let $u(t)$ be the *control variable* and $x(t)$ the *state variable*; and consider the general dynamic optimization problem

$$\max_{u(t)} \int_0^T f[t, x(t), u(t)] \, dt$$

$$\text{st } x'(t) = g[t, x(t), u(t)] \qquad x(0) = x_0 \qquad x(T): \text{some condition.} \tag{7.15}$$

It is easily verified, by looking back, that each of problems A, B and C is expressed in this way, when the appropriate identification of control variable $u(t)$ and state variable $x(t)$ is made. The *terminal condition* on $x(T)$ varies with the problem, and as we have intimated it can be made quite complicated.

The solution to this general problem (however obtained) will be a *function*, say $\hat{u}(t)$, giving the optimal time-path for the control variable. This generates a time-path $\hat{x}(t)$ for the state variable as the solution to the first-order differential equation

$$x'(t) = g[t, x(t), \hat{u}(t)]$$

plus end-point conditions. The maximum value for the problem is then

$$V = \int_0^T f[t, \hat{x}(t), \hat{u}(t)] \, dt. \tag{7.16}$$

We may as well simplify the notation, by dropping the time argument t from control and state variables. Then specification (7.15) becomes:

$$\max_u \int_0^T f(t, x, u) \, dt \tag{7.17}$$

$$\text{st } x' = g(t, x, u) \qquad x(0) = x_0 \qquad x(T): \text{some condition.}$$

The notation can encompass multivariate problems

$$\max_{u_1, u_2 \ldots} \int_0^T f(t, x_1, x_2, \ldots, u_1, u_2, \ldots)\, dt$$

$$\text{st } x_i' = g_i(t, x_1, x_2, \ldots, u_1, u_2, \ldots)$$

with several controls and state variables, simply by regarding x, u and g as vectors in problem (7.17) (or writing them as $\underline{x}$, $\underline{u}$ and $\underline{g}$). This purely cosmetic change widens considerably the range of problems covered, and does not add significantly to the mathematical complexity. It is worth bearing in mind that x, u and g may be vectors in what follows, and we shall return to this. A multivariate problem will be encountered in Exercise 7.7.1(e).

The terminal condition can take several forms. The time of termination T will usually be fixed; it could be infinite. We have seen terminal conditions of the form

$$x_T \text{ free} \qquad x(T) \geqslant x_T \qquad x(T) \leqslant x_T$$

in Problems A, B and C. In other problems we may wish to specify

$$x(T) = x_T$$

and, yet again, T may itself be determined by the model, e.g. as the first point in time that a constraint $x(t) > \bar{x}$ is violated (consider the health-care version of Problem B, and let $\bar{x} = \bar{K}$ be the stock of health that defines death).

7.3 OPTIMAL CONTROL THEORY: A LAGRANGEAN APPROACH

We must now consider how to solve the general problem (7.17). We proceed rather as we did in chapter 5, for inequality-constrained static optimization, by first defining a Lagrangean, and then considering how to maximize it.

Let us leave aside for the time being the end-point constraints, as these merit separate attention. Then we require a multiplier *function* $\lambda(t)$, because there is a constraint at each time t, and the natural way to define the Lagrangean is

$$L = \int_0^T \{f(t, x, u) - \lambda(t)[x' - g(t, x, u)]\}\, dt. \tag{7.18}$$

The multiplier $\lambda(t)$ is, in the terminology of optimal control theory, the *costate variable* for the problem.

(For a vector problem with more than one state variable, there is a costate variable for each of the state variables: replace $\lambda(t)$ by $\underline{\lambda}(t)^t$ in the Lagrangean.)

If we follow the approach taken in chapter 5, then we should consider maximizing L over the variables of the problem. This would be straightforward if the integral defining L was separable across time in u and x: it is not, however, because of the term involving x'. But we may perform integration by parts upon the offending term,

$$\int_0^T -\lambda(t)x'\,dt,$$

yielding an expression for the Lagrangean:

$$L = \int_0^T [f(t,x,u) + \lambda g(t,x,u) + \lambda'x]\,dt - [\lambda(T)x(T) - \lambda(0)x(0)] \quad (7.19)$$

which *is* separable across time in u and x.

Denote the first two terms of the integrand in equation (7.19) by

$$H(\lambda,t,x,u) = f(t,x,u) + \lambda g(t,x,u). \quad (7.20)$$

$H(\lambda,t,x,u)$ is called the *Hamiltonian* for the problem. Thus

$$L = \int_0^T [H(\lambda,t,x,u) + \lambda'x]\,dt - [\lambda(T)x(T) - \lambda(0)x(0)]. \quad (7.21)$$

The term outside the integral is related to the end-point conditions for the problem. The integral is maximized, over x and u, by maximizing $H + \lambda'x$ for each t.

Of course nothing we have said justifies this Lagrangean approach. But the analogy with chapter 5 encourages us to hope that if $\hat{u}(t)$ and $\hat{x}(t)$ maximize $H + \lambda'x$ freely, and satisfy the constraints of the problem, then they may form the solution to the problem. Pontryagin *et al.* (1962) have shown that this is indeed the right approach:

7.3.1 Theorem   Pontryagin's Maximum Principle

If a solution $u = \hat{u}$ exists to the optimization problem (7.17), then there exists a λ such that $\hat{u}$ and $\hat{x}$ maximize $H + \lambda'x$.

The elegant generalized gradient vector approach to optimization, put forward by Clarke (1979) and briefly described in the Appendix to this book, also yields a proof of Theorem 7.3.1.

The result shows that the Lagrangean/Hamiltonian approach, of maximizing $H + \lambda'x$ freely over x and u, will lead to the solution to the problem, if a solution exists. It therefore validates our use of a Lagrangean in this context.

7.4 THE HAMILTONIAN CONDITIONS

Assuming differentiability of $f(t, x, u)$, $\lambda(t)$ and $g(t, x, u)$, the practical conditions we are led to are the first-order conditions for the free maximization of $H + \lambda'x$ over u and x:

$$0 = \frac{\partial H}{\partial u} \tag{7.22}$$

$$\lambda' = \frac{-\partial H}{\partial x} \tag{7.23}$$

A further condition,

$$x' = \frac{\partial H}{\partial \lambda} \tag{7.24}$$

says that the constraint $x' = g(t, x, u)$ holds. These conditions, together with another one – to be specified later – which depends upon the end-point constraint, and is called the *transversality condition* in optimal control theory parlance, form the *Hamiltonian conditions* for the problem. They have the same role as the Arrow–Enthoven conditions (5.14) in static optimization: they are necessary, but in general not sufficient, for the solution to the problem.

In fact the Maximum Principle can be addressed to a wider class of problems than (7.22)–(7.24) suggest. If to our general problem (7.17) we wish to add a *constraint on the control variable*, say $u \in U$, then the Hamiltonian condition (7.22) can be replaced by the first-order condition for

$$\max_{u \in U} H \tag{7.25}$$

plus an appropriate constraint qualification (see Kamien and Schwartz, 1981).

For multivariate problems (7.22)–(7.24) extend readily, to:

$$0 = \frac{\partial H}{\partial u_i} \tag{7.22a}$$

$$\lambda_j' = \frac{-\partial H}{\partial x_j} \tag{7.23a}$$

$$x_j' = \frac{H}{\partial \lambda_j} \tag{7.24a}$$

where i indexes the control variables and j the state variables of the problem. Equations (7.22a) are optimality conditions; (7.23a) are differential equations for the costate variables (the 'costate equations') and (7.24a) are the differential equations for the state variables.

It remains to consider the final element in the solution, namely the transversality condition.

But before doing this, let us address the sufficiency question. Maximization of $H + \lambda'x$ is necessary for the solution to problem (7.17): under what conditions are the Hamiltonian (first-order) conditions sufficient? Are there properties we may impose upon the objective and constraint functions which guarantee sufficiency? The simplest result is:

7.4.1 Theorem   (Mangasarian, 1966)

If $f(t, x, u)$ is concave in x and u, and if $g(t, x, u)$ is linear in x and u, then the Hamiltonian conditions (7.22)–(7.24) are necessary and sufficient for the solution to (7.17).

These conditions will be true of the problems we shall solve. A very much less demanding sufficiency condition is that the maximum value

$$\max_u H$$

be concave as a function of x. This is satisfied if f, g are as in Theorem 7.4.1, or if both f and g are concave in x and u. For a very clear discussion of the sufficiency issue see Arrow and Kurz (1970).

7.5 THE TRANSVERSALITY CONDITION

We turn at last to the transversality condition. This depends, of course, upon the particular end-point constraint dictated by the problem at hand.

Initially we shall confine ourselves to the simplest cases, end-point conditions of the types:

$$x(T) = x_T \qquad x(T) \geqslant x_T \qquad x(T) \text{ free}$$

where T is finite. (This encompasses the other case we have seen, $x(T) \leqslant x_T$, by a simple change of sign of the state variable.) We deal with the infinite horizon case later. More complex specifications, involving target 'terminal surfaces' and/or a variable terminal time T, are treated in detail in specialist texts (see, for example, Kamien and Schwartz, 1981). The results we need are shown in Table 7.1.

The reader will notice immediately the appearance of a familiar complementary slackness relation, between the constraint and the multiplier, in the case of the inequality-constrained end-point.

Table 7.1 Transversality conditions

End-point condition	Transversality condition
$x(T) = x_T$	No condition
$x(T) \geqslant x_T$	$\lambda(T) \geqslant 0$
	$[\hat{x}(T) - x_T]\lambda(T) = 0$
$x(T)$ free	$\lambda(T) = 0$

Let us examine this case more closely. When we defined the Lagrangean for problem (7.17) as

$$L = \int_0^T \{f(t, x, u) - \lambda(t)[x' - g(t, x, u)]\} \, dt \qquad (7.18)$$

we neglected the end-point constraint, in order to be general. In this particular case, we should have added a term

$$-\mu[x_T - x(T)] \qquad (7.26)$$

corresponding to the inequality constraint

$$-x(T) \leqslant -x_T$$

of the problem. Further, following the line of argument developed in chapter 5, we should also have imposed complementary slackness between μ and $[x_T - \hat{x}(T)]$. Then equation (7.19) would have been:

$$L = \int_0^T [H(\lambda, t, x, u) + \lambda'x] \, dt - [\lambda(T)x(T) - \lambda(0)x(0)]$$

$$-\mu[x_T - x(T)]. \quad (7.27)$$

To maximize L over x and u now requires, in particular, that

$$\frac{\partial L}{\partial x(T)} = \mu - \lambda(T) = 0$$

(the effect of a small change in $x(T)$ on the integral, which ends at $t = T$, is negligible). Thus $\mu = \lambda(T)$ and the complementary slack relation already mentioned becomes the transversality condition in Table 7.1.

But we can say more. A term now cancels in equation (7.27):

$$L = \int_0^T [H(\lambda, t, x, u) + \lambda'x]\, dt - \lambda(T)x_T + \lambda(0)x(0) \tag{7.28}$$

and since the optimal path $u = \hat{u}$, $x = \hat{x}$ satisfies the constraints of the problem, the maximum value function

$$V = \int_0^T f[t, \hat{x}(t), \hat{u}(t)]\, dt \tag{7.16}$$

and the Lagrangean at $u = \hat{u}$, $x = \hat{x}$ are equal: thus

$$V = \int_0^T [H(\lambda, t, \hat{x}, \hat{u}) + \lambda'\hat{x}]\, dt - \lambda(T)x_T + \lambda(0)\hat{x}(0). \tag{7.29}$$

Therefore

$$\frac{\partial V}{\partial x_T} = -\lambda(T). \tag{7.30}$$

The nature of this result should not be unexpected. It says that $\lambda(T)$ *can be interpreted as the marginal effect on maximum value of a small reduction in the parameter* x_T.

We can now understand the transversality condition in the light of this interpretation of the multiplier (costate variable) $\lambda(T)$. A reduction in x_T is a relaxation of the constraint, and cannot reduce maximum value: $\lambda(T) \geqslant 0$. Further, if the constraint does not bind (i.e. $[\hat{x}(T) - x_T]$ positive) then a small change in x_T makes no difference to the solution: $\partial V/\partial x_T = -\lambda(T) = 0$ (and conversely if $\partial V/\partial x_T = -\lambda(T)$ is negative then the constraint must bind).

The other transversality conditions in Table 7.1 can be seen in a similar light. If the end-point condition is $x(T) = x_T$, the (sign of the) marginal effect on maximum value of a small change in x_T cannot be argued *a priori*: there is no restriction on $\lambda(T)$. If $x(T)$ is free, then the end-point $\hat{x}(T)$ that is achieved cannot be bettered in maximum value terms, and the marginal value $\lambda(T)$ is zero.

In some problems, the terminal value achieved by the state variable, $\hat{x}(T)$, has value *per se*, and $x(T)$ enters the objective function. For example, consider the problem:

$$\max \int_0^T f(t, x, u)\, dt + \emptyset[x(T)]$$

$$\text{st } x' = g(t, x, u) \qquad x(0) = x_0 \qquad x(T) \text{ free.}$$

(7.17a)

$\emptyset[x(T)]$ is known as the *scrap value function*. In this case the transversality condition for a free end-point, $\lambda(T) = 0$, gets replaced (not unnaturally) by $\lambda(T) = \emptyset'[\hat{x}(T)]$.

Finally we mention the case of an infinite time horizon. Here, it is sufficient to insert 'lim' in the relevant transversality condition from $T \to \infty$

Table 7.1. For example if the end-point condition is $x(\infty) \geqslant x_\infty$, then an appropriate transversality condition is

$$\lim_{T \to \infty} \lambda(T) \geqslant 0 \quad \text{and} \quad \lim_{T \to \infty} [\hat{x}(T) - x_\infty]\lambda(T) = 0$$

etc. For further discussion see Arrow and Kurz (1970, pp. 45–51).

7.6 INTERPRETING THE COSTATE VARIABLE

Recall now that the other end-point constraint for the problem was $x(0) = x_0$. We do not need a multiplier for this: we simply set $x(0) = x_0$ throughout. In particular, equation (7.29) becomes:

$$V = \int_0^T [H(\lambda, t, \hat{x}, \hat{u}) + \lambda' \hat{x}]\, dt - \lambda(T)x_T + \lambda(0)x_0$$

(7.31)

and we see that

$$\frac{\partial V}{\partial x_0} = \lambda(0).$$

(7.32)

The $t = 0$ *multiplier (costate variable) determines the sensitivity of maximum value to a change in the stipulated initial state* x_0. (But contrast with equation (7.30): there is no minus sign here.)

In fact we can show that at each moment s, $0 \leqslant s < T$, the costate variable $\lambda(s)$ *can be interpreted as the marginal effect on maximum value of a small, exogenous increment to the state variable* $\hat{x}(s)$ *at time* s.

By this we mean that if the optimal path $\hat{x}(t)$ is disturbed slightly at time $t = s$, rendering this path non-optimal from $t = s$ to $t = T$, then as a result of the re-optimization from $t = s$ to $t = T$ there is an effect on maximum value, and it is given by $\lambda(s)$.

To see this, we split the original optimization problem into two parts, the break coming at the point $t = s$:

$$\max_{u} \int_0^s f(t, x, u)\,dt \qquad\qquad \max_{u} \int_s^T f(t, x, u)\,dt$$

st $x' = g(t, x, u)$	**PLUS**	st $x' = g(t, x, u)$
$x(0) = x_0$		$x(s) = \hat{x}(s)$
$x(s) = \hat{x}(s)$		$x(T)$: some condition.

It is clear that the solutions to the two sub-problems, taken together, will coincide with the overall solution $u = \hat{u}$, $x = \hat{x}$ (if not, then some other overall solution would have been optimal in the first place). Furthermore the same costate variable will be replicated within the two sub-periods: all differential equations are the same as before.

Since $\hat{x}(s)$ is the initial state for the second sub-problem, it is a parameter for that problem, and we may consider the effect on maximum value of a small exogenous increment Δx to it, which will affect the optimal path for the second sub-problem but leave the first sub-problem unaffected.

If maximum value for the entire problem is

$$V = V_1 + V_2 \tag{7.33}$$

where V_1, V_2 arise from the two sub-periods $0 \leqslant t \leqslant s, s \leqslant t \leqslant T$ respectively, then, following the increment to the initial state of the second sub-problem, we have

$$\Delta V = \Delta V_2 \doteq \left[\frac{\partial V_2}{\partial \hat{x}(s)}\right] \cdot \Delta x. \tag{7.34}$$

Applying equation (7.32) now yields

$$\frac{\Delta V}{\Delta x} \doteq \lambda(s) \tag{7.35}$$

and this is what was claimed.

A final point to note, in this consideration of the costate variables, concerns problems in which a present value integral is being maximized (this was the case for each of our Problems A, B and C). The point to note is that $\lambda(s)$ gives the marginal valuation *at the moment of planning* of the state variable at time $t = s$. That is to say, it measures the effect at time $t = s$ *discounted back to time* $t = 0$. It is often neater mathematically to work with the *current marginal valuation*, say $m(s)$. This is obtained simply by taking $\lambda(s)$ *forward* from $t = 0$ to $t = s$:

$$m(s) = e^{rs}\lambda(s). \tag{7.36}$$

The differential equation for the costate variable λ, equation (7.23) of the Hamiltonian conditions, can be written in terms of m by combining it with the differential equation

$$m' - rm = e^{rt}\lambda' \tag{7.37}$$

satisfied by $m(t)$.

See Dorfman (1969) for an excellent and very readable account of optimal control theory, its interpretations and use in economics.

7.7 USING THE HAMILTONIAN CONDITIONS TO SOLVE PROBLEMS

We now return to Problems A, B and C which were set out in section 7.1, and which motivated the optimal control format (7.17). The problems will be solved using the Hamiltonian conditions, which consist of equations (7.22)–(7.24) together with a transversality condition, to be found in Table 7.1.

Before we begin, let us summarize the position we have reached. For a dynamic optimization problem in the form

$$\max_u \int_0^T f(t, x, u)\, dt$$

$$\text{st } x' = g(t, x, u) \qquad x(0) = x_0$$

and with an end-point condition which is one of:

$$x(T) = x_T \qquad x(T) \geqslant x_T \qquad x(T)\text{ free}$$

the Hamiltonian conditions are

$$0 = \frac{\partial H}{\partial u} \qquad \lambda' = -\frac{\partial H}{\partial x} \qquad x' = \frac{\partial H}{\partial \lambda}$$

plus, of course,

a transversality condition from Table 7.1.

For any dynamic optimization problem we may encounter, it is a simple matter of casting the problem in the right format, and applying these conditions. This will generate differential equations which we may hope to solve for the control, state and costate variables.

We now take each of the three problems A, B and C in turn, and apply the appropriate Hamiltonian conditions.

Problem A   An individual maximizing his discounted utility stream from consumption.

This problem was expressed as

$$\max_{C(t)} \int_0^T e^{-rt} U[C(t)]\, dt$$

$$\text{st } S' = iS - C \qquad S(0) = S_0 \qquad S(T) \text{ free}$$

in equations (7.4)–(7.6).

The control variable is $u = C$ and the state variable is $x = S$. Note that the conditions of Theorem 7.4.1 are satisfied for this problem if $U(C)$ is concave in C (not an unreasonable assumption, in economic terms). In that case, the Hamiltonian conditions are sufficient as well as necessary. The Hamiltonian is

$$H = f + \lambda g = e^{-rt} U(C) + \lambda(iS - C) \qquad (7.38)$$

and the conditions for the optimal path $C = \hat{C}, S = \hat{S}$ are:

$$H_C = 0 \qquad e^{-rt} U'(C) - \lambda = 0 \qquad (7.39)$$

$$H_S = -\lambda' \qquad i\lambda = -\lambda' \qquad (7.40)$$

$$S' = H_\lambda \qquad S' = iS - C \qquad (7.41)$$

$$\text{transversality} \qquad \lambda(T) = 0. \qquad (7.42)$$

Solving equation (7.40), we find

$$\lambda(t) = \lambda_0 e^{-it} \qquad (7.43)$$

see (1.72)

for all t, and the only way equation (7.42) can be satisfied is if $\lambda_0 = 0$, which means that $\lambda(t) = 0$ for all t. Then $U'(\hat{C}) = 0$, from equation (7.39).

Marginal utility is thus driven to zero on the optimal consumption path. If the utility function $U(.)$ has a bliss point, well and good: there is no restriction on the amount of dissaving the individual can effect and, by overdrawing heavily if necessary over the period (recall $S(T)$ is free), the individual can consume to the point where bliss is always achieved.

But more commonly the utility function will be assumed increasing (as well as concave: $U' > 0, U'' < 0$). Then optimal consumption $\hat{C} \to \infty$ in order to satisfy $U'(\hat{C}) \to 0$.

This bizarre result tells us that we have mis-specified the problem; clearly the trouble lies in the lack of end-point constraint, which means that the individual can finance any degree of consumption whatever.

If we re-specify the problem with an end-point constraint

$$S(T) \geqslant 0 \tag{7.44}$$

then the individual cannot end up overdrawn. The transversality condition (7.42) is then replaced by

$$\lambda(T) \geqslant 0 \qquad \lambda(T)S(T) = 0 \tag{7.45}$$

and, assuming $\lambda(T) \neq 0$ (otherwise we return to the bizarre situation) we must have

$$\hat{S}(T) = 0. \tag{7.46}$$

Now equations (7.39) and (7.43) yield

$$U'(\hat{C}) = \lambda_0 e^{(r-i)t}. \tag{7.47}$$

Since $U'' < 0$ this means that optimal consumption grows over the period if and only if the interest rate on savings exceeds the discount rate.

From equation (7.43) savings have a positive, declining marginal valuation, and (from equation (7.46)) are exhausted at the end of the period. The *current* marginal valuation $m(t)$ of savings (see equation (7.36)), satisfies

$$m(t) = \lambda(t)e^{rt} = U'(\hat{C}), \tag{7.48}$$

i.e. consumption is driven to the point at which its marginal utility just equals the current marginal valuation of savings: a familiar marginal result in economic analysis.

If the functional form of the utility function is known then the optimal path for savings could be obtained by inverting equation (7.47), using equation (7.41) and solving a differential equation:

$$C = iS - S' = [U']^{-1}(\lambda_0 e^{(r-i)t}) \tag{7.49}$$

using the end-point information $\hat{S}(0) = S_0$ and, from equation (7.46), $\hat{S}(T) = 0$ (see Exercise 7.7.1(b) ahead). Optimal control problems often reduce, in the end, to solving rather unpleasant-looking differential equations.

Problem B   A firm maximizing its net profit stream.
   This problem was expressed as

$$\max_{I(t)} \int_0^T e^{-rt}[P(K) - C(I)] \, dt$$

$$\text{st } K' = I - bK \qquad K(0) = K_0 \qquad K(T) \geqslant 0$$

in equations (7.7)–(7.9).

The control variable is $u = I$ and the state variable is $x = K$. If, as we shall later assume, $P''(K) < 0$ and $C''(I) > 0$, then the objective function is concave jointly in I and K (recall Exercises 3.7.4(b), p. 84, and 3.7.7(b), p. 85). Then the Hamiltonian conditions are necessary and sufficient to solve the problem. The Hamiltonian is

$$H = f + \lambda g = e^{-rt}[P(K) - C(I)] + \lambda(I - bK) \tag{7.50}$$

and the conditions for the optimal path $I = \hat{I}, K = \hat{K}$ are:

$$H_I = 0 \qquad -e^{-rt}C'(I) + \lambda = 0 \tag{7.51}$$

$$H_K = -\lambda' \qquad \lambda' - b\lambda = -e^{-rt}P'(K) \tag{7.52}$$

$$K' = H_\lambda \qquad K' = I - bK \tag{7.53}$$

$$\text{transversality} \quad \lambda(T) \geqslant 0 \qquad \lambda(T)K(T) = 0 \tag{7.54}$$

Equation (7.51) says, very simply, that

$$C'[\hat{I}(t)] = \lambda(t)e^{rt} = m(t), \tag{7.55}$$

i.e. at each time t, investment is taken to the point where its marginal cost equals the marginal valuation of capital.

Now multiply both sides of equation (7.52) by the integrating factor e^{-bt}. We obtain

$$(\lambda' - b\lambda)e^{-bt} = \frac{d}{dt}[\lambda e^{-bt}] = e^{-(r+b)t}P'(K). \tag{7.56}$$

Integrating from time $t = s$ to $t = T$ we have

$$\lambda(s)e^{-bs} - \lambda(T)e^{-bT} = \int_s^T e^{-(r+b)t}P'[K(t)]\,dt \tag{7.57}$$

(following equation (1.81a), p. 35). Now multiply both sides of equation (7.57) by $e^{(b+r)s}$, and assume for the moment that capital is not exhausted at the end of the period, so that from conditions (7.54) $\lambda(T) = 0$. Equation (7.57) becomes

$$\lambda(s)e^{rs} = m(s) = \int_s^T e^{-(r+b)(t-s)}P'[K(t)]\,dt. \tag{7.58}$$

This says that the marginal valuation of capital at time s equals the discounted stream *to time* s of the marginal profit generated. The discount rate includes the rate of depreciation b of capital.

If $\lambda(T) \neq 0$ then $\hat{K}(T) = 0$, i.e. capital gets exhausted and it cannot be presumed that the obvious marginal condition (7.58) holds: indeed it does not, needing adjusting by a term that involves $\lambda(T)$, the marginal effect on value (discounted profit) if capital stock were able to go negative (recall equation (7.30) and the surrounding discussion).

We could combine equations (7.55) and (7.58) and obtain a quite unpleasant differential equation for the time-path of capital stock:

$$C'[I(s)] = C'[K'(s) + bK(s)] = \lambda(s)e^{rs} = m(s)$$

$$= \int_s^T e^{-(r+b)(t-s)} P'[K(t)] \, dt \tag{7.59}$$

but we shall not attempt to solve it.

It is beginning to become clear that we shall need some sort of ancillary technique if we are to distill, from the optimal control results to our problems, useful information about the time-path of the state variable. For example we would like to be able to carry out comparative analysis, e.g. to consider the effect on the solution of a change in a discount rate or other parameter. The tool-kit we can use to address this sort of question – and very effectively – is *diagrammatic analysis*, and we will come to it after we have considered the Hamiltonian conditions for the remaining problem, Problem C.

Problem C   A society maximizing welfare in the presence of pollution from production.

This problem was given in (7.14) as

$$\max_{E(t)} \int_0^T e^{-rt} U[f(E) - h(M)] \, dt$$

$$\text{st } M' = aE - bM \qquad M(0) = M_0 \qquad M(T) \leqslant M_T.$$

The control variable is $u = E$ and the state variable is $x = M$. Recall that $f(.)$ was assumed concave and $h(.)$ convex. Later we shall assume that $U(.)$ is linear. These assumptions are certainly enough to ensure that the Hamiltonian conditions are sufficient as well as necessary. The Hamiltonian is

$$H = f + \lambda g = e^{-rt} U[f(E) - h(M)] + \lambda(aE - bM) \tag{7.60}$$

and the conditions for the optimal path $E = \hat{E}$, $M = \hat{M}$ are:

$$H_E = 0 \qquad e^{-rt} U'(C) f'(E) + \lambda a = 0 \tag{7.61}$$

$$H_M = -\lambda' \qquad e^{-rt}U'(C)h'(M)+\lambda b = \lambda' \tag{7.62}$$

$$M' = H_\lambda \qquad\qquad aE - bM = M' \tag{7.63}$$

transversality $\qquad \lambda(T) \leqslant 0 \qquad \lambda(T)[M_T - M(T)] = 0. \tag{7.64}$

We have written C for $f(E)-h(M)$ in equations (7.61) and (7.62), for convenience.

The *non-positive* terminal multiplier results from the terminal inequality being of the form $M(T) \leqslant M_T$, and not $M(T) \geqslant M_T$ as in Table 7.1. To see this, simply note that for the $\leqslant$ constraint, μ should be replaced by $-\mu$ in equation (7.26), but otherwise the analysis that justified the transversality condition on pp. 176–177 is the same.

Proceeding very much as for Problem B, multiply both sides of equation (7.62) by the integrating factor e^{-bt} and integrate from $t = s$ to $t = T$:

$$\lambda(T)e^{-bT} - \lambda(s)e^{-bs} = \int_s^T e^{-(b+r)t}U'(C)h'(M)\,dt. \tag{7.65}$$

If $\hat{M}(T) \neq M_T$ then $\lambda(T) = 0$ from conditions (7.64), and the first term in equation (7.65) disappears. This term would also disappear if $T \to \infty$, as assumed by Nordhaus (1982), or if the end-point $M(T)$ were free. Now multiply both sides of equation (7.65) by $e^{(b+r)s}$:

$$m(s) = - \int_s^T e^{-(b+r)(t-s)}U'(C)h'(M)\,dt. \tag{7.66}$$

The current marginal valuation of the 'stock' (concentration) of CO_2 in the air is negative. It is clear why: utility is a negative function of $M(t)$. Indeed equation (7.66) can be written

$$m(s) = \int_s^T e^{-(b+r)(t-s)}\left[\frac{\partial U}{\partial M}\right]dt \tag{7.67}$$

making the economic interpretation perfectly clear.

Now multiply both sides of equation (7.61) by e^{rt}:

$$U'(C)f'(E)+ma = 0 \tag{7.68}$$

and substitute for m from equation (7.66):

$$U'[C(s)]f'[E(s)] = a \int_s^T e^{-(b+r)(t-s)}U'[C(t)]h'[M(t)]\,dt. \tag{7.69}$$

We may eliminate E and C from equation (7.69), by putting $E = (M' + bM)/a$ and $C = f(E) - h(M) = f[(M' + bM)/a] - h(M)$. This yields the usual, unattractive differential equation for the state variable.

7.7.1 Exercises

(a) Show that when $T \to \infty$ equation (7.69) is equivalent to Nordhaus' (1982) equation (5), viz.:

$$U'[C(t)]f'[E(t)] = a \int_0^\infty e^{-(b+r)v} U'[C(t+v)]h'[M(t+v)] \, dv.$$

(b) Modify Problem A to include wage income at a constant rate w, and end-point conditions $S(0) = S(T) = 0$. Further, let the utility function take the specific form $U(C) = \ln(C)$. Obtain a first-order linear differential equation for the optimal savings path $\hat{S}(t)$, and solve it.

(c) From a stock K of capital, output can be produced by society at rate $F(K)$. Assume $F'(K) > 0$ and $F''(K) < 0$. This output can be consumed, yielding a utility flow, or it can be invested. Investment is needed both to maintain the existing capital stock, which decays at a constant proportionate rate b, and to augment it and hence future productive capacity. Society's problem is to maximize utility over some specific period by choosing the proportion of output to be consumed at each time t. Specify this problem in the optimal control format and solve the Hamiltonian conditions.

(d) In a certain goods market there is a dominant, price-setting producer. The rate of entry of rivals is a function of current product price. If the dominant firm sets a high price, to achieve high current profits, it will sacrifice profit in the future through erosion of its market share. Thus its pricing strategy is the solution to a dynamic optimization problem.

Let $p(t)$ be the product price set by the dominant firm, c the (assumed constant) average production cost and $x(t)$ the level of rival sales. Suppose that the dominant firm faces a demand schedule $q[p(t), t] = f[p(t)] - x(t)$, and that the rate of entry of rival producers, $x'(t)$, is determined by the current rate of return in the market: $x'(t) = k[p(t) - \bar{p}]$ where $k > 0$ and $\bar{p}$ is the 'limit price', at which net entry is equal to zero.

Express the dominant firm's pricing problem in the optimal control format, assuming that the firm uses a discount rate of r for assessing the present value of its profit stream.

What is the interpretation of the multiplier (costate variable) $\lambda(t)$? What sign would you expect it to have? Show that current value multiplier $m(t) = \lambda(t) e^{rt}$ satisfies

$$m = -\frac{q(\hat{p}, t) + (\hat{p} - c)f'(\hat{p})}{k}$$

and

$$m' = rm + \hat{p} - c$$

from the Hamiltonian conditions (use also equation (7.37)).

(e) The worth of a firm is the present value of its net revenue stream: $W = \int_0^\infty e^{-rt} R(t) \, dt$. Net revenue at time t is the value of output, less the cost of labour and the cost of investment: $R(t) = p(t)Q(t) - w(t)L(t) - q(t)I(t)$, to use a transparent notation. Worth is to be maximized subject to a production function $Q(t) = F[K(t), L(t)]$ where $K(t)$ is capital stock, which decays at rate b. Set up the firm's problem in the optimal control format, using *two* control variables $u_1 = L$ and $u_2 = I$. Show that the Hamiltonian conditions (7.22a)–(7.24a) imply that on the optimal path: (a) the current marginal valuation of capital is $m(t) = q(t)$, (b) the marginal product of labour is $F_L = w(t)/p(t)$, and (c) the marginal product of capital can be expressed in the form $F_K = c(t)/p(t)$ where

$$c(t) = q(t) \left[b + r - \frac{q'(t)}{q(t)} \right].$$

Interpret this expression carefully: it is the 'imputed rental price for the services of capital'. Finally, show that if the production function is Cobb–Douglas, $F(K, L) = K^e L^f$, then the desired capital–output ratio is $K(t)/Q(t) = ep(t)/c(t)$.

(f) Consider an optimization problem of the form

$$\max_{x(t)} \int_0^T f[t, x(t), x'(t)] \, dt$$

$$\text{st } x(0) = x_0 \qquad x(T) = x_T.$$

Write this problem in the optimal control format, and show that at the solution value $\hat{x}(t)$ the equation

$$\frac{\partial f}{\partial x} = \frac{d}{dt} \left(\frac{\partial f}{\partial x'} \right)$$

is satisfied. (*Hint*: introduce a control variable.)

Exercise 7.7.1(c) is a version of the *Ramsey problem*. Hadley and Kemp (1971) examine many versions of this problem, in great detail. Exercise 7.7.1(d) is taken from Gaskins (1971), which contains a useful intuitive discussion of the Hamiltonian. Exercise 7.7.1(e), due to Jorgenson (1963), provides an outline of what is known as the neoclassical theory of investment behaviour. The equation in Exercise 7.7.1(f) is known as the *Euler equation*: see ahead to section 7.9 for more on this.

Optimal control theory has found wide application. Kamien and Schwartz (1981) is an excellent reference work, containing many interesting examples. For example, problems can be found there which deal with advertising, fishing, machine maintenance, road building, human capital, and land use.

7.8 THE PATH TO THE STEADY STATE: DIAGRAMMATIC ANALYSIS

The Hamiltonian conditions determine the optimal control $\hat{u}(t)$ and the optimal path for the state variable $\hat{x}(t)$. They also determine the costate variable $\lambda(t)$, as the marginal valuation at the moment of planning of the state variable $\hat{x}(t)$ along the optimal path. The *current* marginal valuation, $m(t)$, satisfies

$$m(t) = e^{rt}\lambda(t) \tag{7.36}$$

and

$$m' = rm + e^{rt}\lambda'. \tag{7.37}$$

For many problems the terminal time T is infinite. We discussed briefly the appropriate transversality conditions for an infinite time horizon at the end of section 7.5, but we have not otherwise paid much attention to this case. If the duration of the problem stretches out to infinity, we may look for the emergence of a steady state in the state variable, when the time-path $\hat{x}(t)$ settles down asymptotically to a constant value, say x^*, and, in essence, the solution to the problem becomes timeless.

Of course a steady state need not exist: the solution $\hat{x}(t)$ to the first-order differential equation $x' = g(t, x, \hat{u})$ may not be stable. Or, the steady state could be achieved exactly in a finite period of time. But for the sort of problem we are interested in, it becomes important to analyse the steady state, and the path to it, when the horizon is infinite and under the assumption that stability exists. What, then, are the characteristics of the path to the steady state? And how is the steady state affected by changes in parameters (e.g. the discount rate or a decay rate)?

As we have seen, the differential equation for the state variable that emerges from the Hamiltonian conditions is not always tractable, although its economic interpretation may be transparent. However, steady-state information can be derived readily enough using a diagrammatic approach.

Formally, we define the steady state as that path for the state variable $x(t)$ *and current marginal valuation* m(t) on which

$$x' = m' = 0. \tag{7.70}$$

Thus the current marginal valuation of the timeless asymptotic value $x(t) = x^*$ must also be timeless.

How do we set about solving equation (7.70)?

First, differential equations expressing x' and m' in terms of x and m may be obtained from the Hamiltonian conditions (7.23)–(7.24):

$$x' = \frac{\partial H}{\partial \lambda}$$

$$m' = rm + e^{rt}\lambda' = rm - e^{rt}\left(\frac{\partial H}{\partial x}\right)$$

using equations (7.36)–(7.37) and appropriate substitutions to remove the control and co-state variables.

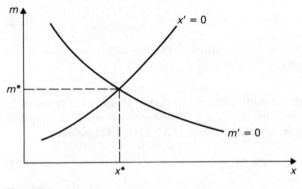

Figure 7.1

Then, the steady state may be identified as the intersection of the two loci $x' = 0$ and $m' = 0$ in (x, m)-space, e.g. as in figure 7.1. The (x, m)-plane in this diagram is known as *phase-space* in some texts. Parameter changes shift the phase-space loci and enable us to argue the effect on the steady state (x^*, m^*) just as, in the simplest and most familiar piece of economic analysis, we argue from shifts in demand and supply schedules to changes in equilibrium prices and quantities.

But we shall be able to take this diagrammatic analysis further. The differential equations in x and m will determine the *signs* of x' and m' when $x' \neq 0$ and $m' \neq 0$, i.e. at points in the quadrants of the (x, m)-plane formed by the two loci. This dictates the directions taken by paths $[x(t), m(t)]$ through the (x, m)-plane in time, and in particular allows us to identify paths to the steady state.

Diagrammatic analysis can be used in this way to explore the asymptotic behaviour of any pair of simultaneous first-order differential equations in two variables. The equations do not need to be linear (as they did in chapter 2). However, we are anticipating somewhat the effectiveness of diagrammatic analysis when geared to the Hamiltonian conditions for dynamic optimization; let us now return to our worked examples.

All three problems, A, B and C, had finite time horizons T as specified, but by letting $T \to \infty$ steady-state analysis becomes relevant. Indeed Nordhaus's original formulation of Problem C had an infinite horizon. Since Problem A can be solved directly for the path of the state variable, savings, using an explicit function (Exercise 7.7.1(b)), we put this problem to one side.

Problem B   The state variable is capital stock K and the simultaneous equations for K' and m' in terms of K and m are

$$C'(K' + bK) = m \tag{7.71}$$

$$m' = (r + b)m - P'(K). \tag{7.72}$$

Equation (7.71) comes from equations (7.55) and (7.53); equation (7.72) follows from equations (7.52) and (7.37).

Problem C   Tractable simultaneous equation for M' and m' in terms of M and m are not so readily derived in this case: we use a simplifying assumption. First, from equations (7.61), (7.62) and (7.37) we have

$$U'(C)f'(E) + ma = 0 \tag{7.73}$$

$$U'(C)h'(M) + m(b + r) = m'. \tag{7.74}$$

Now suppose $U(C)$ is linear, in fact, without loss of generality, that $U'(C) = 1$. This simplifying assumption makes equations (7.73) and (7.74) tractable, and means that welfare is being measured as the present value of the consumption stream (see expression (7.11)). Now substitute $E = (M' + bM)/a$, from equation (7.63), into equation (7.73) and re-arrange slightly:

$$f'\left(\frac{M' + bM}{a}\right) = -ma \tag{7.75}$$

$$m' = (b + r)m + h'(M). \tag{7.76}$$

These are the equations for M' and m' that we require.

For each of Problems B and C we have found a pair of simultaneous differential equations in terms of x (the relevant state variable) and m *only*. We eliminated the control variable u and costate variable λ. The differential equations are not linear, at least not without further simplifying assumptions, but this will not matter.

We shall now analyse Problem C in detail, diagrammatically, using equations (7.75) and (7.76). In an exercise to follow, the reader will be invited to do the same for Problem B.

Problem C: diagrammatic analysis. Equations (7.75) and (7.76) yield the loci in (M, m)-space on which $M' = 0$ and $m' = 0$. These are given by

$$M' = 0 \qquad m = \frac{-f'(bM/a)}{a} \qquad\qquad (7.77)$$

$$m' = 0 \qquad m = \frac{-h'(M)}{(b+r)}. \qquad\qquad (7.78)$$

They remind us that m is negative: $-m$ is the marginal cost (or damage) in terms of consumption of an increment to the concentration of CO_2 in the atmosphere along the optimal path $M(t)$.

In equation (7.77), m and M are positively related (recall that $f'' < 0$), whilst in equation (7.78) they are negatively related ($h'' > 0$): see figure 7.2.

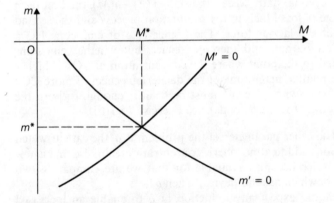

Figure 7.2

A steady state exists if and only if the two loci cross. They cannot cross twice because of their slopes, so assuming existence the steady state $M = M^*$, $m = m^*$ is unique. The effect upon it of a change in one of the parameters of the problem (namely, one of r, b and a) can be analysed in terms of the induced shifts in the two loci.

Increase in r   If r is increased, the $m' = 0$ locus shifts vertically upwards, whilst the $M' = 0$ locus is unaffected (consider equations (7.77) and (7.78)).

Hence M^* rises and m^* rises. Since m^* is negative, this means it gets smaller in absolute terms. The rate of emissions at the steady state is determined from the constraint $E = (M' + bM)/a$ by setting $M' = 0$:

$$E^* = bM^*/a \qquad (7.79)$$

and hence E^* also rises when r increases. With a higher discount rate, more CO_2 is emitted in the steady state. The concentration of CO_2 in the atmosphere is higher, and the marginal damage from further CO_2 in the air is reduced.

Increase in b   For any fixed value $M = M_1$, the value of m on the $M' = 0$ locus, namely $-f'(bM_1/a)/a$, *rises* when b increases, because the argument in $f'(.)$ increases and f' is decreasing ($f'' < 0$). Hence the $M' = 0$ locus shifts upwards when b increases. The $m' = 0$ locus also shifts upwards. Thus m^* is increased (marginal damage $-m^*$ falls) but the effect on M^* is not determined.

It is clear that this increase in the decay rate of CO_2 into the outer atmosphere enables an increased steady state rate of emission (we have $f'(E^*) + m^*a = 0$ from equation (7.73)). But we cannot say from this whether the steady state concentration of CO_2 will be higher or lower. There are two conflicting considerations to be taken into account in setting the new optimal path. Recall that $C = f(E) - h(M)$, the first term proxying the role of fossil fuels in the production process and the second term the role of the labour force. The higher rate of emissions has a positive effect on output, and thereby welfare, but whether emissions should be pushed to the point where the concentration of CO_2 is higher depends on the relative magnitude of the deleterious effect of more CO_2 on the labour force (who, after all, must be healthy enough to burn the extra fuel, to produce the extra goods). See Exercise 7.8.1(b).

Change in a   The other parameter of the problem is a, the rate at which new CO_2 emissions add to atmospheric concentration. Suppose that a new anti-pollution device becomes available (or that we are comparing two economies, one of which has this device). Then a falls.

Clearly we should expect any reduction in a to enable an increased steady-state rate of emission. This is indeed the case (see Exercise 7.8.1(c)).

But the effect on steady-state CO_2 concentration is, once again, more difficult to argue. Briefly, the $m' = 0$ locus is unaffected, whilst the $M' = 0$ locus shifts up/down, i.e. M^* decreases/increases, according as the elasticity of the marginal consumption from emission schedule $f'(E)$ is less than/ greater than unity (see Exercise 7.8.1(d)). If this elasticity is high, then f is 'very concave', i.e. decreasing returns to the use of fossil fuels set in very rapidly, and in order to optimize the consumption stream emissions are pushed to the point at which, despite the anti-pollution device, steady-state CO_2 concentration is increased.

We could also examine the effect on the steady state of shifts in the schedules f' and h'. These are easily translated into shifts in the $M' = 0$ and $m' = 0$ loci, and could, for example, represent the effects of new technology and protective breathing apparatus respectively.

7.8.1 Exercises

(a) Use equations (7.73) and (7.74) to show that, whatever the utility function $U(C)$, the steady state is characterized by the equation

$$f'(E^*) = \frac{ah'(M^*)}{(b+r)}. \tag{7.80}$$

This is Nordhaus's (1982) equation (4). Interpreting the left-hand side of this as the marginal benefit to consumption of an extra unit of emission, what economically meaningful property of the steady state does this equation convey?

(b) Eliminate E^* from equation (7.80) using equation (7.79). This yields an equation that defines M^* implicitly in terms of the parameters a, b and r. Show by differentiating that

$$\frac{\partial M^*}{\partial b} = \frac{ah'(M^*)/(b+r)^2 + M^*f''(E^*)/a}{ah''(M^*)/(b+r) - bf''(E^*)/a}.$$

What determines the sign of $\partial M^*/\partial b$?

(c) Now eliminate M^* from equation (7.80) using equation (7.79), to obtain an equation defining E^* implicitly in terms of r, b and a. Prove that $\partial E^*/\partial a < 0$.

(d) Determine the effect on the $M' = 0$ locus (7.77) of a change in the parameter a: show that for a fixed value $M = M_1$,

$$\partial m/\partial a = \frac{(1-v)f'(bM_1/a)}{a^2}$$

where, letting $bM_1/a = e$ for convenience, $v = -ef''(e)/f'(e) > 0$.

We have now seen, at least for the infinite-horizon Nordhaus problem, how to carry out comparative static analysis on the (timeless) steady state using diagrammatic analysis. The more complicated question is that of *comparative dynamics*, concerning the effect of parameter changes on the time-path to the steady state. We cannot go into this issue to any significant extent here, but we can make some observations about the nature of the time-path to the steady state.

Consider the $M' = 0$ locus. In figure 7.3 it is denoted AA. Points (M, m) on it satisfy

$$m = \frac{-f'(bM/a)}{a}. \tag{7.77}$$

Points (M, m) *above* AA plainly satisfy $m > -f'(bM/a)/a$, i.e.

$$-ma < f'\left(\frac{bM}{a}\right). \tag{7.81}$$

Now recall the differential equation (7.75) for M':

$$f'\left(\frac{M' + bM}{a}\right) = -ma. \tag{7.75}$$

Combining equation (7.75) and inequality (7.81) we find that, above line AA in figure 7.3, $f'[(M' + bM)/a] < f'(bM/a)$. Since f' is decreasing ($f'' < 0$) this implies $M' > 0$, i.e. M is increasing. An identical argument shows that below the line AA, $M' < 0$.

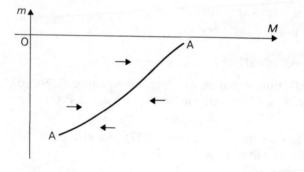

Figure 7.3

The arrows in figure 7.3 show direction of movement of M through time, above and below the locus AA (where M is stationary by definition).

Let BB be the $m' = 0$ locus. It is specified by

$$m = \frac{-h'(M)}{(b+r)}. \tag{7.78}$$

Hence above BB we have $m > -h'(M)/(b+r)$, i.e. using equation (7.76), $m' = (b+r)m + h'(M) > 0$. Similarly we can infer that below BB $m' < 0$. Adding this information to figure 7.3, we obtain figure 7.4.

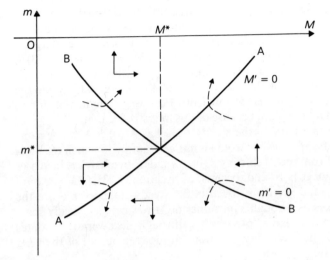

Figure 7.4

If $[M(t), m(t)]$ is a point on the optimal time-path, we know the overall direction of movement from the direction of the arrows in the component M- and m-directions. Near the $M' = 0$ or $m' = 0$ locus, this implies a movement across the locus (dotted arrows). The only stable point is, of course, the steady state value (M^*, m^*).

Furthermore, *the steady state can only be approached from two directions*: see figure 7.5.

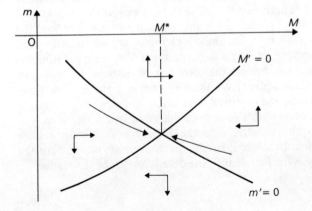

Figure 7.5

The two feasible paths to the steady state correspond to the cases $M(0) < M^*$ and $M(0) > M^*$.

The first of these would plausibly arise as the optimal path from pre-industrial society to a steady-state industrialized society. The CO_2 concentration M increases, and its marginal valuation m falls (i.e. marginal damage $-m$ increases) towards the steady state. From equation (7.73) E falls along this time-path. That is, the optimal policy involves high initial emissions, decreasing through time. The rate of dissipation of CO_2 into the outer atmosphere is, however, insufficient to outweigh the increments to concentration that take place because of this industrial activity.

The other feasible path to the steady state has $M(0) > M^*$: the same steady state can be approached from an initial situation in which the air is 'over-polluted'. From such a starting point, M falls (obviously), m increases (i.e. marginal damage falls) and (because of equation (7.73)) CO_2 emission E starts out low and increases towards the steady-state level. Since the optimal path takes us through *high* values of M towards the steady state, there is a continuing, large loss of CO_2 through decay into the outer atmosphere, and the increasing emissions do not replace all of the CO_2 being leaked away.

We have thus identified the broad characteristics of time paths to the steady state. We have also seen how the steady state itself is influenced by changes in parameters. But a treatment of *comparative dynamics*, i.e. of the effect of parameters on the optimal time-path, is beyond our scope. See Kamien and Schwartz (1981) for a useful exposition.

Let us summarize what we have done. We began with a pair of simultaneous, first-order, differential equations in the state variable M and current marginal valuation m. They were not linear. (This is not vital for diagrammatic analysis, although linearity was crucial for the solution technique for such equation systems in chapter 2.) The steady state is characterized by the equations $M' = m' = 0$. We derived the loci $M' = 0$ and $m' = 0$ in the (M, m)-plane, and from their intersection deduced the steady state values (M^*, m^*). Parameter changes shifted the two loci, enabling the effect upon the steady state to be argued. By manipulating the differential equations, we showed the direction of motion through time from points in the (M, m)-plane. We thereby obtained the feasible time-paths to the steady state, and explored their characteristics.

Judging by our success with Problem C, diagrammatic analysis may in general be geared quite effectively to the Hamiltonian conditions for dynamic optimization problems. In the next exercise we outline the corresponding analysis for Problem B; the details are left to the reader.

7.8.2 Exercise

(a) Assume that in Problem B the cost of investment $C(I)$ is increasing and convex, and the rate of profit $P(K)$ is increasing and concave. Given the differential equations (7.71) and (7.72) for K and its current marginal valuation m, deduce that in (K, m)-space the locus $K' = 0$ is upward-sloping whilst the locus $m' = 0$ is downward-sloping. Identify the steady state values K^*, m^* and show that, (i) an increase in the discount rate engenders a lower steady-state capital stock, marginal valuation of capital and rate of investment; (ii) an increase in the depreciation rate of capital reduces steady-state capital stock but has an indeterminate effect on the rate of investment; (iii) an investment credit leads to a higher steady-state stock of capital and a higher steady-state rate of investment (replace $C(I)$ by $C(I)-tI$); and (iv) two approaches to the steady state are possible. If $K(0) = 0$ then $K(t)$ increases towards the steady state, investment taking place at a declining rate that is sufficient to outweigh depreciation.

(b) Refer back to the Exercise 7.7.1(c) (the Ramsey problem). Show that the simultaneous first-order differential equations for the state variable K and its current marginal valuation m are

$$U'[-K'+F(K)-bK] = m$$
$$m' = m[r+b-F'(K)]$$

where U is the utility function. Carry out diagrammatic analysis on the effect on parameter changes on the steady state, and identify feasible paths to the steady state, assuming that $U' > 0$, $U'' < 0$ and $F'(K) > b$.

(c) Recall Exercise 7.7.1(d), concerning the pricing decision of the dominant firm in a market. Let $f(p) = a-bp$ ($f(p)$ is market demand for the good in question). Show that the $x' = 0$ and $m' = 0$ loci are

$$x' = 0 \qquad k\beta m = \beta x - \alpha + \bar{p}$$
$$m' = 0 \qquad (r+k\beta)m = \beta x - \alpha + c$$

where $\alpha = \dfrac{(a+bc)}{2b}$ and $\beta = \dfrac{1}{2b}$. Draw these loci in the (x, m)-plane and deduce that there are two possible paths to the steady state (x^*, m^*), depending on the original size of the 'competitive fringe' $x(0)$. Show that if $x(0) < x^*$ the dominant firm gradually lowers its price towards the limit price $\bar{p}$, inducing rival entry, whilst if $x(0) > x^*$ the optimal strategy is to price below the limit price, continuously driving out rivals.

Either by diagrammatic argument, or by solving $x' = m' = 0$ for the steady state values, show that $\partial x^*/\partial \bar{p} < 0$ and $\partial x^*/\partial c > 0$ and interpret.

Show also that $\partial x^*/\partial k \leq 0$ if $\bar{p} \geq c$. How do you explain this?

If $\bar{p} = c$, show that $x^* = f(\bar{p})$ and explain.

The reader is referred to Yohe (1984, pp. 39–49), for discussion of the dynamic effects of the anticipated/unanticipated introduction and removal of an investment credit as in Problem B. Gaskins (1971) discusses comparative dynamics for the limit-pricing example: see also Ireland (1972).

7.9 OTHER APPROACHES TO DYNAMIC OPTIMIZATION

As we have now seen, the Lagrangean approach to constrained optimization can be fruitfully extended from the static to the continuous-time dynamic case.

There are other approaches to dynamic optimization in continuous time. We shall outline here, albeit briefly, two: the *calculus of variations* and *dynamic programming* approaches. The latter provides an important line of attack for discrete-time dynamic optimization, and we point to this at the end of the chapter.

The calculus of variations   This is a line of approach which preceded the Lagrangean approach historically. It is applied to problems in the format

$$\max_{x} \int_0^T f(t, x, x') \, dt$$
$$\text{st } x(0) = x_0 \qquad x(T) = x_T \tag{7.82}$$

although other forms of end-point condition can be accommodated.

This format is not very far removed from the optimal control theory format (7.15). There, we had a control variable u in the objective function and a constraint $x' = g(t, x, u)$. If this constraint could be inverted, i.e. solved for u in terms of t, x and x', then we could eliminate u from the objective function and the optimal control problem would be in precisely the right format for the calculus of variations approach.

7.9.1 Exercise

Write each of Problems A, B and C in the format (7.82). Similarly, put the problems in Exercises 7.7.1(c) and 7.7.1(d) into this format.

The idea behind the calculus of variations method of solving dynamic optimization problems is very simple.

Suppose that a solution to problem (7.82) exists, and is of the form $x(t) = \hat{x}(t)$. Now let $h(t)$ be any differentiable function for which $h(0) = h(T) = 0$, and consider the path

$$x_a(t) = \hat{x}(t) + ah(t) \tag{7.83}$$

for $x(t)$. Then x_a is *feasible* for problem (7.82), because it satisfies the end-point conditions. It is in fact a *variation* from the optimal path, approaching optimality when $a \to 0$. Therefore

$$I(a) = \int_0^T f(t, x_a, x_a') \, dt \tag{7.84}$$

is maximized at $a = 0$. This must be true whatever the function $h(t)$ (provided it satisfies $h(0) = h(T) = 0$).

The first-order condition $I'(a) = 0$ must therefore be satisfied *for all* $h(t)$ *satisfying* $h(0) = h(T) = 0$.

This fact will yield a necessary condition, the *Euler equation*, which forms the basis of the calculus of variations solution technique.

Let us examine $I'(a)$. Differentiating under the integral sign in equation (7.84) with respect to a (recall our discussion of this in Example 1.8.3, p. 29), we have

$$I'(a) = \int_0^T \left[f_2(t, x_a, x_a') \left(\frac{\partial x_a}{\partial a} \right) + f_3(t, x_a, x_a') \left(\frac{\partial x_a'}{\partial a} \right) \right] dt$$

$$= \int_0^T [f_2(t, x_a, x_a')h(t) + f_3(t, x_a, x_a')h'(t)] \, dt$$

assuming differentiability of h, from equation (7.83). We use f_2 and f_3 for the derivatives $\partial f / \partial x$ and $\partial f / \partial x'$ respectively. Then

$$I'(0) = \int_0^T [f_2(t, \hat{x}, \hat{x}')h(t) + f_3(t, \hat{x}, \hat{x}')h'(t)] \, dt.$$

Now integrate the second term by parts, using $h(0) = h(T) = 0$:

$$I'(0) = \int_0^T \left\{ f_2(t, \hat{x}, \hat{x}') - \frac{d}{dt} [f_3(t, x, x')] \right\} h(t) \, dt.$$

If this is to be zero for all $h(t)$ then we require

$$f_2(t, x, x') = \frac{d}{dt} [f_3(t, x, x')] \tag{7.85}$$

at the optimum $x = \hat{x}$ (see Exercise 1.6.4(c), p. 24).

Equation (7.85) is a necessary condition for the solution of the problem in hand and is known as the *Euler equation*. If $f(t, x, x')$ is concave in x and x' it is also sufficient. The Euler equation is more often to be seen in the form:

$$\frac{\partial f}{\partial x} = \frac{d}{dt} \left(\frac{\partial f}{\partial x'} \right). \tag{7.86}$$

Historically the Euler equation preceded the Hamiltonian conditions for solving dynamic optimization problems. The Euler equation may be derived from the Hamiltonian conditions: this was the substance of

Exercise 7.7.1(f). But not only does optimal control theory address a rather wider class of problems than the calculus of variations; it also yields the co-state variable with its economically very informative interpretation. For detailed treatments of the calculus of variations, see Hadley and Kemp (1971) and Kamien and Schwartz (1981).

7.9.2 Exercise

Apply the Euler equation to any one of the following: Problem A, Problem B, Problem C, Exercises 7.7.1(c) and (d). Compare the outcome with the Hamiltonian conditions. What is lost by adopting the Euler equation approach?

Finally, we note that the Euler equation applies equally to multivariate problems. We may regard x as a vector $\underline{x}$ in problem (7.82), and $h(t)$ as a vector of deviations from the optimal path $\underline{x}(t)$. Then replace $ah(t)$ by $\underline{a}'\underline{h}(t)$. The function $I(\underline{a})$ is maximized at $\underline{a} = 0$. Replace $I'(a)$ by $\partial I/\partial a_i$. The mathematics hardly changes and the Euler equations are $(1 \leqslant i \leqslant n)$:

$$\frac{\partial f}{\partial x_i} = \frac{\mathrm{d}}{\mathrm{d}t}\left(\frac{\partial f}{\partial x_i'}\right). \tag{7.87}$$

7.9.3 Exercise

Express the Jorgenson investment problem of Exercise 7.7.1(e) in a format suitable for applying the Euler equations (7.87). Derive the results in Exercise 7.7.1(e), parts (ii)–(iii), for the marginal products of labour and capital along the optimal path.

Dynamic programming   Dynamic programming is the name given to a line of approach to problems in the optimal control theory format. By simple manipulation of the maximum value function, a condition emerges, known as *Bellman's equation*, which is necessary for the optimal time-path of the control variable u. Bellman's equation is intimately linked with the Hamiltonian conditions, and for continuous time problems it is more difficult to solve. Thus dynamic programming does not offer any advantages over optimal control theory for continuous time problems, but as we shall see the discrete time version can be very useful and illuminating. Dynamic programming is essentially the only technique available to the economist for discrete time optimization.

   We begin by outlining the approach in continuous time. We confine ourselves to fixed end-point problems. Recall that in section 7.6 we split up the optimization problem

$$\max_{u} \int_0^T f(t, x, u)\,\mathrm{d}t$$
$$\text{st } x' = g(t, x, u) \qquad x(0) = x_0 \qquad x(T) = x_T \tag{7.17}$$

into two parts:

$$\max_{u} \int_0^s f(t,x,u)\,dt \qquad\qquad \max_{u} \int_s^T f(t,x,u)\,dt$$

st $\quad x' = g(t,x,u)$ PLUS st $\quad x' = g(t,x,u)$

$\qquad x(0) = x_0 \qquad\qquad\qquad\qquad x(s) = \hat{x}(s)$

$\qquad x(s) = \hat{x}(s) \qquad\qquad\qquad\qquad x(T) = x_T$

and we wrote the maximum value as

$$V = V_1 + V_2. \tag{7.33}$$

We argued that this was legitimate, and would lead to the same solution as the undivided problem, because of the nature of the optimization. Actually, our argument rested upon the basic principle of dynamic programming, known as the *principle of optimality*. This is defined, perhaps most succinctly, by Kamien and Schwartz (1981, p. 238):

> An optimal path has the property that whatever the initial conditions and control values over some initial period, the control...over the remaining period must be optimal for the remaining problem, with the state resulting from the early decisions considered as the initial condition.

Let us adopt a more sophisticated notation for the maximum value function. Specifically, let $V[s,x\,|\,T,y]$ be the maximum value for the more general problem

$$\max_{u} \int_s^T f(t,x,u)$$

st $x' = g(t,x,u) \qquad x(s) = x \qquad x(T) = y.$

Then equation (7.33) can be written

$$V[0,x_0\,|\,T,x_T] = V[0,x_0\,|\,s,\hat{x}(s)] + V[s,\hat{x}(s)\,|\,T,x_T] \tag{7.88}$$

and the result that gives us the interpretation of the co-state variable is

$$\lambda(s) = \frac{\partial V[s,\hat{x}(s)\,|\,T,x_T]}{\partial \hat{x}(s)} \tag{7.89}$$

(see equations (7.32)–(7.35)).

The principle of optimality may be applied again, to the second term in equation (7.88), breaking up the interval $[s,T]$ into subintervals $[s,s+ds]$

and $[s+ds, T]$;

$$V[s, \hat{x}(s) \mid T, x_T] = V[s, \hat{x}(s) \mid s+ds, \hat{x}(s+ds)]$$
$$+ V[s+ds, \hat{x}(s+ds) \mid T, x_T]. \quad (7.90)$$

We now explore this result; it yields a fundamental proposition in dynamic programming. The first term on the right-hand side of equation (7.90) is the integral of $f(t, x, u)$ over the very small range $[s, s+ds]$. Now any integral is an area = height × base; and in this case, base = ds and height $\doteq f[s, \hat{x}(s), \hat{u}(s)]$. Thus equation (7.90) becomes, approximately:

$$V[s, \hat{x}(s) \mid T, x_T] = f[s, \hat{x}(s), \hat{u}(s)] ds + V[s+ds, \hat{x}(s+ds) \mid T, x_T]. \quad (7.91)$$

The next step is to recall the maximization process that defines the optimal control $\hat{u}(s)$: we claim that equation (7.91) may be written

$$V[s, \hat{x}(s) \mid T, x_T] = \max_u \{ f(s, \hat{x}(s), u) ds$$
$$+ V[s+ds, \hat{x}(s)+g(s, \hat{x}(s), u) ds \mid T, x_T] \}. \quad (7.92)$$

This is because if u had been chosen in the time period $(s, s+ds)$, and not $\hat{u}$, then the right-hand side of equation (7.91) would have been equal to the maximand in equation (7.92): the state variable at time $s+ds$ would have been, not $\hat{x}(s+dx)$, but

$$x(s+ds) \doteq \hat{x}(s)+x'(s) ds = \hat{x}(s)+g[t, \hat{x}(s), u]$$

because of the constraint $x' = g(t, x, u)$ (which ensures that $x(.)$ is differentiable). The value $\hat{u}$ is defined as the best possible choice of u: hence the maximization in equation (7.92).

We may write equation (7.92) as:

$$V[s, \hat{x} \mid T, x_T] = \max_u \{ f(s, \hat{x}, u) ds + V[s+ds, \hat{x}+dx \mid T, x_T] \} \quad (7.93)$$

where $\hat{x}+dx$ is the value of the state variable at time $s+ds$ if the control is $u(s) = u$. This is known as the *fundamental recurrence relation of dynamic programming*. It has an illuminating discrete-time analogue, which we come to very soon.

But we can take equation (7.93) further. Dropping the T, x_T arguments from V for convenience, we may expand

$$V(s+ds, \hat{x}+dx) = V[s+ds, \hat{x}+dx \mid T, x_T]$$

about $V(s, \hat{x})$ using the first-order approximation of Taylor's theorem (see

p. 10). Now cancel terms, and (noting that $dx = g(t, \hat{x}, u \, ds)$ divide throughout by ds:

$$V_1(s, \hat{x}) + \max_u \left[V_2(s, \hat{x})g(t, \hat{x}, u) + f(t, \hat{x}, u) \right] = 0. \tag{7.94}$$

This result is known as *Bellman's equation*. It is a 'partial differential equation' which, in principle at least, can be solved for the maximum value function V.

The importance of dynamic programming as a solution technique is primarily through its applicability to discrete-time problems. But before we turn to this, let us note a simple relation between Bellman's equation and the Hamiltonian. Substitute $\lambda = V_2(s, \hat{x})$ into equation (7.94) from equation (7.89), and recall the definition of the Hamiltonian, $H(\lambda, s, x, u) = f(s, x, u) + \lambda g(s, x, u)$. Thus equation (7.94) is

$$V_s + \max_u H(\lambda, s, \hat{x}, u) = 0. \tag{7.95}$$

This is another version of Bellman's equation; as in Pontryagin's Maximum Principle, maximization of the Hamiltonian is involved.

We now turn to dynamic programming in discrete time. Consider the problem

$$\max_{u_t} \sum_{t=0}^{T} f_t(x_t, u_t) \tag{7.96}$$

$$\text{st } x_{t+1} = g_t(x_t, u_t) \qquad x(0) = x_0 \qquad x(T) \text{ free}$$

(where T may be infinite). Given the state variable x_s in period s, the choice of control u_s in that period determines the value of the state variable in the next period, x_{s+1}. This affects the time $(s+1)$ choice of control. How do we choose the optimal time path for the control variable?

Let $V(s, x_s)$ be the maximum value obtainable from time $t = s$ to time $t = T$ given an initial (time s) state variable x_s. The discrete-time version of the fundamental recurrence relation of dynamic programming is

$$V(s, x_s) = \max_{u_s} \left[f_s(x_s, u_s) + V(s+1, x_{s+1}) \right] \tag{7.97}$$

(compare equation (7.93)). It says that the maximum value obtainable from date s onwards equals the maximized sum of the value obtained at date s and the future optimal value $V(s+1, x_{s+1})$. We do not, however, choose u_s to maximize the current contribution to value, $f_s(s, u_s)$: the right-hand side of equation (7.97) makes clear the trade-off between this and the value obtainable in future periods.

One can use the fundamental recurrence relation to obtain a step-by-step solution to problem (7.96) by backward induction.

First, consider the time $s = T$ version of equation (7.97). There is only one term to maximize: let $\hat{u}_T$ be the value of u_T that maximizes $f_t(x_T, u_T)$ conditional on the value of x_T. Now consider the time $s = T - 1$ problem. Let $\hat{u}_{T-1}$ solve the problem

$$\max_{u_{T-1}} \left[f_{T-1}(x_{T-1}, u_{T-1}) + V(T, x_T) \right]$$

conditional on x_{T-1} and x_T. In fact $\hat{u}_{T-1}$ determines the optimal x_T conditional upon x_{T-1}:

$$\hat{x}_T = g_{T-1}(x_{T-1}, \hat{u}_{T-1}). \tag{7.98}$$

Thus the solution for the last two periods is actually conditional only upon x_{T-1}. Continuing backwards, we reach the beginning, at time $t = 0$. Now the entire solution has been traced out, conditional only upon x_0 – *which is known*.

Backward induction can be handled easily by computer; this provides a practicable means of solving many discrete-time, finite-horizon dynamic programming problems.

For problems with an infinite time horizon, backwards induction is, of course, inapplicable.

In Hey (1979, pp. 47–55), there is an interesting survey and theoretical analysis of certain discrete-time versions of Problem A, concerning an individual's consumption and savings decision through time. Both finite and infinite horizon problems are addressed.

The reader is also referred to Bellman (1957), Bellman and Dreyfus (1962) and Larson and Casti (1982), for more detailed material on dynamic programming.

Appendix   The Generalized Gradient Vector and Constrained Optimization

We saw in chapter 1 (Example 1.1.1(b), p. 3) that the function $h(x) = |x|$ is not differentiable at the point $x = 0$. Similar restrictions are true of some multivariate functions. For example $h(x_1, x_2) = |x_1| + x_2$ is not differentiable with respect to x_1 at any point of the form $(0, x_2)$. Directional (left and right) derivatives exist at the points of non-differentiability of these functions, and they convey useful information; but there are many non-differentiable functions for which directional derivatives do not exist.

In this appendix, we extend the differential calculus to a certain class of non-differentiable functions, and report an application to constrained optimization, both static and dynamic, recently made by Clarke (1979).

Not only does Clarke's approach widen the class of functions for which we may use calculus to solve optimization problems (and this in itself is important); but for differentiable functions too, his method provides an elegant alternative way of deriving the Arrow–Enthoven and Hamiltonian conditions.

First, let us define a *distance function* that measures 'how far apart' two n-tuples $\underline{x} = (x_1, x_2, \ldots, x_n)$ and $\underline{z} = (z_1, z_2, \ldots, z_n)$ are in n-dimensional space. Specifically, let

$$d(x, z) = \|\underline{x} - \underline{z}\| = \sqrt{\left[\sum_{i=1}^{n} (x_i - z_i)^2 \right]}. \tag{A1}$$

When $n = 1$, x and z are two points on the real line (e.g. on the x-axis of the graph in figure A1(a)); then $d(x, z) = \|x - z\|$ is the distance $|x - z|$ between these two points. For $n = 2$, we have

$$\|(x_1, x_2) - (z_1, z_2)\| = \sqrt{[(x_1 - z_1)^2 + (x_2 - z_2)^2]}.$$

By Pythagoras' rule, this is the distance apart of two points P and Q whose co-ordinates in two-dimensional space are (x_1, x_2) and (z_1, z_2): see figure A1(b).

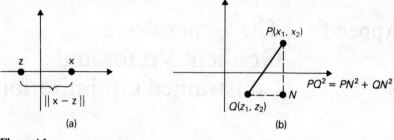

Figure A1

The distance function $d(.,.)$ is known as the *Euclidean metric* in n-dimensional space, and $\|.\|$ is the *Euclidean norm*.

We can now define a class of functions to which the differential calculus may be extended. A function $h(x_1, x_2, \ldots, x_n) = h(\underline{x})$ of n variables is said to be *locally Lipschitz* if, for every point $\underline{x}_0$, there exists a small number $\varepsilon > 0$ and a (possibly big) number $K > 0$ such that whenever $\|\underline{x} - \underline{x}_0\| < \varepsilon$ and $\|\underline{z} - \underline{x}_0\| < \varepsilon$, it is the case that

$$|h(\underline{x}) - h(\underline{z})| < K . \|\underline{x} - \underline{z}\|. \tag{A2}$$

It can be shown that differentiable functions are locally Lipschitz. We can illustrate this very easily for $n = 1$ in the special case that $h(x)$ is *twice* differentiable, using Taylor's theorem. We can write

$$h(x) - h(x_0) = (x - x_0)h'(x_0) + (x - x_0)^2 h''(x_0 + \theta_1[x - x_0])/2!$$

$$h(z) - h(x_0) = (z - x_0)h'(x_0) + (z - x_0)^2 h''(x_0 + \theta_2[z - x_0])/2!$$

where $\theta_1, \theta_2 \in (0, 1)$ (see equations (1.11) and (1.12), p. 9). Subtracting, we get

$$h(x) - h(z) = (x - z)h'(x_0) + R$$

where

$$R = \{(x - x_0)^2 h''(x_0 + \theta_1[x - x_0]) - (z - x_0)^2 h''(x_0 + \theta_2[z - x_0])\}/2!$$

If $h'(x_0) \neq 0$ then by taking x and z close enough to x_0 (closer than some ε), R becomes negligible in relation to the other term. We can certainly ensure, for example, that

$$|h(x) - h(z)| < 2|x - z| . |h'(x_0)|$$

by suitable choice of ε. Now put $K = 2|h'(x_0)|$ for condition (A2). The extension to the case $h'(x_0) = 0$, and more generally to once-differentiable functions of $n \geqslant 1$ variables, is not hard.

However, the class of locally Lipschitz functions is considerably wider than the class of differentiable functions. For example, it includes the functions $h(x) = |x|$ and $h(x_1, x_2) = |x_1| + x_2$. (As an exercise, verify condition (A2) in these cases: you only need to do so for points $\underline{x}_0$ of non-differentiability.) In fact all continuous and concave or convex functions are locally Lipschitz: this is an important class of functions in economics.

An extended calculus for the class of locally Lipschitz functions is defined as follows. Let $h(\underline{x})$ be locally Lipschitz. At any point $\underline{x} = \underline{x}_0$ where $h(\underline{x})$ is not differentiable, we may detect sequences $\underline{x}_i$ of points at which $h(\underline{x})$ *is* differentiable and such that $\underline{x}_i \to \underline{x}_0$. The gradient vector at one of these points $\underline{x}_i$, $\nabla h(\underline{x}_i)$ as defined in equation (3.8), p. 78, is an $n \times 1$ column vector. Let $\mathbf{R}^n$ be the set of all $n \times 1$ column vectors. As $\underline{x}_i \to \underline{x}_0$, $\nabla h(\underline{x}_i)$ may or may not approach a limit in $\mathbf{R}^n$. We discard sequences $\underline{x}_i$ approaching $\underline{x}_0$ for which the gradient vector $\nabla h(\underline{x}_i)$ does not approach a limit in $\mathbf{R}^n$. Now define the *generalized gradient vector* of $h(\underline{x})$ at $\underline{x}_0$ as

$$\partial h(\underline{x}_0) = \text{the smallest convex subset of } \mathbf{R}^n \text{ that contains all limits}$$

$$\lim_{\underline{x}_i \to \underline{x}_0} \nabla h(\underline{x}_i).$$

This construction is known as the *convex hull* of the limits.

Recall the definition of a convex set in the proof of Theorem 5.2.3, p. 120. In fact $\partial h(\underline{x}_0)$ consists of all points in $\mathbf{R}^n$ which are 'convex combinations' of limits of gradient vectors:

$$\underline{u} \in \partial h(\underline{x}_0) \Leftrightarrow \underline{u} = \sum_i \lambda_i \cdot \left[\lim_{\underline{x}_i \to \underline{x}_0} \nabla h(\underline{x}_i) \right] \tag{A3}$$

where each λ_i is non-negative and $\sum_i \lambda_i = 1$.

If $h(\underline{x})$ is differentiable at $\underline{x} = \underline{x}_0$, then, fairly clearly,

$$\partial h(\underline{x}_0) = \nabla h(\underline{x}_0). \tag{A4}$$

In this case the generalized gradient vector (a set) contains a single point in $\mathbf{R}^n$, the gradient vector itself. If $h(\underline{x})$ is not differentiable at $\underline{x} = \underline{x}_0$, then $\partial h(\underline{x}_0)$ can be quite large.

For example, consider the $n = 1$ case $h(x) = |x|$ and let $x_0 = 0$. If a sequence x_i approaches zero from the left, then the gradient vector ($=$ ordinary derivative) at x_i is -1; for sequences approaching from the right, the gradient vector is $+1$. Thus the generalized gradient vector of $h(x)$ at $x = 0$ is the interval $\partial h(0) = [-1, 1]$. The reader may like to convince himself that in the $n = 2$ case of the function $h(x_1, x_2) = |x_1| + x_2$, the generalized gradient vector at the origin equals the set of all points in

$\mathbf{R}^2$ of the form $\begin{bmatrix} t \\ 1 \end{bmatrix}$ where $-1 \leqslant t \leqslant 1$.

Two important properties of the generalized gradient vector are as follows. We do not prove them here. The first extends a familiar condition for maximum and minimum points of differentiable functions:

P1. If $h(\underline{x})$ has a maximum or minimum at $\hat{\underline{x}}$, then $\underline{0} \in \partial h(\hat{\underline{x}})$.

Here, $\underline{0}$ is the zero vector. Recall that the function $h(x) = x$ has a minimum at $x = 0$; we have already seen that $\underline{0} \in \partial h(0)$.

The second property is, perhaps, harder to grasp:

P2. If $h_1, h_2, \ldots, h_m$ are m locally Lipschitz functions and if for each $\underline{x}$ we define

$$h(\underline{x}) = \max\{h_1(\underline{x}), h_2(\underline{x}), \ldots, h_m(\underline{x})\}$$

then $h(\underline{x})$ is locally Lipschitz, and for each $\underline{x}_0$ the generalized gradient vector $\partial h(\underline{x}_0)$ is equal to the smallest convex subset of $\mathbf{R}^n$ containing the generalized gradient vectors $\partial h_j(\underline{x}_0)$ for all those j such that $h_j(\underline{x}_0) = h(\underline{x}_0)$.

The reader could verify that if $h_1(x_1, x_2) = |x_1| + x_2$ and if $h_2(x_1, x_2) = x_1 + |x_2|$ then $h = \max\{h_1, h_2\}$ is defined by

$$h(x_1, x_2) = \begin{cases} h_2(x_1, x_2) & \text{if } x_2 \leqslant 0 \quad \text{and} \quad x_2 \leqslant x_1 \\ h_1(x_1, x_2) & \text{otherwise,} \end{cases}$$

and $\partial h(0,0)$ is the set of all points $\begin{bmatrix} u \\ v \end{bmatrix}$ in $\mathbf{R}^2$ for which $-1 \leqslant u \leqslant 1$, $-1 \leqslant v \leqslant 1$ and $u + v \geqslant 0$.

We have outlined enough properties of the generalized gradient vector now to demonstrate Clarke's (1979) derivation of the Arrow–Enthoven conditions (5.14), p. 122, for constrained static optimization.

Consider, then, the problem

$$\max_{\underline{x}} f(\underline{x})$$

$$\text{st } \underline{g}(\underline{x}) \leqslant \underline{b} \tag{5.5}$$

and assume only that $f(\underline{x})$ and all of the $g_j(\underline{x})$ are locally Lipschitz. This would be true, for example, if $f(\underline{x})$ and each $g_j(\underline{x})$ were differentiable, or if, as in Theorem 5.2.3, $f(\underline{x})$ were concave and each $g_j(\underline{x})$ convex. But given P1 and P2 above, we do not need any of these specific assumptions to establish the existence of Lagrange multipliers as in Theorem 5.2.3.

Suppose that $\underline{x} = \hat{\underline{x}}$ is the unique solution to maximization problem (5.5), and let

$$h(\underline{x}) = \max\{f(\hat{\underline{x}}) - f(\underline{x}), g_1(\underline{x}) - b_1, g_2(\underline{x}) - b_2, \ldots, g_m(\underline{x}) - b_m\}.$$

It is immediately clear that

$$h(\hat{\underline{x}}) = 0 \tag{A5}$$

and that if $h(\underline{x}) < 0$ then, (i) $\underline{x}$ is feasible for the optimization problem, because $g_j(\underline{x}) < b_j$ for each j; and (ii) $f(\hat{\underline{x}}) - f(\underline{x}) < 0$. But taken together (i) and (ii) contradict the fact that $\hat{\underline{x}}$ was defined as the optimum. Therefore we must have:

$$\text{for all } \underline{x}, \ h(\underline{x}) \geqslant 0. \tag{A6}$$

From equation (A5) and property (A6) $\hat{\underline{x}}$ is a minimum point of the function $h(\underline{x})$. Therefore, by P1 we have

$$\underline{0} \in \partial h(\hat{\underline{x}}). \tag{A7}$$

Also, by P2 $\partial h(\hat{\underline{x}})$ is the smallest convex subset of $\mathbf{R}^n$ containing the generalized gradient vectors at $\hat{\underline{x}}$ of those functions among $[f(\hat{\underline{x}}) - f(\underline{x})]$, $[g_1(\underline{x}) - b_1]$, $[g_2(\underline{x}) - b_2], \ldots, [g_m(\underline{x}) - b_m]$ which, evaluated at $\hat{\underline{x}}$, are zero. This is trivially true of the first of these functions, $[f(\hat{\underline{x}}) - f(\underline{x})]$; it is also true of those $[g_j(\underline{x}) - b_j]$ which represent binding constraints at the optimum. Since, fairly clearly,

$$\partial[f(\hat{\underline{x}}) - f(\underline{x})] = -\partial f(\underline{x})$$

and

$$\partial[g_j(\underline{x}) - b_j] = \partial g_j(\underline{x})$$

for all $\underline{x}$, we have the following: there exists a non-negative number λ_0, and non-negative numbers λ_j, one for each constraint $g_j(\underline{x}) < b_j$ which binds at the optimum, such that

$$\underline{0} \in -\lambda_0 \partial f(\hat{\underline{x}}) + \Sigma \lambda_j \partial g_j(\hat{\underline{x}}) \tag{A8}$$

and such that $\lambda_0 + \Sigma \lambda_j = 1$. The summation is over the binding constraints.

Let us assume for the moment that $\lambda_0 \neq 0$. Then (A8) can be written

$$\underline{0} \in \partial f(\hat{\underline{x}}) - \Sigma \left(\frac{\lambda_j}{\lambda_0}\right) \partial g_j(\hat{\underline{x}})$$

or as:

$$\underline{0} \in \partial f(\hat{\underline{x}}) - \sum_{j=1}^{m} \hat{\lambda}_j \partial g_j(\hat{\underline{x}}) \tag{A9}$$

where $\hat{\lambda}_j = 0$ if the constraint is slack.

This says that $\underline{0} \in \partial L(\hat{\underline{x}})$, where $L(\underline{x})$ is the Lagrangean function for the optimization problem; and that the complementary slackness condition holds between multipliers and constraints. It is a direct generalization of the Arrow–Enthoven conditions (5.14).

We stipulated that $\lambda_0 \neq 0$ in order to derive (A9). This is in fact a *constraint qualification*, needed to validate the Lagrangean approach. It says that there should not exist non-negative numbers λ_j, one for each binding constraint, such that

$$\underline{0} \in \Sigma \lambda_j \partial g_j(\hat{\underline{x}}).$$

Suppose that there are k binding constraints, and that the relevant functions g_j are differentiable. Then the constraint qualification is satisfied if the $k \times n$ matrix $A = (\partial g_j / \partial x_i)$ of partial derivatives of the binding constraint functions has rank equal to k, the number of binding constraints at the optimum. In particular (and intuitively reasonably) this requires $k \leqslant n$: the number of binding constraints must not exceed the number of variables (recall section 2.5 of chapter 2, especially equation (2.11), p. 50). Constraint qualifications of this form are. discussed in Kamien and Schwartz (1981).

Optimal control problems in the format (7.17) can also be addressed using Clarke's generalized gradient vector approach. This is helpful for problems with non-differentiable Hamiltonians. A continuous version of the convex hull property P2 is needed; the mathematics goes beyond the level of this book. For more details, see Clarke (1979), and associated references. Clarke's approach is also described in the chapter on non-differentiable optimization in Fletcher (1981).

References

Apostol, T. (1974) *Mathematical Analysis: A Modern Approach to Advanced Calculus*. Reading, Mass.: Addison-Wesley.

Arrow, K. J. and Enthoven, A. C. (1961) Quasi-concave programming. *Econometrica*, **29**, 779–800.

Arrow, K. J. and Kurz, M. (1970) *Public Investment, the Rate of Return and Optimal Fiscal Policy*. Baltimore: Johns Hopkins.

Bellman, R. (1957) *Dynamic Programming*. Princeton, N.J.: Princeton University Press.

Bellman, R. and Dreyfus, S. (1962) *Applied Dynamic Programming*. Princeton, N.J.: Princeton University Press.

Buiter, W. H. (1980) Walras' law and all that: budget constraints and balance sheet constraints in period models and continuous time models. *International Economic Review*, **21**, 1–16.

Burrows, P. and Hitiris, T. (1974) *Macroeconomic Theory: A Mathematical Introduction*. London: John Wiley.

Casson, M. (1973) *Introduction to Mathematical Economics*. London: Nelson.

Chiang, A. C. (1984) *Fundamental Methods of Mathematical Economics*. London: McGraw-Hill.

Clarke, F. H. (1979) Optimal control and the true Hamiltonian. *SIAM Review*, **21**, 157–66.

Cowell, F. A. (1977) *Measuring Inequality*. Oxford: Philip Allan.

Deaton, A. and Muellbauer, J. (1980) *Economics and Consumer Behavior*. Cambridge: University Press.

Dixit, A. K. (1976) *Optimization in Economic Theory*. Oxford: University Press.

Dorfman, R. (1969) An economic interpretation of optimal control theory. *American Economic Review*, **49**, 817–31.

Fletcher, R. (1981) *Practical Methods of Optimization*, Volume 2: *Constrained Optimization*. Chichester: John Wiley.

Fries, A., Hutton, J. P. and Lambert, P. J. (1982) The elasticity of the U.S. individual income tax: its calculation, determinants and behavior. *Review of Economics and Statistics*, **64**, 147–51.

Gandolpho, G. (1980) *Economic Dynamics: Methods and Models*. Amsterdam: North-Holland.

Gaskins, D. W. (1971) Dynamic limit pricing: optimal pricing under threat of entry. *Journal of Economic Theory*, **3**, 306–22.

Glaister, S. (1984) *Mathematical Methods for Economists*. Oxford: Blackwell.

Hadley, G. (1962) *Linear Programming*. Reading, Mass.: Addison-Wesley.

Hadley, G. (1964) *Nonlinear and Dynamic Programming*. Reading, Mass.: Addison-Wesley.

Hadley, G. and Kemp, M. C. (1971) *Variational Methods in Economics*. New York: North-Holland.

Henderson, J. M. and Quandt, R. E. (1980) *Microeconomic Theory: A Mathematical Approach*. London: McGraw-Hill.

Hey, J. D. (1979) *Uncertainty in Microeconomics*. Oxford: Martin Robertson.

Hutton, J. P. and Lambert, P. J. (1979) Income tax progressivity and revenue growth. *Economics Letters*, 3, 377–80.

Hutton, J. P. and Lambert, P. J. (1982) Modelling the effects of income growth and discretionary change on the sensitivity of U.K. income tax revenues. *Economic Journal*, 92, 145–55.

Intrilligator, M. D. (1971) *Mathematical Optimization and Economic Theory*. Englewood Cliffs, N.J.: Prentice-Hall.

Ireland, N. J. (1972) Concentration and the growth of market demand: a comment on Gaskins limit pricing model. *Journal of Economic Theory*, 5, 303–5.

Jorgenson, D. W. (1963) Capital theory and investment behavior. *American Economic Review, Proceedings*, 53, 247–59.

Kamien, M. I. and Schwartz, N. L. (1981) *Dynamic Optimization: The Calculus of Variations and Optimal Control in Economics and Management*. New York: North-Holland.

Karlin, S. (1959) *Mathematical Methods and Theory in Games, Programming and Economics*. Reading, Mass.: Addison-Wesley.

Katzner, D. W. (1970) *Static Demand Theory*. New York: Macmillan.

Keating, G. (1985) *The Production and Use of Economic Forecasts*. London: Methuen.

Lambert, P. J. and Poskitt, D. S. (1983) *Stationary Processes in Time Series Analysis: the Mathematical Foundations*. Gottingen: Vandenhoeck & Ruprecht.

Lancaster, K. (1968) *Mathematical Economics*. New York: Macmillan.

Larson, R. E. and Casti, J. L. (1982) *Principles of Dynamic Programming* (in two parts). New York: Dekker.

Madden, P. (1985) *Concavity and Optimization*. Oxford: Basil Blackwell.

Mangasarian, O. L. (1966) Sufficient conditions for the optimal control of nonlinear systems. *SIAM Control Journal*, 4, 139–52.

Meyer, P. A. (1983) Money multipliers and the slopes of IS–LM. *Southern Economic Journal*, 49, 226–9.

Nordhaus, W. (1982) How fast should we graze the global commons? *American Economic Review, Proceedings*, 72, 242–6.

O'Nan, M. (1977) *Linear Algebra*. New York: Harcourt Brace Jovanovich.

Patinkin, D. (1965) *Money, Interest and Prices: An Integration of Monetary and Value Theory*. New York: Harper and Row.

Pontryagin, L. S., Boltyanskii, V. G., Gamkrelidze, R. V. and Mischenko, E. F. (1962) *The Mathematical Theory of Optimal Processes*, translated by K. N. Trirogoff. New York: Wiley.

Robinson, A. (1974) *Non-standard Analysis*. Amsterdam: North-Holland.

Samuelson, P. A. (1972) Maximum principles in analytical economics. *American Economic Review*, 57, 249–62.

Silberberg, E. (1971) The le Chatelier principle as a corollary to a generalized envelope theorem. *Journal of Economic Theory*, 3, 146–55.

Tobin, J. (1947) Liquidity preference and monetary policy. *Review of Economics and Statistics*, **29**, 124–31; reprinted as chapter 3 in Tobin, J. (1971) *Essays in Economics*, Volume I: *Macroeconomics*. Amsterdam: North-Holland.

Widder, D. (1961) *Advanced Calculus*. Englewood Cliffs, N.J.: Prentice-Hall.

Yohe, G. W. (1984) *Exercises and Applications for Microeconomic Analysis*. New York: Norton.

Answers to Exercises

Chapter 1

1.2.3(a) $y = x^4$ is convex; $y = -x^4$ is concave; both have zero second derivative at $x = 0$.

1.2.3(b) Maximum value $y = 21$ when $x = 2$ and when $x = 5$. Minimum value $y = 1$ when $x = 0$.

1.2.3(c) Both second derivatives are zero where they exist.

1.3.1(a) Put $a = b$, $x = c - b$ and $n = 2$ in equation (1.11).

1.3.1(b) If $y > x$ then there exist v, w such that $0 < v < x < w < y$ and

$$\frac{t(y) - t(x)}{(y - x)} = t'(w) > t'(v) = t(x)/x.$$

1.4.2(a) $f^{(n)}(x) = (-1)^{n-1}(n-1)!x^{-n}$.

1.4.2(b) No, because (1.13) is violated.

1.3.3(a) The first non-zero derivative of $y = \pm x^n$ at $x = 0$ is $y^{(n)} = \pm n!$ If n is odd, the turning point is an inflection. If n is even, $y = x^n$ has a minimum, and $y = -x^n$ a maximum, at $x = 0$.

1.3.3(b) $\sqrt{(100 + x)} = 10 + x/20 - x^2/4000 + 3x^3/800000 - \ldots$; 10.148.

1.7.2(a) For $x < 0$,

$$\frac{d}{dx}[\ln(-x)] = \frac{d}{d(-x)}[\ln(-x)] \cdot \frac{d(-x)}{dx} = \frac{1}{x}.$$

Hence when $a, b < 0$ we have

$$\int_a^b \left[\frac{1}{x}\right] dx = \ln(-b) - \ln(-a) = \ln\left(\frac{b}{a}\right)$$

just as for $a, b > 0$. If $ab < 0$ then $\int_a^b [1/x]\, dx$ is a divergent improper integral.

1.7.2(b) $\ln(2)/4$; $4^{123}/123$; the substitution implies $t = 0$ at each limit of integration, i.e. a trivial integral, and is invalid since the precondition for equation (1.49) is violated for $-4 \leqslant x \leqslant 1$.

214

1.7.2(c) $1; 4(1+\sqrt{2})/15$.

1.8.4(a) The formula for $\theta(p)$ follows from:

$$p = 1-[e/y]^a, \ X(p) = aeP(1-[e/y]^{a-1})/(a-1) \text{ and } \theta(p) = X(p)/X(1).$$

1.8.4(c) $\theta''(p) = \dfrac{1}{\mu f(y)}$.

1.9.1(b) $x(t) = e^{-P(t)}\int_0^t c(u)e^{-P(u)}\,du + d.e^{-P(t)}$. This is the analogue of (1.83a).

Chapter 2

2.1.2 1 and 3 have no solution, whilst 1 and 2 have ∞ solutions.

2.2.1(a) By Theorem 2.1.1 $A\underline{x} = \underline{0}$ has 0 or ∞ solutions. Since $\underline{x} = \underline{0}$ is one obvious solution, we must have ∞ solutions.

2.2.1(b) $A\underline{h} = \underline{b}$ and $A\underline{g} = \underline{0}$, so $A(\underline{h}+k\underline{g}) = A\underline{h}+kA\underline{g} = \underline{b}$.

2.2.1(c) If $A\underline{x} = \underline{b}$ then $A(\underline{x}-\underline{h}) = A\underline{x}-A\underline{h} = \underline{b}-\underline{b} = \underline{0}$, so $\underline{x}-\underline{h}$ is a vector $\underline{g}$ satisfying $A\underline{g} = \underline{0}$.

2.2.2(c) $AB = \begin{bmatrix} 18 & 36 & 6 \\ 6 & 10 & 2 \end{bmatrix}$; $A^tB = \begin{bmatrix} 18 & 24 & 6 \\ 30 & 38 & 10 \end{bmatrix}$;

BA and $C^t - AC^tB^t$ are impossible; $B^tA = (A^tB)^t$; and

$$C^t - B = \begin{bmatrix} 3 & -6 & -2 \\ 3 & 4 & 0 \end{bmatrix}.$$

2.2.2(d) $3x_1^2 + x_2^2 + 6x_1x_2$; $A = \begin{bmatrix} 1 & -\frac{3}{2} & 0 \\ -\frac{3}{2} & 2 & \frac{1}{2} \\ 0 & \frac{1}{2} & 0 \end{bmatrix}$.

2.2.2(e) $\underline{x}^tA\underline{y} = \Sigma\Sigma a_{ij}x_ix_j = (\underline{x}^tA\underline{y})^t = \underline{y}^tA^t\underline{x}$.

2.2.2(f) $B = IB = (A^{-1}A)B = A^{-1}I = A^{-1}$, so $BA = I$.

2.2.2(g) $I+A^{-1}B = A^{-1}(A+B) = $ a product of invertible matrices $= $ invertible.

2.2.2(h) $A+B = A(I+A^{-1}B) = AC^{-1} = $ the product of two invertible matrices.

2.2.2(i) No. For example, $A = -B = I$.

2.3.4(b) Zero.

2.3.4(c) Zero.

2.3.4(d) If you multiply the first row of A by -1, and also the first column, then the determinant is multiplied by $(-1) \times (-1) = 1$; the first element a_{11} is unaffected.

2.4.2(a) No: zero determinant.

2.4.2(b) The equation is $A(A-I) = 0$. If $\det A \neq 0$, A is invertible and $A - I = A^{-1}0 = 0$.

2.4.2(c) $\det AB = \det A \cdot \det B = \det I = 1$, therefore $\det A \neq 0$.

2.4.2(d) If $\det A \neq 0$ or $\det B \neq 0$ then A or B is invertible and this implies $B = A^{-1}0 = 0$ or $A = 0B^{-1} = 0$.

2.5.4(a) Third row = first row $+ 2 \times$ (second row).

2.5.4(b) $\Sigma a_i \underline{e}_i = \underline{a} = \underline{0}$ if and only if $a_i = 0$ for each i.

2.5.6 $3 \times$ (third row $-$ second row) $- 2 \times$ (fifth row) = row of zeros.

2.6.1(a) (i) Suppose for a contradiction rk $A = n$ and $A\underline{x} = \underline{b}$ has more than one solution. Then by Exercise 2.2.1(c), $A\underline{x} = \underline{0}$ has a non-zero solution, say $A\underline{a} = \underline{0}$ where $\underline{a} \neq 0$. This shows a linear dependence among the columns of A, i.e. rk $A < n$, a contradiction.

(ii) If $A\underline{x} = \underline{b}$ has a unique solution then $A\underline{x} = \underline{0}$ has no non-zero solution by Exercise 2.2.1(b). Thus the columns of A are linearly independent and rk $A \geqslant n$. By (2.12) rk $A \leqslant \min[m, n] = n$, hence rk $A = n$. Therefore there are also n linearly independent *rows* in A: the $m - n$ equations corresponding to the other rows are redundant.

2.6.2 $x_2 = -3$.

2.8.3(a) No other real eigenvalues. The eigenvectors are of the form

$$\underline{x} = a \begin{bmatrix} 1 \\ -6 \\ 9 \end{bmatrix}.$$

2.8.3(b) Characteristic polynomial $r^2 - (a+d)r + ad - bc = (r_1 - r)(r_2 - r)$ where $r_1 + r_2 = a + d = \text{tr } A$ and $r_1 r_2 = ad - bc = \det A$.

2.8.3(d) The only eigenvalue is $r = 1$ and its eigenvectors are of the form

$$a \begin{bmatrix} 0 \\ 1 \end{bmatrix}.$$

2.8.6(a) The general eigenvectors corresponding to $r = 0$, $r = 1$ and $r = -1$ are

$$a \begin{bmatrix} 0 \\ 1 \\ 0 \end{bmatrix}, b \begin{bmatrix} 1 \\ 0 \\ 1 \end{bmatrix} \text{ and } c \begin{bmatrix} 1 \\ 0 \\ -1 \end{bmatrix}$$

respectively. Those satisfying $\underline{x}^t\underline{x} = 1$ are in the columns of P.

$$P^t A P = \begin{bmatrix} 0 & 0 & 0 \\ 0 & 1 & 0 \\ 0 & 0 & -1 \end{bmatrix}.$$

2.8.6(b) The general eigenvector for $r = 0$ is

$$\begin{bmatrix} 2a \\ b \\ a \end{bmatrix},$$

the sum of

$$\underline{x}_1 = \begin{bmatrix} 0 \\ b \\ 0 \end{bmatrix} \text{ and } \underline{x}_2 = \begin{bmatrix} 2a \\ 0 \\ a \end{bmatrix}.$$

The general eigenvector for $r = 5$ is

$$\underline{x}_3 = \begin{bmatrix} c \\ 0 \\ -2c \end{bmatrix}.$$

The particular values of $\underline{x}_1$, $\underline{x}_2$ and $\underline{x}_3$ satisfying $\underline{x}_i^t\underline{x}_i = 1$ are obtained by putting $a = 1/\sqrt{5}$, $b = 1$ and $c = 1/\sqrt{5}$.

2.8.6(c) $\det(A - rI) = (r_1 - r)(r_2 - r)\dots(r_n - r)$. Now put $r = 0$.

2.9.1 If $A = \begin{bmatrix} -p & -q \\ 1 & 0 \end{bmatrix}$ then

$$\begin{bmatrix} y_p \\ x_p \end{bmatrix} = -A^{-1} \begin{bmatrix} c \\ 0 \end{bmatrix} = \begin{bmatrix} 0 \\ c/q \end{bmatrix},$$

i.e. $x_p = c/q$. The characteristic equation of A is $r^2 + pr + q = 0$. If $p^2 > 4q$ there are two real roots r_1 and r_2. If $p^2 = 4q$ there is a single eigenvalue $r = -p/2$ whose eigenvectors take the form

$$a \begin{bmatrix} 1 \\ -2/p \end{bmatrix}.$$

2.9.2 $A = \begin{bmatrix} -p & -q \\ 1 & 0 \end{bmatrix}$ and $\underline{k} = \begin{bmatrix} c \\ 0 \end{bmatrix}$,

as in Exercise 2.9.1. $\text{Det}(I - A) = 1 + p + q$.

$$(I - A)^{-1}\underline{k} = \begin{bmatrix} c/(1+p+q) \\ c/(1+p+q) \end{bmatrix}.$$

Results follow as in Exercise 2.9.1.

2.10.2(a) (i) $A = \begin{bmatrix} 0 & 0 & 1 \\ 0 & 0 & 0 \\ 1 & 0 & 0 \end{bmatrix}$; (ii) $A = \begin{bmatrix} 1 & 0 & -2 \\ 0 & 0 & 0 \\ -2 & 0 & 4 \end{bmatrix}$;

(iii) $A = \begin{bmatrix} 4 & 2 & 2 \\ 2 & 4 & 2 \\ 2 & 2 & 4 \end{bmatrix}$; (iv) $A = \begin{bmatrix} 3 & 1 & 0 & 0 & 0 \\ 1 & 3 & 0 & 0 & 0 \\ 0 & 0 & 2 & 1 & 1 \\ 0 & 0 & 1 & 2 & 1 \\ 0 & 0 & 1 & 1 & 2 \end{bmatrix}$.

2.10.2(b) $\underline{x}^t B^t \underline{x} = \underline{x}^t B \underline{x}$ from Exercise 2.2.2(e). Hence $\underline{x}^t A \underline{x} = \underline{x}^t B \underline{x}$ and $\underline{x}^t C \underline{x} = 0$.

2.10.6 (i) $r = 0, 1, -1$: indefinite. (ii) $r = 0, 0, 5$: positive semi-definite. (iii) $r = 2, 2, 8$: positive definite. (iv) $r = 1, 1, 2, 4, 4$: positive definite.

Chapter 3

3.1.2(a) $\dfrac{\partial y}{\partial x_1} = 6x_1 - 3x_2 \qquad \dfrac{\partial y}{\partial x_2} = 3x_2^2 - 3x_1.$

3.1.2(b) $\dfrac{\partial y}{\partial x_i} = x_j x_k \qquad (i \neq j \neq k = 1, 2, 3).$

3.1.2(c) $\dfrac{\partial y}{\partial x_1} = \dfrac{1}{x_1} \qquad \dfrac{\partial y}{\partial x_2} = 1 \qquad \dfrac{\partial y}{\partial x_3} = \dfrac{1}{x_3}.$

3.1.2(d) $\dfrac{\partial y}{\partial x_1} = x_2 x_1^{x_2 - 1} \qquad \dfrac{\partial y}{\partial x_2} = y \cdot \ln(x_1) \text{ if } x_1 > 0.$

3.1.2(e) $\dfrac{\partial Q}{\partial K} = \dfrac{aQ}{K} \qquad \dfrac{\partial Q}{\partial L} = \dfrac{bQ}{L}.$

3.1.2(f) $\dfrac{\partial Q}{\partial K} = \left(\dfrac{Q}{K}\right)^{r+1} \qquad \dfrac{\partial Q}{\partial L} = a\left(\dfrac{Q}{L}\right)^{r+1}.$

3.1.3(b) $\dfrac{\partial^2 Q}{\partial K^2} = \dfrac{a(a-1)Q}{K^2} \qquad \dfrac{\partial^2 Q}{\partial L^2} = \dfrac{b(b-1)Q}{L^2} \qquad \dfrac{\partial^2 Q}{\partial K \partial L} = \dfrac{abQ}{KL}.$

3.3.2(a) No turning points.

3.3.2(b) Turning points at $(x_1, x_2, x_3) = (a, 0, 1)$ and $(0, b, 1)$, for all $\dot{a}$ and all b.

3.3.2(c) See Exercise 3.5.1.

3.5.1 Putting $\underline{a} = (0, 1)$, the second-order Taylor series approximation is $f(\underline{x} + \underline{a}) \doteq -1 + 3x_1^2 + 4x_2^2 \geqslant -1 = f(\underline{a})$ suggesting a minimum at $\underline{a} = (0, 1)$.

3.6.2(c) Minimum at $(1, 1)$.

3.6.2(d) $\hat{x} = 40, \hat{y} = 24$.

3.6.2(e) $H(q) = 2D; \hat{q} = D^{-1}\underline{e}/2; \pi(\hat{q}) = -\underline{e}^t D^{-1}\underline{e}/4$.

3.7.4(a) If $\underline{x}' = (0, 0)$ then

$$f[k\underline{x} + (1-k)\underline{x}'] - [kf(\underline{x}) + (1-k)f(\underline{x}')] = -k(1-k)x_1 x_2 \lessgtr 0$$

according as $x_1 x_2 \gtrless 0$.

3.7.4(b) Trivial from definitions.

3.7.4(c) Apply Exercise 3.7.4(b) to Example 3.7.3(b).

3.7.7(a) $\det H(x_1, x_2) = 36x_2 - 9 \gtrless 0$ according as $x_2 \gtrless \frac{1}{4}$.

3.7.7(b)
$$H(x_1, x_2) = \begin{bmatrix} f''(x_1) & 0 \\ 0 & g''(x_2) \end{bmatrix}$$

is negative semi-definite. If $f''(x) < 0$ and $g''(x) < 0$ for all x, then y is strictly concave. The generalization is straightforward.

3.7.7(c) Let $g(y_1) = f(x_1, y_1)$ and $g(y_2) = f(x_2, y_2)$ (i.e. $x_1 = x_0(y_1)$ and $x_2 = x_0(y_2)$). Then

$$g[ky_1 + (1-k)y_2] \geqslant f[x, ky_1 + (1-k)y_2]$$

for all x. Then in particular,

$$g[ky_1 + (1-k)y_2] \geqslant f[kx_1 + (1-k)x_2, ky_1 + (1-k)y_2] \geqslant kf(x_1, y_1)$$
$$+ (1-k)f(x_2, y_2) = kg(y_1) + (1-k)g(y_2)$$

by the concavity of $f(x, y)$. This proves concavity of $g(y)$.

3.7.11(a) Clear from the contour map.

3.7.11(b) Clear from the definitions.

3.7.13 No.

3.8.3(a) $dy = 3dx_1 + 2dx_2 - dx_3$.

3.8.3(b) $dy = x_2(x_3 - 1)dx_1 + x_1(x_3 - 1)dx_2 + (x_1 x_2 + 2 - 2x_3)dx_3$.

3.8.3(c) $dy = 6x_1 dx_1 + 4(x_2 - 1)dx_2$.

3.8.5(a) Put $d\bar{M} = d\bar{G} = 0$ in equation (3.31);

$$\frac{\partial Y}{\partial P} = \frac{-\bar{M}(C_r + I_r)}{P^2 D} < 0.$$

3.8.5(b) When $L_r \to -\infty, D \to -\infty$ and $\partial Y/\partial P \nearrow 0$.

3.8.5(c) Equation (3.29) becomes

$$[1-C_Y(1-T_Y)-I_Y]\,dY-(C_r+I_r)\,dr = d\bar{G}+C_A\left(\frac{d\bar{M}}{P}-\frac{\bar{M}\,dP}{P^2}\right);$$

equation (3.30) is unchanged; equation (3.31) becomes

$$dY = [(d\bar{M}/P-\bar{M}\,dP/P^2)(C_r+I_r+C_AL_r)+L_r\,d\bar{G}]/D;$$

equation (3.32) becomes

$$dr = \{(d\bar{M}/P-\bar{M}\,dP/P^2)[1-C_Y(1-T_Y)-I_Y-C_AL_Y]-L_Y\,d\bar{G}\}/D;$$

$$\frac{\partial Y}{\partial P} = \frac{-\bar{M}(C_r+I_r+C_AL_r)}{P^2D};$$

as $L_r \to -\infty$,

$$\frac{\partial Y}{\partial P} \to \frac{-\bar{M}C_A}{P^2(1-C_Y(1-T_Y)-I_Y)} < 0.$$

Yes.

3.8.8 (a) $\dfrac{\partial y}{\partial x_1} = \dfrac{\partial y}{\partial x_2} = y;$

(b) $\dfrac{\partial y}{\partial x_i} = \dfrac{-y^{4-i}}{3y^2x_1+2yx_2+x_3}, i = 1, 2, 3.$

Chapter 4

4.3.2(a) Same solution as in Example 4.3.1: the utility function is the logarithm of that in Example 4.3.1 (maximizing the logarithm of a function is same as maximizing the function).

4.3.2(b) For the problem $\max x_1^{a_1}x_2^{a_2}\ldots x_n^{a_n}$ st $\Sigma p_i x_i = m$, the optimal values are given by $p_i\hat{x}_i/m = a_i/\Sigma a_j$.

4.3.2(c) $\hat{x}_1 = \hat{x}_2 = \frac{1}{2}$, $\hat{\lambda} = 1$. The contours of the objective function are circles, centre $(0,0)$.

4.3.2(d) $(\hat{x}_1, \hat{x}_2, \hat{x}_3, \hat{\lambda}) = (-1, -\frac{3}{2}, \frac{7}{2}, -6)$. When $x_3 = 1$ and the constraint is satisfied, $x_2 = -x_1$ and the objective function has value $5x_1^2$. There is no maximum (let $x_1 \to \infty$).

4.3.2(e) $(\hat{x}_1, \hat{x}_2, \hat{\lambda}, \hat{y}) = (0, 4, \frac{3}{2}, 17)$, $(0, -4, \frac{5}{2}, 49)$, $(2\sqrt{3}, -2, 3, 53)$ and $(-2\sqrt{3}, -2, 3, 53)$.

4.3.3(c) Minima when $y = 17, 49$. Maxima when $y = 53$.

4.4.2(a) Follow Example 4.4.1, putting $x_i^2 = a_i/\Sigma a_j$ into the inequality $f(\underline{x}) \le V$.

4.4.2(b) The first-order conditions $\partial L/\partial x_i = 0$ yield $a_i\hat{x}_i = p\hat{\lambda}\hat{x}_i^p$. Summing, $V = \Sigma a_i\hat{x}_i = p\hat{\lambda}$. The result follows from the value of $\hat{\lambda}$ implied by the constraint.

4.4.5 If H is the bordered Hessian then $H_2 = -F_K^2 < 0$ and $H_3 = \hat{\lambda}[F_K^2 F_{LL} + F_L^2 F_{KK}]$. By Theorem 4.4.3,

$$V'(Q) = \hat{\lambda} = r/MP_K = w/MP_L = \text{marginal cost.}$$

4.4.6 $\hat{x}_1 = b - \ln(c), \hat{x}_2 = c = \hat{\lambda}, V = c[b - \ln(c)] + c, \partial V/\partial c = b - \ln(c) = \hat{x}_1,$

$$H = \begin{bmatrix} 0 & -1 & -1/c \\ -1 & 0 & 0 \\ -1/c & 0 & 1/c \end{bmatrix}$$

and det $H < 0$: a minimum.

4.5.3(a) The minimum subject to the equality constraint is $y = 17$. The overall minimum is $y = -1$, achieved at $(x_1, x_2) = (0, 1)$ which satisfies the inequality constraint.

4.5.3(b) $\hat{x}_1 = p_2/p_1, \hat{x}_2 = (m - p_2)/p_2, \hat{\lambda} = \partial V/\partial m = 1/p_2$. If $m < p_2$ this implies a negative demand $\hat{x}_2 < 0$. A more appropriate specification would be to include an *inequality* constraint $x_2 \geq 0$ in the individual's utility maximization problem.

Chapter 5

5.2.5(b) The Lagrangean conditions include

A. $1 - 4\lambda_1 + 2\lambda_1 x_1 - 2\lambda_2 = 0$

B. $\qquad 1 + \lambda_1 - 3\lambda_2 = 0$

B implies $\lambda_2 > 0$, i.e. the second constraint binds. If $\lambda_1 = 0$ then $\lambda_2 = \frac{1}{2}$ from A and $\lambda_2 = \frac{1}{3}$ from B. Thus $\lambda_2 > 0$, i.e. both constraints bind. We can reject $(x_1, x_2) = (4, 0)$ since A and B imply $\lambda_1 < 0$ in this case.

5.4.4(a) Maximum profit is $\pi = \frac{19}{6}$ when $Q = \frac{5}{3}$. Thus if $\pi_0 > \frac{19}{6}$ there is no solution. From 1, $\lambda = (10 - 2Q)/(3Q - 5) \to \infty$ as $Q \to \frac{5}{3}$.

5.4.4(b) The objective function is linear, as is one constraint. The other constraint is convex by Example 3.7.3(b). The solution is $(\hat{x}_1, \hat{x}_2, \hat{\lambda}_1, \hat{\lambda}_2) = (\frac{1}{2}, \frac{3}{4}, 1, 0)$. All other possibilities can be eliminated.

5.4.4(c) The K–T conditions include

A. $x_1 \geq 0 \quad [1 - 4\lambda_1 + 2\lambda_1 x_1 - 2\lambda_2] \leq 0 \quad x_1[1 - 4\lambda_1 + 2\lambda_1 x_1 - 2\lambda_2] = 0$

B. $x_2 \geq 0 \quad [1 + \lambda_1 - 3\lambda_2] \leq 0 \quad x_2[1 + \lambda_1 - 3\lambda_2] = 0.$

From B $\hat{\lambda}_2 > 0$, i.e. the second constraint binds. Suppose $\hat{\lambda}_1 = 0$. Then A and B imply $\hat{x}_2 = 0$. A solution is $(\hat{x}_1, \hat{x}_2, \hat{\lambda}_1, \hat{\lambda}_2) = (4, 0, 0, \frac{1}{3})$. If

$\hat{\lambda}_1 > 0$ then both constraints bind. It can be shown that if $(\hat{x}_1, \hat{x}_2) = (4, 0)$ then any positive value of $\hat{\lambda}_1$ satisfies A and B, and then $\hat{\lambda}_2 = (1 + 4\hat{\lambda}_1)/2$. If $(\hat{x}_1, \hat{x}_2) = (\frac{2}{3}, \frac{20}{9})$ then $\hat{\lambda}_1 = \frac{1}{10}$ and $\hat{\lambda}_2 = \frac{11}{30}$.

5.4.4(d) Profit is $\pi(r) = pq - brq = ar^2(p - br)$. This is increasing with r for $0 < r < r_1 = 2p/3b$ and decreasing for $r > r_1$. If $r = r_1$ is feasible, i.e. if $ar_1^2 \leqslant q_0$, the firm sets $r^* = r_1$ and obtains maximum profit. Entire capacity may or may not be used ($ar_1^2 = q_0$ or $ar_1^2 < q_0$). If r_1 is not feasible the firm's problem is to maximize $\pi(r)$ st $0 \leqslant r \leqslant \sqrt{(q_0/a)}$ ($< r_1$). Since $\pi(r)$ is increasing in this range the firm uses its entire capacity, setting $r^* = \sqrt{(q_0/a)}$. A correct question would have been: 'Show that if the firm does not use its entire capacity then $br^* = 2p/3$'. The implication was the wrong way round, as given.

The K–T conditions could be used (but since the objective function is neither concave nor convex in r, a unique solution is not guaranteed). With $L = \pi(r) - \lambda(ar^2 - q_0)$, $\partial L/\partial r = 0$ implies $r = 0$ or $r = 2(p - \lambda)/3b$. Rejecting $r = 0$, we see that if $\lambda = 0$ (i.e. if the marginal profit from additional capacity is zero) then $r^* = 2p/3b$. But we cannot infer from $r^* = 2p/3b$ (i.e. from $\lambda = 0$) that the capacity constraint is non-binding: it may 'just' bind.

5.4.6 This problem is in the format given in Definition 5.4.5, with $f(x_1, x_2) = (x_1 - 1)^2 + (x_2 - 1)^2$, $g_1(x_1, x_2) = x_2 - x_1^2$, $g_2(x_1, x_2) = 2 - x_2$ and $\underline{b} = \underline{0}$. The objective function f is convex (follow the approach used in either Example 3.7.3(b) or Exercise 3.7.7(b)); g_1 is concave (Exercise 3.7.4(c)) and g_2 is linear. Hence the K–T conditions are necessary and sufficient. The Lagrangean is

$$L^* = (x_1 - 1)^2 + (x_2 - 1)^2 - \lambda_1(x_2 - x_1^2) - \lambda_2(2 - x_2).$$

The K–T conditions imply (i) $\hat{x}_2 = 1 + (\hat{\lambda}_1 - \hat{\lambda}_2)/2$; and (ii) $\hat{x}_1 = 0$ or $\hat{x}_1 = (1 + \hat{\lambda}_1)^{-1}$. From (ii) $0 \leqslant \hat{x}_1 \leqslant 1$. If $\hat{\lambda}_2 > 0$ then $\hat{x}_2 = 2$ and $\hat{\lambda}_1 > 0$ from (i), whence $\hat{x}_1^2 = \hat{x}_2 = 2$ which contradicts $0 \leqslant \hat{x}_1 \leqslant 1$. Thus $\hat{\lambda}_2 = 0$. If $\hat{\lambda}_1 > 0$ then $\hat{x}_1^2 = \hat{x}_2 = 1 + \lambda_1/2 > 1$ from (i), another contradiction. So $\hat{\lambda}_1 = 0$. Thus $(\hat{x}_1, \hat{x}_2) = (1, 1)$. This point is the overall minimum of the objective function, whose contours are circles centre $(1, 1)$.

5.5.2(a) The Lagrangean is

$$L = 3x_1 + 2x_2 - \lambda_1(6x_1 + 5x_2 - 6000) - \lambda_2(3x_1 + x_2 - 2400)$$
$$- \lambda_3(x_1 + 2x_2 - 2000).$$

The solution implies $\hat{\lambda}_1 = \hat{\lambda}_2 = \frac{1}{3}$ and $\hat{\lambda}_3 = 0$. Thus there is a net decrease in profit of 16.7 pence from the use of an extra machine hour; and a net increase in profit of 16.7 pence from the use of an extra 2 lb of raw material A.

5.5.7(a) It is the dual of the problem: $\max x_1 + x_2$ st $3x_1 + 2x_2 \leqslant 34$, $x_1 + 2x_2 \leqslant 18$, $x_1 + 6x_2 \leqslant 48$, $x_1 \leqslant 10$ and $x_1, x_2 \geqslant 0$. This maximum occurs at $\hat{x}_1 = 8$, $\hat{x}_2 = 5$ where constraints III and IV are slack. Hence the minimum value of the original problem is 13 and $\hat{y}_3 = \hat{y}_4 = 0$. Since both $\hat{x}_1$ and $\hat{x}_2$ are non-zero, the two constraints of the original problem bind. This is enough to determine $\hat{y} = (\frac{1}{4}, \frac{1}{4}, 0, 0)$. The K–T conditions for the original problem yield $\hat{\lambda}_1 = 8$, $\hat{\lambda}_2 = 5$.

5.5.7(b) $(\hat{x}, \hat{y}, \hat{z}) = (4, 0, 0)$.

Chapter 6

6.2.4 $V(\underline{c}^i) = f(\underline{x}^i, \underline{c}^i) \geqslant f(\underline{x}, \underline{c}^i)$ for all $\underline{x}$ st $\underline{g}(\underline{x}) \leqslant \underline{0}$ $(i = 1, 2)$. Since $\underline{g}(\underline{x}^j) \leqslant \underline{0}$ by assumption $(j = 1, 2)$, $V(\underline{c}^i) \geqslant f(\underline{x}^j, \underline{c}^i)$ for $j \neq i$.

6.2.5 By assumption $\underline{x}^1$ is feasible when $\underline{c} = \underline{c}^2$, so $f(\underline{x}^1) \leqslant V(\underline{c}^2) = f(\underline{x}^2)$. Suppose for a contradiction that $\underline{x}^2$ is feasible when $\underline{c} = \underline{c}^1$. Then $f(\underline{x}^2) \leqslant V(\underline{c}^1) = f(\underline{x}^1)$. This forces $f(\underline{x}^2) = f(\underline{x}^1)$, the required contradiction.

6.3.1 The minimum of $\Sigma p_i x_i$ st $Q = \Pi x_i^{a_i}$ is achieved when $p_i \hat{x}_i / V = a_i / \Sigma a_j$, $1 \leqslant i \leqslant n$, where $V = \Sigma p_i \hat{x}_i$; this budget–shares property of the Cobb–Douglas production function parallels that of the Cobb–Douglas utility function derived in Example 4.3.1 and Exercise 4.3.2(b). Hence for the problem at hand we have

A $\quad r_1 \hat{K}_1 = r_2 \hat{K}_2 = \hat{L} = \dfrac{V}{3}$.

Substituting these values into the production constraint, we find

B $\quad V = V(Q) = 3(r_1 r_2)^{\frac{1}{3}} Q^2$.

The restricted problem may be expressed as $\min[r_1 K_1 + L]$ st $\bar{Q} = (K_1 L)^{\frac{1}{6}}$, where $\bar{Q} = Q / K_2^{\frac{1}{6}}$. Hence its solution is given by $r_1 \tilde{K}_1 = \tilde{L} = (\tilde{V} - r_2 \bar{K}_2)/2$, where $\tilde{V}$ is the full cost, $\tilde{V} = r_1 \tilde{K}_1 + r_2 \bar{K}_2 + \tilde{L}$. Substituting into the production constraint, we find

C $\quad \tilde{V} = \tilde{V}(Q, \bar{K}_2) = r_2 \bar{K}_2 + 2(r_1 / \bar{K}_2)^{\frac{1}{2}} Q^3$.

Now substitute $\bar{K}_2 = \hat{K}_2(Q_0) = V(Q_0)/3r_2$ from A into C: we have

D $\quad \tilde{V} = V(Q_0)/3 + 2QV(Q)/3Q_0$

from which all of the results, and a graph like figure 6.6, follow easily.

6.4.1(a) Euler's theorem applied to $V(\underline{p}, m)$ yields

$$\Sigma p_k \frac{\partial V}{\partial p_k} + m \frac{\partial V}{\partial m} = 0.$$

From Roy's identity this is

$$\frac{\partial V}{\partial m} \cdot (-\Sigma p_k \hat{x}_k + m) = 0$$

which is the familiar complementary slack relation. For the equality-constrained utility maximization we may assume $\partial V / \partial m > 0$. Euler's theorem applied to $E(\underline{p}, u)$ yields $\Sigma p_k \, \partial E / \partial p_k = E$. From Shephard's lemma this is $\Sigma p_k x_k^* = E$, which is equation (6.44).

6.4.1(b) $\dfrac{\partial V}{\partial p_k} + \dfrac{\partial V}{\partial m} \cdot \dfrac{\partial E}{\partial p_k} = 0.$

From (i)–(iii) this is equivalent to $-\hat{\lambda} x_k + \hat{\lambda} x_k^* = 0$. Assuming $\hat{\lambda} \neq 0$ we have $\hat{x}_k = x_k^*$. But x_k is a function of $\underline{p}$ and m, whilst x_k^* is a function of $\underline{p}$ and u. Only when $V(\underline{p}, m) = u$ do they coincide.

Chapter 7

7.7.1(b) The constraint becomes $S' = iS - w + C$. The solution for C is $\hat{C} = \lambda_0^{-1} e^{(i-r)t}$ for some λ_0 (as in equation (7.47)) and the differential equation for S is $S' - iS = w - \lambda_0^{-1} e^{(i-r)t}$. The integrating factor is e^{-it}. Using the end-point conditions $S(0) = S(T) = 0$, we find

$$\lambda_0^{-1} = \frac{rw(e^{iT} - 1)}{i e^{iT}(1 - e^{-rT})}$$

and the optimal savings path is

$$\hat{S}(t) = \frac{w e^{it}[(1 - e^{-rT})(1 - e^{-it}) - (1 - e^{-rt})(1 - e^{-iT})]}{i(1 - e^{-rT})}.$$

7.7.1(c) The problem is max $\int_0^T e^{-rt} U(C) \, dt$ st $C = F(K) - I$, $K' = I - bK$ plus end-point conditions. This may be put into the optimal control format in two ways:

Control variable C: max $\int_0^T e^{-rt} U(C) \, dt$ st $K' = F(K) - C - bK$.

Control variable I: max $\int_0^T e^{-rt} U[F(K) - I] \, dt$ st $K' = I - bK$.

In either case the Hamiltonian conditions yield $\lambda = e^{-rt} U'(\hat{C})$ and $\lambda' + \lambda[F_K - b] = 0$. Therefore $U'(\hat{C}) = \lambda e^{rt} = m$. Also $m' = \lambda' e^{rt} + rm$ (see equation (7.37)), whence $m' + [r + b - F_K]m = 0$. This is readily integrated, using the integrating factor $e^{P(t)}$ where $P(t) = \int_0^t [b + r - F_K] \, d\tau$. The result is the differential equation

$$U'[F(K) - bK - K'] = m = A e^{\int_0^t (b + r - F_K) \, d\tau}.$$

7.7.1(d) The problem is

$$\max_{p} \int_0^T e^{-rt}(p - c)[f(p) - x] \, dt \text{ st } x' = k(p - \bar{p})$$

with state variable x, control p. The multiplier $\lambda(t)$ is the marginal effect on the dominant firm's profits of a small increase in $x(t) = $ rival sales; the effect of such entry should be negative. The Hamiltonian is $H = e^{-rt}(p-c)[f(p)-x] + \lambda k(p-\bar{p})$ and $\partial H/\partial p = 0$ yields $m = \lambda e^{rt} = -[(\hat{p}-c)f'(\hat{p}) + f(\hat{p}) - x]/k$. From $\partial H/\partial x = -\lambda'$ we have $(\hat{p}-c)e^{-rt} = \lambda'$, i.e. $\hat{p} - c = m' - rm$ as required.

7.7.1(e) The problem is

$$\max_{L,I} \int_0^\infty e^{-rt}[pF(K,L) - wL - qI]\,dt \text{ st } K' = I - bK.$$

The Hamiltonian conditions $\partial H/\partial L = \partial H/\partial I = 0$ and $\partial H/\partial K = -\lambda'$ imply the results given.

7.7.1(f) The problem can be written

$$\max \int_0^T f[t, x(t), u(t)]\,dt \text{ st } x'(t) = u(t).$$

The Hamiltonian is $H = f(t, x, u) + \lambda u$; $\partial H/\partial u = 0$ implies $f_3 = -\lambda$, so $d/dt[f_3] = -\lambda' = \partial H/\partial x = f_2$.

7.8.1(a) Set $m' = 0$ in equation (7.74) and eliminate $U'(C)/m$ from equations (7.73) and (7.74). The right-hand side of equation (7.80) is the discounted cost in terms of consumption of the atmospheric concentration arising from an extra unit of emission. See Nordhaus (1982) for further discussion.

7.8.1(b) The numerator determines the sign. It depends upon 'how concave' $f(E)$ is, i.e. whether the negative term $M^*f''(E^*)/a$ dominates or not.

7.8.1(c) Differentiate $f'(E^*) = ah'(aE^*/b)/(b+r)$ with respect to a:

$$\partial E^*/\partial a = \frac{h'(M^*) + M^*h''(M^*)}{(b+r)f''(E^*) - a^2 h''(M^*)/b} < 0.$$

7.8.2(a) The two loci are

$$K' = 0 \qquad m = C'(bK)$$

$$m' = 0 \qquad m = \frac{P'(K)}{(r+b)}.$$

The $K' = 0$ locus is upward-sloping and the $m' = 0$ locus is downward-sloping in (K, m)-space. Steady-state investment is $I^* = bK^*$. In case (i) if r is increased, the $m' = 0$ locus shifts down; (ii) if b is increased the $m' = 0$ locus shifts down and the $K' = 0$ locus shifts up – hence K^* falls but since $I^* = bK^*$ the effect on I^* is not determined; (iii) the $K' = 0$ locus becomes $m = C'(bK) - t$, i.e. it shifts down.

7.8.2(b) See the answer to Exercise 7.7.1(c). The $K' = 0$ and $m' = 0$ loci are

$$K' = 0 \qquad\qquad m = U'[F(K) - bK]$$
$$m' = 0 \qquad (r + b - F_K)m = 0.$$

The $K' = 0$ locus is downward-sloping if $F_K > b$, $U'' < 0$ and the $m' = 0$ locus is vertical in (K, m) – space.

7.8.2(c) From Exercise 7.7.1(d) the $x' = 0$ and $m' = 0$ loci are

$$x' = 0 \qquad p = \bar{p}$$
$$m' = 0 \qquad rm = c - p.$$

Substituting $f(p) = a - bp$ into the expression for m given in Exercise 7.7.1(d) yields $p = (km + a + bc - x)/2b$. The equations for the $x' = 0$ and $m' = 0$ loci in the (x, m)-plane follow; both are upward-sloping.

When p is increased, the $x' = 0$ locus shifts up. When c is increased, the $x' = 0$ locus shifts down and the $m' = 0$ locus shifts up. The steady-state values are $m^* = -(\bar{p} - c)/r$ and $x^* = km^* + a + bc - 2b\bar{p}$. Hence

$$\partial x^*/\partial \bar{p} = -2b - \frac{k}{r} < 0 \qquad \text{and} \qquad \partial x^*/\partial c = b + \frac{k}{r} > 0.$$

The dominant firm's cost advantage is $\bar{p} - c$; its pricing strategy allows less entry the higher this cost advantage.

We have $\partial x^*/\partial k = m^* \leqslant 0$ assuming $\bar{p} \geqslant c$. The more rapidly rivals can respond to price signals, the larger will be the dominant firm's long-run market share: see Gaskins (1971) for discussion of this apparently counter-intuitive result.

7.9.1 The problem is:

$$\max_{K, L} \int_0^\infty f(t, K, K', L, L') \, dt$$

where

$$f(t, K, K', L, L') = e^{-rt}[pF(K, L) - wL - q(K' + bK)].$$

The Euler conditions are $d/dt[\partial f/\partial K'] = \partial f/\partial K$ and $0 = \partial f/\partial L$.

Index